MAN of GLORY
SIMÓN BOLÍVAR

SIMÓN BOLÍVAR
1783–1830

*"The eyes, deep-set, dark and brilliant, impressed
at once all who ever saw him"*

Man of Glory: Simón Bolívar

Thomas Rourke

Simon Publications

2001

Printed by Lightning Source Inc. La Vergne, TN

Published by Simon Publications, P. O. Box 321, Safety Harbor, FL 34695

CONTENTS

PREFACE

✤

HOW revealing it is, when contemplating the causes of a century of misunderstandings and suspicions between the two Americas, to consider that North Americans know absolutely nothing about the South American Liberator, the national hero of five republics. Such, though, is what it amounts to, generally speaking—absolutely nothing. Familiarity with the life and achievements of Simón Bolívar is limited in the United States of North America to specialists and historians. A few able English-language writers have tried, even quite recently, to remedy that situation; but all of them have failed, through no fault of their own, to gain a wide hearing among their countrymen. This work, then, is merely one more effort in the same direction.

As well as interpreting the man himself, the author hopes also, in view of the dangers that threaten the principles of democracy throughout the world today, to bring the reader a clear conception of that sympathy toward dictatorships which has always been inherent in Latin Americans, and thus to warn him how very formidable that danger is in the countries south of us.

I remember one morning in Caracas six weeks after the death of Juan Vicente Gómez, the man who ruled Venezuela in ruthless tyranny for twenty-seven years. The city was in howling confusion. Eleazar López Contreras, the head of the army under Gómez, had taken over the presidency; but he had, surprisingly, emptied the prisons of political offenders, invited back the political exiles, reestablished the constitutional rights of free speech, press

ix

and assembly. The people were exercising their new liber-
ties to the fullest, indulging in a veritable orgy of mass
meetings and speech-making; and there had been some
mob violence and looting. Everyone was delighted with
the reaction of Contreras against the old régime. Hopes
for a democratic government were high. I was sitting with
a Venezuelan gentleman in the patio of his house, a few
blocks from the Plaza Bolívar. My host was an educated
man, a liberal who had suffered under Gómez, who had
been exiled by him and who had just returned to his
country under the new amnesty. The cheers of the crowds
in the Plaza and the high-pitched voices of the speech-
makers came faintly through the latticed windows. We
were talking politics, naturally, and my friend was enthusiastic about the democratic reforms he and his fellow
liberals were planning for their country. Suddenly, as we
talked, the voices from the Plaza were drowned by a great
roar. It was a dull, harsh sound that echoed among the
buildings out in the street. We both automatically stood
up and looked at each other. There was a dead silence
for a moment and then the roar came once more. Another moment of silence and again the roar. Then the air
was filled with other sounds, awful, human sounds,
screaming and moaning. They went on and on.

I knew what it was; but I asked anyway, without thinking, "What is it?"

I shall never forget the smile that came over the face
of that man—that idealistic, liberal, democratic man.
There was satisfaction in it and a kind of pride, but most
of all, relief—infinite relief.

"Contreras has put his pants on at last," he said.

The troops had fired three volleys from the balcony of
the Government House pointblank into the crowd in the
Plaza, slaughtering men, women and children.

It must be stated in justice to President Contreras that
he had had no responsibility in the affair; and he ordered
the arrest, on the charge of murder, of Félix Galaviz, the
Governor of Caracas, the man who had given the order to
fire.

But there you have it. Even this liberal-thinking man felt instinctively, when his guard was down, that there were occasions when the brutal, repressive methods of totalitarianism were desirable for his people.

That tendency toward dictatorships in the Hispano-American, peon and don alike, is more than a mere acceptance of it; it is, in times of trouble and insecurity, a definite yearning, a sort of despairing, fatalistic desire for it, as a narcotic to relieve his mind, tired with the unaccustomed effort of social struggle. It is a definite racial disease. It is born in the Latin American of his feeling of inadequacy, his lack of self-confidence, his confused and uneducated idealism. It has roots far back in history—in the peon, in his enslavement by the Spaniards and the padron system practiced by the landed creoles after independence; in the don, in the centuries under Spanish rule which permitted him wealth and property but gave him no part whatever in government, yet at the same time instilled in him ideas of autocracy by providing him with the example of its efficacy as a working system.

Bolívar, more clearly than anyone else, saw this weakness in his people. It governed largely the whole course of his life. He wrote and spoke of it constantly, harped on it. He deplored it, cast about for educational means to remedy it; but he temporized with it and built his whole political philosophy around it. It was the rock upon which his dreams for a great union of South American states foundered; it might also become the principal factor in the collapse of democratic ideology in the Latin American countries.

It is this attitude, more than any other one thing, that gives the present Nazi-Fascist drive against democracy in Latin America a definite possibility of success. Whether or not it can happen *here*, it most certainly can happen *there*—and with a violent suddenness that would leave us reeling in the ruins of our cherished isolation.

T. R.

Miami Beach
July, 1939.

I: GUAPO

Chapter I

POLVORÍN

✤

FERNANDO, Prince of the Asturias, heir to the throne of Spain, was playing at lances in the garden of the summer palace at Aranjuez. His opponent was a young South American with a slender, graceful body and a handsome head, a sub-lieutenant of colonial militia. From a shaded bower Queen María Luisa watched the bright blades flashing in the clear sunlight and her eyes, none the less keen for their fifty years, followed the movements of her son's companion with sensual interest. The tight white trousers of his uniform showed the play of every muscle; his straight back moved in quick arcs of rhythmic grace. His waist and thighs were slender almost to delicacy, but they were corded with hard sinew; and above them his chest swelled like a young stallion's and his shoulders were square and wide.

The South American had learned to use the lance among the cattlemen of his haciendas in the wild llanos, and he could wield it with either hand as though it were a willow wand. The prince was no match for him. The young colonial toyed with him, grinning, tricked him into awkward and helpless postures. Then, at last, when he had him done in, weak and panting for breath, with superb impudence he lifted the velvet cap neatly from the royal head.

The Prince of the Asturias was furious. He turned to his mother and complained violently of the outrage to his dignity. She, devouring the debonair figure of the young colonial officer with her eyes, said, laughing, "Don't be a

3

fool, Fernando, it's only a game. You must learn to play it better if you wish to triumph."

Simón Bolívar was seventeen then. Years later, when he had liberated all of northern South America from Spanish rule, he said, "How was the prince to know then that I was also to strike from his head the fairest jewel of his crown with my sword?"

Varying details of this legend are given by different writers; but the comment of Bolívar is recorded as authentic by Daniel O'Leary in his memoirs.

His own beginnings and the conditions of the class he was born into contributed greatly to what he became; but they do not explain him, for there were many, with similar beginnings, born into the same conditions. It was his own spark of genius, fed by the influences of those beginnings and flaming out into the tinder of those conditions, which made him one of the great men of history. Nevertheless, these things should be studied briefly in order to understand the personality and career of this man, Simón Bolívar.

The creole aristocracy of the South American colonies of Spain, enjoying great wealth and almost limitless power over their Indian and negro slaves, suffered, paradoxically, a collective and intense inferiority complex. Descendants of the Conquistadores and proud of their clear lineage, they inherited the will to dominate, a desire for a free scope for their driving ambition—qualities which the mother country, in her glorious era of empire a few centuries before, had encouraged and rewarded in their forebears, and which she now, in her decadence, ruthlessly surpressed. The result was frustration—frustration in a whole class, a class that embraced the best brains and courage of nearly a whole continent.

The colonial policy of Spain in the eighteenth century was shortsighted in the extreme. Panicky over her own safety among the dangers that threatened her in Europe,

she neglected her colonies shamefully and looked upon
them only as a source of revenue with which to conduct
her wars, preserve her existence and maintain her ruling
class in its accustomed luxury. The ruling class in the
American colonies, or what should have been the ruling
class by ancestral right, was entirely disregarded. It was
made subject to ignorant and avaricious officials sent out
from Spain for the tacit purpose of enriching themselves
as a reward for some service to the crown—officials who
were changed often and who had no interest whatever in
the welfare of the colonies they governed. It had no voice
whatever in its own affairs. All officials of government,
high and low, and all the higher clergy, were sent out
from Spain, willy-nilly. Educational facilities for this intelligent, wealthy class were provided only to a limited
degree, under religious auspices; and efforts of its own to
increase them were discouraged and sometimes suppressed
outright. In addition, their commercial enterprises were
subject to the limits placed upon them by the Spanish
crown. Landowners, their wealth lay in coffee, cacao,
sugar, indigo, hides and minerals. Not only was the sale of
these products restricted to Spain alone and all trade for-
bidden, even with other Spanish colonies, but a monopoly
had been granted by the crown to a single company; a
company which had the exclusive privilege not only of
buying from the colonies but of selling to them as well.
Everything produced in the colonies for export had to be
sold to one company and everything imported from abroad
had to be purchased from it also; both transactions subject to the company's own arbitrary prices. These prices
were almost always several hundred per cent below the
current European prices in the one case, and the same
amount above them in the other. The colonial producers
were beautifully taken, coming and going.
    Besides these abuses, there was great social discrimina-
tion; and it was this, perhaps, which created the greatest
resentment in the breasts of a people aristocratic by blood

and haughty by race. With intelligence, they were denied education. With wealth, they were denied even the right to travel about without royal permission. With business instincts, they were deprived of the possibility of trade with the world. With an inherited urge to govern others, they had no voice even in their own affairs. But what galled most the sensitivities of the "mantuano," or creole aristocrat in the American colonies, was the wide social gulf which existed between him and his foreign-born neighbors. Even the most ignorant Spanish-born or Canary Island adventurer or the most bloodthirsty deserter from a Spanish privateer enjoyed social privileges which were denied the creole aristocrat. Forms of address, location of seats in church, at theaters and other public gatherings—all were regulated with the place of birth as the first consideration.

Spain's greatest error in her policy of oppression in her American colonies lay in her failure to deprive the landed creoles of their wealth. Inexplicably, she never went in for confiscation on a wide scale. By restriction of trade, she placed insurmountable obstacles in the way of the accumulation of wealth; but in South America land and slaves meant wealth, and these she never confiscated. She respected her old laws of inheritance. She acknowledged and protected legally the orderly succession to the "vínculo," the entailed estates of the descendants of the Conquistadores; and in so doing, she permitted power to remain in the hands of those in whom she was breeding hatred. She permitted an aristocracy to exist and denied it the privileges an aristocracy always demands.

And besides all this, at the end of the eighteenth century a lusty young republic was thriving in North America, while in France the people had stormed the Bastille and overthrown their king. The seed of independence had flowered on the earth, and its odor was being borne by the four winds even to the remote cities in the Andes.

Spain, in her Indian colonies, was sitting on a powder keg to which she herself had applied the slow match.

Two years before Bolívar was born there were several premature sputterings of revolution, but they were quickly snuffed out by the iron heel of Spain. In the town of Socorro in the captain-generalcy of New Granada one José Antonio Galán raised the cry of rebellion. They got to him fast, quartered him and exhibited the various parts of his body in iron cages on the highways. In the viceroyalty of Perú, Tupac-Amarú, a descendant of Inca kings, gathered together a sizable army of forty thousand Indians and attempted to re-establish the empire which had been conquered by Pizarro two centuries before. He didn't get far. The Spaniards pulled out his tongue and then bound him to a stake and forced him to watch while his wife and son and six kinsmen were stretched out on the ground and pulled apart by four horses driven in different directions. Then he himself was served the same way.

These pleasant events took place in the Year of Our Lord 1781.

Such were the conditions in South America when Simón José Antonio de la Santísima Trinidad Bolívar y Palacio was born. His own beginnings were of a nature to intensify the influences of those conditions and to develop still further the personality which they would be expected to produce.

He was the spoiled youngest child of one of the wealthiest families of Venezuela. From his birth he enjoyed a personal income of twenty thousand pesos [1] yearly. His father, Don Juan Vicente Bolívar y Ponte, died when the boy was three and his mother only twenty-seven. She, Doña Concepción Palacio y Sojo, an intelligent and gentle woman, adored him, pampered him and had her hands

[1] Approximately twenty thousand dollars.

full with him. His sisters, María Antonia, five and a half years older, Juana María, four years older, and his brother, Juan Vicente, two years older, adored him and pampered him too.

Some writers claim that Doña María Concepción despaired of trying to discipline her wayward son and, when he was six, sent him to live with the distinguished Caracas jurist, Miguel José Sanz; but it is probably not true. It is true, though, that she called upon Sanz for aid in educating him. Sanz reports that young Simón was "insupportable, restless, imperative, audacious, willful, heedless to all counsel, intolerable before his own family and strangers." But with it all the boy had a sharp wit and an endearing charm. Sanz told him once that he was a "polvorín"—a horn of gunpowder. Bolívar replied, "Then be careful not to come near me—I might explode." And once, riding in the outskirts of Caracas with his pupil who was mounted on a burro, Sanz said, "Simoncito, I'm afraid you'll never be a caballero." (A gentleman, but literally a horseman.) "How do you expect me to be a caballero, mounted on this mangy burro?" said the boy.

Then, when he was nine (some historians say seven), his mother died; and within a few months his sisters, María Antonia, then fifteen, and Juana, not yet fourteen, married and went to live with their husbands in other parts of the city. Young Simón [1] and his brother were left alone in the handsome house on the Plaza de San Jacinto under the care of the household slaves and the guardianship of their maternal uncle, Don Carlos Palacio. Juan Vicente, a serious, quiet boy, was the direct opposite of his vivacious, daring younger brother. He was his devoted slave. Everyone, in fact, seemed to fall victim to the precocious youngster. He was warmly generous, and impetu-

[1] Spanish Americans long, I know, for some miracle which would suddenly bestow upon all English-speaking people a knowledge of how properly to pronounce the name of the Liberator. And that knowledge would go far to promote better feeling between us. Therefore, not *Sigh*-mun *Ball*-a-ver, but See-*moan* Bow-*lee*-var, please.

ous in his affections. Uncle Carlos succumbed to him quickly and even his Uncle Esteban in Spain wrote suggesting that young Simoncito be sent over to him, apparently feeling that the boy's charm would be an asset to him at court. (Esteban was trying his hand at winning the favors of the lascivious old Queen María Luisa.) Bolívar's negro nurse, Hipólita, and the young slave girl, Matea, scolded and caressed him alternately, unable to deny him anything.

Bolívar never, all his life, in the midst of the terrific whirlwind of affairs which involved him, forgot any of these. In 1825, when he was busy establishing a new government in far-off Perú, learning that his old nurse was destitute in Caracas, he found time to write to María Antonia, "I send you a letter from my 'mother,' Hipólita. Give her everything she desires; do for her as though she were your own mother, for her milk has fed my life and I have never known another father than her."

Physically he was slight of build, wiry, incredibly energetic. He had a beautiful smile, brilliant dark eyes and a shock of black curls. In appearance and in temperament he resembled his older sister, María Antonia, and all their lives, however far apart they were, these two were very close. The other two, Juan Vicente and Juana, were of another type—fair, blue-eyed, quiet. They always regarded their younger brother with adoring awe.

Bolívar was born on July 24, 1783. The first of his line to come to America was also a Simón Bolívar, a native of Vizcaya, who came to Caracas in 1589, thirty-nine years after the city was founded. He had been Procurador General in the court and he was named by the Spanish king Regidor Perpetuo of Caracas and Oficial Real of the province. He acquired wealth and great tracts of land, as did all the early Spanish gentlemen. He married a Spanish girl of gentle birth; and when he died the vínculo was handed down intact from generation to generation in accordance with Spanish law. The vínculo was increased by

the property of the women who married the Bolívar men.
There was considerable intermarriage with rather close
relatives, and somewhere along the line it is claimed that
two titles were acquired, "Marqués de Bolívar" and "Vis-
conde de Cocorote"; but these had been discarded, apparently, when the last Simón Bolívar was born. Somewhere,
too, it is probable that some touches of Indian blood were
introduced, for few colonial families were without it, de-
spite their proud claims to pure white blood. The Venezuelan historian, Gil Fortoul, says that Indian blood had
"penetrated even to the family of the Liberator." This is
most probable; the Conquistadores brought few Spanish
women with them, and along the "Main," the north coast
of South America, the Indians were gentle and friendly.
They welcomed the white men with trust and childlike
eagerness. "The men opened their hearts to them; the
women, their arms."

Doña María Concepción brought to her marriage with
Juan Vicente Bolívar a considerable estate of her own as
well as an equally aristocratic lineage. In fact, the two
family lines had crossed frequently before, and the names
Blanco, Sojo, Ponte, Palacio and Aristiguieta appear in
both. Young Simón Bolívar was related by blood to almost
all the distinguished families of Venezuela, for both his
lines were prolific and had spread widely. His grand-
father, Capitán Feliciano Palacio Sojo y Gil Aguirre, had
ten uncles and eleven brothers.

When Bolívar's father and mother died, the estate they
left to their four children included interests in nearly
every type of business enterprise in the colony. Besides
the house of residence in the Plaza San Jacinto there were
two other houses in the city of Caracas and a block without buildings. In La Guaira, the port city of Caracas,
there were nine houses rented out; and the whole near-by
valley of Aroa, with valuable mineral deposits, largely
unworked, belonged to the estate. In the valley of Aragua,
some fifty miles from Caracas, there was the beautiful

hacienda of San Mateo. This hacienda was always Bolívar's favorite country place; while his mother lived and
his sisters were unmarried, the whole family with all their
personal servants would go there two or three times a
year. San Mateo had vast acres of sugar cane, a water-
power mill, a rum distillery, fruit orchards and all the
men, animals and buildings necessary to its running. On
this one farm alone there were over twelve hundred slaves.
In the valley of Taguaga there was a cacao plantation; in
the valley of Suata, one of indigo; and far off in the llanos
there were three "hatos," or cattle farms, with great herds
roaming the trackless plains.

At Don Vicente's death a bastard son presented himself,
a youth named Augustín, born of a woman of the city of
Maracaibo. This created no undue disturbance in the old
man's family. Concubinage was practically a universal
custom and even the women of the best families sometimes produced questionable offspring. This was particularly true in the Bolívar family, on both sides. The unexpected kinsman was provided for to some extent; but even
so the shares of all four children in the estate of Juan
Vicente and Doña María Concepción were very sizable
for those times.

Uncle Carlos, as guardian of young Simoncito, did his
best to provide good instruction for him. For tutors he
obtained the services of some of the best minds in the
captain-generalcy. Besides the jurist Sanz, there were
Padre Negrete, Guillermo Pelgrón and Padre Andújar, a
priest whom the great German naturalist, Alexander von
Humboldt, praised for his scientific knowledge. Later
there was young Andrés Bello, recognized even today as
one of South America's great poets. Most important of all
was the eccentric savant, Simón Rodríguez. He was the
only one who exerted any real influence on the future of
Simón Bolívar. That influence was considerable indeed,
and calls for more detailed comment later on.

The best efforts of his tutors, it appears, failed to ac-

complish much with young Simoncito in the way of education. He had a quick mind and an uncanny memory
when he chose to exert them; but he just wasn't interested
at that time. He acquired a smattering of the sciences, an
elementary knowledge of mathematics, grammar, geog-
raphy, history, literature and church doctrine. He picked
them up "porque si," just because, for his mind was really
occupied with the highly imaginative and mischievous
affairs he planned for his gang of young city ruffians
around the Plaza San Jacinto. He was a constant headache
to the good Padre Andrés, pastor of the little church
across the street. And the priest, too, was a victim of Bolívar's charm, as were to be so many, many others in the
Liberator's short, flaming life.

Chapter II

VULTURES MARK THE WAY

✤

SIMÓN CARREÑO or Rodríguez or Samuel Robinson —all of which names he used as his fancy dictated— was a constitutional nonconformist, a half-cracked intellectual who wandered about, sometimes in rags, spouting quotations from the Roman and Greek philosophers and carrying a copy of Rousseau's *Emile* in his pocket. "It is the only book," he said, "which, during any long period, should compose your library." He was a bastard son of a Caracas gentleman who raised a legitimate son to become a priest. Rodríguez ran away from home when he was a boy because he couldn't stand the stuffy religious atmosphere. He roamed all over Europe and came back to his native city full of learning and revolutionary ideas. He was just the man to appeal to young Bolívar, and to set a course for his restless mind and driving energy.

The Rodríguez method of instruction met with young Bolívar's approval immediately. It was somewhat after the Peripatetic system of Aristotle. The master believed in the sacredness of the human body and its accord with nature. If he had had his way he would have dispensed with clothes entirely—which he did sometimes and got into trouble over it. He was probably the first doctrinal nudist in the New World.

The two of them hied off at once to the Bolívar hacienda, San Mateo. There they roamed the forest trails, swam in the clear streams, climbed the shaly peaks that shimmered in the tropic heat; and Rodríguez talked of the glories of the French Revolution, of "the Rights of

Man," of the doctrines of his beloved Rousseau. True to the philosophy of the Sage of Geneva, he sought "to teach one's child to protect himself, once a man, to stand the blows of fate, to adapt himself to wealth or poverty, to support life, if necessary, in the bitter cold of Iceland or on the burning rock of Malta." Bolívar, delighted, drank it all in, absorbed it without effort. Bonaparte was his hero; he plied his teacher with eager questions about the little corporal. They made long journeys on muleback to the Bolívar hatos in the great llanos, and young Simón learned from the vaqueros how to capture and tame wild horses, how to use the lasso and lance, how to "colear" a bull—ride up at full gallop on his flank, grasp his tail with one hand and throw him with a quick, powerful twist. That sort of life went on for six years. Young Bolívar developed an amazingly hard body so that, years after, these same wild llaneros were to call him "Culo de Hierro," "Iron Arse." He developed, too, a sort of confused jumble of idealistic, liberal philosophy which didn't jibe so well with his imperious nature and inherited sense of class superiority.

Things were happening throughout the South American colonies in those days—more preliminary little sputterings of the Spanish powder keg. From the islands of Trinidad and Jamaica and Haiti books had been smuggled in for some time—the works of Helvetius and Montesquieu, *The Social Contract,* Paine's *Rights of Man,* the Jesuit Vizando y Guzman's *Exposition of Complaints and Grievances.* In Santa Fé de Bogotá in the province of New Granada a wealthy intellectual named Antonio Nariño smuggled in a small printing press, made Spanish translations of these works and began to pass them about surreptitiously. They caught him and sent him to Cádiz in chains.

In 1795, when Bolívar was twelve, there was an uprising of slaves in Venezuela in the Valley of Curimagua;

a rebellion probably instigated by white creoles, for the
slaves had no particular complaint against the Spaniards,
no interest in the hatred between the Spanish-born and
the native-born whites. Their complaints, if any, would
naturally be against the latter, their owners. There were
at that time in Venezuela some 12,000 Spaniards and
Canary Islanders, 200,000 white creoles and 400,000 colored. These colored were called, collectively, "pardos,"
and comprised mestizos (mixture of white and Indian),
mulattoes (mixture of white and black) and zambos (mixture of black and Indian). Besides, there were several hundred thousand pure Indians and pure blacks; and of the
latter more were freemen than slaves. The trouble which
was brewing in the colony was purely between the two
small upper classes—the Spaniards and the white creoles.
The leader of the uprising in '95 was a zambo named
José Chiriños. The authorities suppressed the movement
easily and Chiriños was beheaded in the principal plaza
of Caracas. Young Bolívar and Rodríguez were among the
crowd that watched the execution. The two of them discussed all these affairs, and Rodríguez, at least, was considerably worked up about them; but Bolívar wasn't particularly interested. He was much more concerned just
then with his love affairs with his beautiful cousins, the
Aristiguietas. There was a whole bevy of them and Simón
appears to have enjoyed the favors of all alike. Some years
later he said that he'd rather go to purgatory than heaven,
for there he'd be sure to find the Aristiguietas, "beautiful
girls of happy and very independent natures."

Two years later, however, there was an affair which
brought about the separation of Bolívar and his master.
Rodríguez couldn't keep out of this one. Three famous
intellectuals of Spain, Piconel, Cortés and Andrés, had
been arrested for conspiring against the crown, sent across
the sea and imprisoned in La Guaira. Two Venezuelans,
Manuel Gual and José María España, formed a plot to
liberate them. The authorities got wind of it, swooped

down upon the conspirators at a meeting in the woods near La Guaira and captured most of them. Gual and España got away to the British island of Trinidad. Among the papers found in Gual's desk were the plans for the establishment of a republic, complete even to the design for a white, blue, yellow and red flag. Seventy-two persons were found to be involved in the plot and among them was Simón Rodríguez. However, there was little proof against him, and through the influence of Bolívar's Uncle Carlos and the able defense of Miguel Sanz he was released with the stipulation that he leave the country.

Of the others brought up to Caracas for trial, all were sent to prison except seven. These were condemned to death. The sentence which the Spanish captain-general passed upon them was that they should be "brought from the jail at dawn, tied to the tail of a beast and dragged to the gallows; that, dead naturally upon this at the hands of the executioner, the head be cut off and the body quartered; that the head be carried in an iron cage to the port of La Guaira and placed at the high extremity of a thirty-foot post fixed in the ground at the entrance to that port from Caracas; that, upon another equal post, one of the quarters be similarly placed at the entrance of the town of Macuto, where had hid many of the enemies of the State; on another, another quarter at the lookout post of Chacón; on another, another quarter in the place called Quitacalzón . . . ; on another, another quarter at La Cumbre . . . ; that all the properties of the condemned be confiscated."

Young Bolívar, riding about on his horse, saw these things along the roads. Clouds of carrion birds hung over them, thwarted by the iron cages. He didn't think about the happy and independent Aristiguietas any more. He was thinking about some of the things Simón Rodríguez had said to him.

Without his friend and teacher now, Bolívar went back to San Mateo and became a cadet in the regiment of the

Militia of Whites of Aragua, the regiment of which his father, as gran señor of the district, had been colonel. For two years, in the beautiful country around his favorite hacienda, he applied himself to the study of waging war, and then he was commissioned "alférez," sub-lieutenant. He returned to the capital city wearing his splendid uniform. The Aristiguieta girls were very glad to see him. One of them seems to have got the idea that he ought to marry her.

The two titles which had supposedly been conferred upon the Bolívar family somewhere along the line, and later discarded, were involved also in the estates of the Palacios because of the crossing of the blood lines. The men of Doña María Concepción's family felt that they had a just right to have them reinstated. So, on the death of Simón's mother, his uncle, Esteban Palacio, went to Madrid for the purpose of placing the claim before the Royal Tribunal.

Esteban was young, "guapo"—that is, of fine figure and handsome bearing—and, while he didn't get far with his case, he took at once to the brilliant life at the Spanish court. In Madrid there was one Don Manuel Mallo, a New Granadan by birth, a young adventurer, personable, "guapo" also, of questionable antecedents, whom Esteban had known in Caracas. Mallo had supplanted, for the time at least, the famous Prime Minister Manuel Godoy, Príncipe de la Paz, in the affections and bedchamber of Queen María Luisa. He wielded great influence at court, for María wore the royal pants. Carlos IV, weak and crowned only with the horns of cuckoldry in the eyes of his subjects, was a sorry king who spent his time tending the flower gardens at Aranjuez. This Mallo had a gift for intrigue and a surprising loyalty to his South American countrymen. He created a sort of vogue for them at court. Queen María spoke of them affectionately as her "Indios." Mallo secured posts in Madrid for a whole flock of South

Americans. He welcomed Esteban at once, and before long had him commissioned an officer in the Royal Guard. He took him in to share his house in Madrid.

Esteban, exuberant and anxious to secure some of the advantages of his position for his kinsmen, wrote his brother Carlos repeatedly, urging that their young nephews, Simón and Juan Vicente, be sent over.

When he was seventeen, Alférez Simón Bolívar prevailed upon his guardian to permit him to go to Spain. Perhaps the demands of that particular one of the happy and independent Aristiguietas for his hand had a lot to do with his urgency. He sailed from La Guaira on January 19, 1799, aboard the brigantine *San Ildefonso*.

Three months after he had gone, the city of Caracas was stirred by the news that José España had attempted to sneak in from Trinidad and had been captured with six companions in La Guaira. Again the citizens stood in silent crowds about the Plaza while bodies were quartered and blood filled the gutters. Again the little iron cages appeared on the roadsides and the vultures hovered. The people held their breath in passing to avoid the stink.

Chapter III

AN OATH IN ROME

✤

THE *San Ildefonso* was delayed for seven weeks in the
port of Vera Cruz and Bolívar made the two-hun-
dred-and-sixty-mile journey on horseback into the mountains to Mexico City, carrying letters to the archbishop
and the viceroy. He learned of unrest in that Spanish
colony too, and of the uprisings that had occurred there,
affairs similar to those in his own country—abortive little
attempts that had met the same quick defeat, that brought
down the same terrible punishments. He was beginning
to take considerable interest in these things now. He is
said to have spoken out rather indiscreetly to the viceroy
on political questions, but that is doubtful; not because
of timidity, for that quality was completely absent in his
makeup, but simply because he does not seem to have developed any strong, definite opinions or ambitions as yet.
Out of the natural resentment of his class, the effects of
his undisciplined early life and the teachings of Rodríguez, they were still fluxing and just beginning to take
shape.

The next landfall was Cuba; and Bolívar visited the
governor there and learned still more of Spain's treatment of her colonies—not from the governor, of course,
but from creoles with whom he talked. Talking was one
of his great addictions. He talked to everyone, always,
everywhere, throughout his life.

He landed in Bilbao and for the first time in two and a
half centuries a direct descendant of old Simón Bolívar
returned to set foot on Vizcayan soil. He took the dili-

gence to Madrid. He had never ridden in one before. In
the Andean cities, for all their luxuries and for all the
marvels of construction which the Spaniards had accomplished, there were no wheeled vehicles; the distances between them were too great and the country was too mountainous for road building.

The surroundings which Bolívar settled into in the
Spanish capital were very much to his liking, but hardly
conducive to the furthering of his scholastic education—
the principal object of his trip abroad. He went to live
with Mallo and his Uncle Esteban in their bachelor
household in the section of the city inhabited by the fashionable courtesans. He learned a lot of things very quickly
but not from books. His charm and wit and natural elegance won him a place immediately in the gay life of the
capital. His growing interest in the oppressed state of his
homeland suffered an interlude of neglect which was to
last for a long period.

There is a story told, of doubtful authority, of his first
meeting with the queen. One night, dining with Mallo
in their house, a visitor arrived, apparently a young Capuchín monk. However, Mallo tenderly drew aside the
monk's cowl and cloak to reveal the person of the Queen
of Spain. María Luisa is said to have been very attractive
still at fifty years of age. She looked with approval upon
the young colonial officer with the extraordinary, brilliant
eyes. When the time came for the queen to leave, Mallo
suggested that it would be safer if Bolívar, rather than
himself, conduct her back to the palace. So, their way
lighted by a servant's lantern, María Luisa wrapped in
her monk's cloak, and Bolívar muffled in his military
cape, stole silently through the dark, twisting streets of
Madrid. This event is even said to have been the beginning of an affair between the queen and Bolívar himself.
It is probably not true, but it might well have been, for
neither of them is known ever to have passed up anything
in the way of amorous opportunity.

It is probably true, however, that Bolívar did know the queen and her son Fernando, a youth of his own age; and he did attend the court functions. He was the intimate of Mallo, and he had family connections among the Spanish nobility.

Fortunately for Bolívar, his arrival in Spain coincided with the decline of Mallo's reign as queen's favorite, and of the vogue for colonials which he had created in the fickle court. The astute Godoy, worming his way back into the royal affections, was constantly working underground against Mallo. Bolívar's term as playboy was rather short-lived—only seven months in all. Had it continued, its influences might have had a lasting effect on his character and the course of history might have been changed. As it was, the bachelor establishment on Atocha Street had to be broken up and Bolívar went to live in the home of the Marqués de Ustáritz, a scholarly and kindly man, a kinsman of the influential Toro family of Caracas. There he settled at once into an entirely different life. With the good Marqués as his friend and counselor, he secured tutors and devoted himself to study with wholehearted energy. He learned to read and speak French fluently, to understand Italian and English. His reaction to his former life was so complete that he fell in love with the gentle María Teresa del Toro y Alaysa, niece of the Marqués, a type of girl who wouldn't have interested him in the least a few months before. Her father, Bernardo Toro, had brought her from their home in Bilbao to visit the Marqués while he sought to arrange some of his affairs with the government. As a former Caraqueño, he was suffering the effects of the colonials' fall from grace along with their chief mentor, Mallo. Bolívar, impetuous as always, sought permission to marry the girl at once. Don Bernardo objected on the grounds of Bolívar's youth. He was only nineteen then. Anyway, another incident arose which caused a delay in the romance. Bolívar had to flee the country for a while.

The Prince of the Peace, Godoy, was bending every effort to destroy Mallo completely. He had succeeded in arousing the queen's suspicions that Mallo was untrue to her. Bolívar, as Mallo's confidant, was suspected of being his go-between in these extra little affairs. One day, riding his horse along a city street, Bolívar was halted by civil guards who seized his reins and ordered him to dismount. He did so quickly, drawing his sword and preparing to fight. Friends who accompanied him interfered and that probably saved his life. The guards searched him, presumably for contraband diamonds—an excuse to cover their real object, the seizing of letters damning to Mallo. They found no such letters and Bolívar was released. Shortly after, he had word that his Uncle Esteban was in prison and that Mallo had disappeared. Incidentally, Mallo never appeared again in Madrid. Some say he was put to death, others that he was imprisoned and afterwards escaped. Bolívar, feeling that his own liberty was in danger, went to Bilbao and from there took the boat to Marseilles.

It was the spring of 1802 when Bolívar arrived in Paris. The Treaty of Amiens had just been signed and Bonaparte, as First Consul, was at the height of his glory. The city was in the midst of wild enthusiasm and Bolívar was carried away by it and by admiration for his great hero, Bonaparte. He mixed with the crowds and listened to the glowing words pronounced in honor of the savior of the French Republic. Within a few weeks he received word from Spain that his Uncle Esteban had been released from prison, that the way was clear for his own return. He hurried back to Bilbao and continued his suit for the hand of María Teresa del Toro.

It is interesting to note that here for the first time he met Fanny Trobriand du Villars. She was a distant cousin of his and, of all people, an Aristiguieta—a relative of his old playmates of Caracas, having some of their happy and independent traits. Bolívar wasn't interested in her just then, for he was in love; but later she came to figure in one phase of his career. She was twenty-six then, and married to an elderly French officer.

Bolívar and María Teresa del Toro were married in Madrid at the end of May, 1802, and they went to La Coruña the same day and sailed for La Guaira on the *San Ildefonso,* the vessel Bolívar had come over on.

They landed at the Venezuelan port in July and his gentle, Spanish-born wife got her first rude shock. Riding her horse along the rocky, mountainous road to the capital, she saw the whitened skull of José España in its iron cage. Bolívar himself didn't pay much attention. He was still in the midst of that interruption to the course of his development which had begun with the distractions of the Spanish court and continued with his courtship and marriage.

The well-defined strain of exhibitionism which characterized Simón Bolívar throughout his whole life was, in his youth, revealed in a crude sort of theatricalism, an often foolish self-dramatization. Later on, as we shall see, he learned to control his flair, to bend it to his purposes and to produce carefully planned and magnificent effects which were masterpieces of showmanship. He learned the value of restraint, the necessity for timing. And that quality, which he possessed perhaps more than any other figure in history, certainly more than any other warrior, played an important part in his achievements. Time and again it saved his aims and his career from total failure. Always, in his darkest moments, he was able to produce something unexpected, impossible, dramatic, which would re-establish his prestige, revive enthusiasm among his followers and faith in him among foreign governments.

In considering this, his first and only romance to end in marriage, we must regard it in the light of logic rather than on the strength of his own dramatic version given later on.

Bolívar's short and tragic love affair with Teresa del Toro could not possibly have had the tremendous effect upon his career which he attributes to it. His own youth, his reaction to the licentiousness and over-sophistication of the Spanish court, and perhaps a natural response to homely virtues amid strange surroundings can well account for his infatuation—but, in logic, such a puppy-love affair cannot be credited with exerting any great influence upon a man of his stature. It was a case of jenny wren married to an eagle. Nowhere, in any description of Bolívar's young bride, is she spoken of as anything but "sweet" and "gentle." Those qualities alone would never have long satisfied the Liberator. They were in those days, perhaps, valued very highly; but Bolívar had known strong-willed and intelligent women such as his sister María Antonia and the Queen of Spain. Later he was to know Fanny Villars and many more, and even women who went into battle with him. None of them ever really influenced him. Teresa del Toro certainly didn't. It suited his purpose and satisfied his urge for self-dramatization to make it appear so, later.

In Caracas there was a month of fiesta in honor of young Bolívar and his bride. She was the niece of the Marqués del Toro, an amiable, luxury-loving man, one of the first citizens of the colony. Bolívar, with Hipólita and Matea, took Teresa to the hacienda at San Mateo and there he, at least, enjoyed a brief period of idyllic happiness among the beautiful hills and valleys he loved so much. We can only suppose that Teresa must have been a little frightened in what to her would seem a tropical wilderness. Within five months she was stricken with a malignant fever. Bolívar, distraught, carried her in all haste back to the capital. A litter was made of a hammock, Teresa was placed upon it and, borne by slaves, her husband riding at her side, the fifty-mile journey was made over the rough mountain trails. The sad little caravan traveled without halt and at night the path was lighted by flaring torches. In Caracas nothing could be done for the sweet and gentle Teresa. She died on January 22, 1803, eight months after her marriage.

Bolívar said later that in his grief he swore never to marry again. Whether he did or not, there were certainly occasions when he found that oath very convenient as an excuse for avoiding matrimony with other women. He claimed also that the death of his wife was the turning point in his career, that it was for relief from his great loss that his mind turned to the problems of his country, that from it was born his determination to dedicate his life to the cause of liberation. His immediate actions do not bear this out. It was some time yet before he actually showed any such determination.

He said dramatically, "I looked upon my wife as an emanation of the Divine Being who gave her life. Heaven believed that she belonged there and tore her from me because she was not created for this earth."

The young widower stayed in Caracas only long enough to place his affairs in the hands of his older brother Juan. Then he returned to Spain. The life of dissipation into which he plunged there and later in France can be attributed to a desire to escape from his sorrow, as he claimed; but there was little sign of any dedication to noble purpose evident in it.

His meeting with Bernardo del Toro, Teresa's father, in Bilbao was, as he describes it, typically dramatic. They "fell into each other's arms and mingled their tears." Bolívar said of it, "Never shall I forget that scene of delicious torment, for the pain of love is delicious." Very touching indeed. The beautiful gesture of an exhibitionistic, bereaved young husband, wearing his bleeding heart on his sleeve. He wore that bleeding heart on his sleeve pretty publicly for a long time in the cities of Europe.

In Madrid in 1803 there was quite a group of those wealthy, frustrated young South American aristocrats.

Definitely out of favor at court now, jobless, their sense
of inferiority was intensified, their resentment against
Spain at the boiling point. Secretly, they had definitely
declared among themselves for the cause of complete independence from the motherland for their countries.
There was the New Granadan, Francisco Zea, old companion of Nariño, the translator of *The Rights of Man*
who had been sent to prison in Cádiz. There was the
Quiteño, Carlos Montúfar, the Caraqueños, Mariano
Montilla and José Félix Ribas, a close kinsman of Simón
Bolívar. Ribas, perhaps the most colorful of all, was so
enthusiastic for the cause of liberty that he always wore
the little red cap of the French Revolution at their secret
meetings.

Bolívar knew and associated with all these men, attended their meetings, listened to their words and shared
their sentiments; but there is no evidence that he took
any active part in their plans or enjoyed any prestige
among them. Montilla was definitely suspicious of him
for many years after, and later, when this same group
formed an organization in Caracas and Bolívar was proposed as leader by his brother Juan Vicente, he was voted
down unanimously. There is no doubt that Bolívar was
as yet far from ready to devote his life to independence
for his country.

The Spanish Government became intolerant of the
mere presence of these colonials and that same year a
royal edict ordered all South Americans out of Madrid.
The group of plotters dispersed and Bolívar went to Bilbao and thence once more to Paris. This time Fanny Villars, that cousin of his and of the captivating Aristiguieta
girls, was ready to welcome him. That was in January,
1804.

Nearly all the data there is regarding Bolívar's relations
with Fanny and for the period during which they lasted
is found in letters and papers which are claimed to have
been discovered much later in the family records of a

descendant of Fanny's. Many historians deny their authenticity and certainly it is open to doubt. However, nearly all are agreed that Bolívar was on intimate terms with the lady for some time, and there are some points in his own statements elsewhere that jibe with information contained in these dubious records.

Bolívar was then approaching twenty-one. Of only medium height, his slender, wiry figure, good proportions and extraordinary presence gave an impression of greater stature. Above his high, broad forehead the hair rose in curls, and down beside the cheeks it grew in long side-whiskers, their blackness making the skin appear chalky-white by contrast, as it often is with Spaniards of his type. His face was long and thin, the cheeks rather sunken, the nose long, straight—classic Castillian. The eyes, deep-set, dark and brilliant, impressed at once all who ever saw him. His teeth were white and even, his mouth large, mobile, beautiful when smiling or in repose, but growing ugly with anger when the lower lip protruded to hide the teeth. In his dress he was always meticulous, elegant. At that time he usually wore dark green, and his tunic had the high Napoleonic collar heavily embroidered in gold.

Fanny was pretty, round and bosomy and seven years older than Bolívar. Her elderly husband was away at Bologne building armaments for Bonaparte.

Just how important in the high life of the French capital was the salon which Fanny Villars conducted is a matter of conjecture. Some claim that it was one of the most brilliant in the city and that Bolívar met in her drawing-room and came to know intimately practically everyone of any importance in France, among them Madame Récamier, Madame de Staël, Talleyrand, the great French actor François Talma, the scientist von Humboldt, Marshals Ney and Oudinot, General Duroc and the young Beauharnais, son of Josephine. Beauharnais is said to have been Bolívar's rival for Fanny's affections, and a story is told that Bonaparte's stepson, in Bolívar's presence, once asked Fanny what animal the young Venezuelan reminded her of. When Beauharnais said it was a sparrow, Bolívar mistook the French word "moineau" for the Spanish word "mono," monkey, and, insulted, drew his sword. Peace was restored by Fanny's explanation and the Frenchman's apologies.

It is told, too, that Bolívar asked Baron von Humboldt, who had just returned from his famous expedition to South America, if he thought that the country was ready for independence. Humboldt replied that it was; that all that was needed was a great leader, and that the country would produce that leader.

Bolívar wore his bleeding heart to a shred in his affair with Cousin Fanny. She, consoling him on her ample bosom, wept with him over his sorrow, took to calling herself his "Teresa." It was a rôle perfectly suited to a neglected wife; and Bolívar was quite a feather in her cap. He was a brilliant and fiery talker, a fine dancer. She sighed with delight over his acquisition. When his funds were held up from Caracas and he incurred a large gambling debt, Fanny paid it gladly.

On December 2, 1804, Napoleon crowned himself emperor and Bolívar is said to have witnessed the ceremony in the Cathedral of Nôtre Dame. This act of his hero may have given Bolívar a jolt. He claimed so afterward. "His very glory appeared to me as the fulmination of hell, as the flames of the volcano which covered the imprisoned world." But it impressed him, too. "That magnificent act filled me with enthusiasm," he said, adding, "but less for its pomp than for the sentiments of love which an immense populace expressed for its hero. . . . It seemed to me, for the one who received the ovation, the final summit of human aspiration, the supreme desire and the supreme ambition of man. The crown which Napoleon placed upon his head was a thing of no importance, a relic of the Dark Ages; what was great to me was the universal acclamation and the interest which the person of Napoleon inspired. I confess this made me think of my unhappy country and the glory which he would win who should liberate it. . . ." Glory. He was beginning to think of it then, he claims. Not quite yet, if we judge by his actions; but soon now.

Bolívar continued to go the pace in Paris. He became a figure in the fashionable world; and it is said a type of hat he affected was called the chapeau Bolívar and that a box at the opera was named chambre de Bolívar. According to one of the doubtful letters of the Villars collection, his health began to fail under the strain and he located his old teacher Rodríguez working with a scientist in Vienna and went to him. Rodríguez is supposed to have revealed to Bolívar his sudden acquisition of 4,000,-000 francs on his twenty-first birthday and to have got a promise from him to devote this wealth and the rest of his life to that cause of which we have spoken so much. If there is any truth in it, Bolívar must have decided upon another little fling first, for, by the same letter, we find him in London spending 150,000 francs in three months. He is supposed to have been a great success in London, frequenting the clubs, showing his great skill at fencing with either hand, sitting for his portrait to the famous Gill. Wherever he went—Lisbon, Madrid, Paris, Vienna—"he lived like a prince."

However it came about, this phase of Bolívar's life did end at last, and quite suddenly. His health was failing and he was growing bored. Where he found Rodríguez isn't certain but find him he did. Rodríguez, after his expulsion from Venezuela, had gone to Kingston, Jamaica, learned English, and moved on to Baltimore, where he made a living as a typesetter for three years. Then he had gone to Europe and wandered about until Bolívar found him and brought him to Paris.

This marks the beginning of Bolívar's real development into a full-fledged working patriot. It also marks the end

of that long interlude which began with his first trip to
Spain. Rodríguez was the one who had set his course in
the beginning and it was he who now directed it when
progress was resumed.

The old influence of Rodríguez had its effect, and at
once a new life began for Bolívar. He left his luxurious
quarters in an hotel and went to live with his old teacher
in a modest house. Rodríguez, first off, drummed into
him that he must "understand that there are other things
in the life of man besides love." Then he produced his
beloved books—Rousseau, Montesquieu, Hobbes, Helvetius, Holbach, Hume and Spinoza. Bolívar settled down
to study in earnest. His fine mind opened, absorbing
knowledge in great draughts, rapidly, like a thirsty animal
at a cool spring.

An interesting feature of this new phase of Bolívar's
was Fanny's reaction to it. She fell in with it heartily,
made herself a part of it. She saw herself in a new rôle
now, one more pleasing even than the old—the rôle of
the lovely woman inspiring and encouraging a brilliant
young mind to great thoughts, to dreams of great deeds.
She too forsook her old way of life. She encouraged Bolívar in his studies, gushed over him, took part in the long,
ardent discussions of social and political problems. Soon
she was visualizing for Bolívar, under her patronage, "a
glory even greater than the glory of Napoleon himself."
Bolívar enjoyed this, undoubtedly, but, always remark-
ably cool-headed and clear-sighted in his relations with
Fanny, he wasn't taken in by it. There is a faintly satirical
note always evident in his letters to her, even in their
most glowing passages.

Early in the year 1805 Bolívar and his master set out
on a walking tour of southern Europe. Walking was
Rodríguez's favorite mode of travel, his recipe for the
curing of all physical and mental ills. So the old "sabio,"
his head bare and his hair wild in the wind, his ragged
pockets stuffed with books and his aristocratic young pro-

tégé beside him, strolled down the valley of the Saône to Lyons, crossed to Chambery, crossed the Alps into Italy by the pass at Mt. Cenis. About the same time Napoleon set out from Paris on his triumphal journey to crown himself King of Italy. His route followed that of Bolívar and Rodríguez, and they found their path strewn with flowers in honor of the little Corsican. At Turin Napoleon caught up with them and they followed to Alessandria where they witnessed a review of the army on the battlefield of Marengo. Bolívar reports, "What a brilliant and numerous staff Napoleon had and how simple were his own clothes! All those around him were in uniforms covered with gold and rich embroidery while he wore only epaulets, a hat without trimmings, a coat without ornament. That pleased me." It impressed him, too, and he remembered it; for he used the same little gesture of simplicity himself to good advantage years later.

For three months the two men wandered over Italy, visiting the cities, sitting by the roadside, reading and talking—always talking. Finally they arrived at Rome.

There is a story told that Bolívar had an audience with the Pope, that he refused to kiss the Pope's ring, which was worn on his sandal. The Pope, smiling, is said to have removed the ring, handed it to Bolívar to be kissed, saying, "Let the Indian youth do as he pleases." Outside, Bolívar remarked, "The Pope can have little respect for the symbol of Christianity if he wears it on his sandal." The story is obviously untrue, since anyone granted an audience with the Pope would have been instructed in the required ritual; but it is a gesture that would be typical of the arrogant, foolish young show-off of that time.

One day the two foot-travelers climbed the low hill of Monte Sacro, overlooking a branch of the Tiber. It was there that Bolívar uttered his famous oath. He lay on the ground for a long time while Rodríguez delivered a particularly stirring dissertation on the past glories of the city that lay below them, of the noble experiments in republican government which had been tried there. Bolívar, carried away, rose to his knees and, "his eyes moist, his breast palpitating, his face flushed with a feverish animation," he spoke.

His words, as later reported, were, "I swear by the God of my forefathers, I swear by my forefathers, I swear by my native land, that I shall never allow my hands to be idle nor my soul to rest until I have broken the shackles which bind us to Spain!" Fernando González suggests that his words really were, "Rodríguez, I swear that I'll free America from the Spaniards and not leave one of the *carajos* there!" We should like to believe that González is right. Perhaps he is, for history has a way of going pompous on us.

It is a difficult task for a historian to capture the real essence of the personality of his characters, for that essence is found only in their everyday speech, their simple, workaday utterances. But what the historian has to go on is only the written word, embellished—or sometimes castrated—by each repetition.

A marked psychic change, perhaps a chemical change, seems to occur in a man the moment he takes up his pen or mounts a rostrum. He clothes himself in a new personality and his words fall strangely on the ears of those who know him. This is true today among educated people; but it becomes particularly so the farther back into time you go, when learning was a rarer thing and the ability to write or to speak in public was looked upon with respect. That respect automatically creates responsibility and the words of the writer or speaker become heavy with it. That is why, perhaps, the writing of Latin Americans even today is generally over-ornate. It abounds in all the artificialities of rhetoric—the classic allusion, the poetic metaphor and simile. Most of it would put an old-time Southern senator to shame.

The recorded words of Bolívar, fine and clear as they often are, considering his time, race and exalted position, are certainly not to be taken as a clue to his everyday speech, as holding any of the real essence of his personality. They are words spoken to a world audience. Actually, as a man of action, a compañero of soldiers in the field, he was probably terse, colloquial, profane; and we know from evidence that he was humorous.

Bolívar wrote prodigiously. He sometimes dictated to three secretaries at a time and when he died there were ten trunks full of documents among his effects. These became scattered and the part of their contents which was later located and published by Daniel O'Leary filled thirty-two large volumes. But none of this great output can be said to reflect much of his real personality. Bolívar himself seemed to have felt something of that, for he asked, before he died, that all his papers be burned. He gave as his reasons that much of his writing had been to create an effect, for expediency, to take care of certain circumstances. Some of it, he implied, was even deliberate untruth.

Simón Bolívar undoubtedly vowed on Monte Sacro to liberate his native land from Spain, whatever his words actually were. There is definite purpose in all his actions from now on. He left Rodríguez, returned to Paris almost immediately. There he declared to Fanny his intention of sailing for Venezuela and devoting his life to the glorious cause.

It was a wild, presumptuous resolve, surely. He was twenty-three years old, enjoyed no particular prestige in the land he proposed to liberate, had never accomplished anything which should give him reason to believe that he possessed qualities beyond those of other men. But those facts seemed never to have entered his head. He was born with a vast sense of confidence in himself and of self-importance. He had a capacity for great dreams; and dreams, with him, always demanded immediate efforts toward realization.

Fanny was taken considerably aback. She hadn't

counted on anything of the sort. Her idea of a great hero was one who would stay nicely at home and take it all out in words, in long hours of thrilling talk. Apparently she had never really recognized the quality of the lion she thought she had tamed. She wept and pleaded with Bolívar to give up his purpose, to remain with her; but he went calmly about his preparations. Probably he didn't even hear her. He took a boat from Hamburg in September, 1806. In a last letter to Fanny he said, "Yours shall be the last palpitations of my life, the last vision of my consciousness." It was only to appease her, apparently, for he never bothered to write to her again for many years.

The boat he sailed on took him to Boston. After visiting New York, Philadelphia, Baltimore and Washington, where he had an opportunity to study at first hand the workings of a true, going democracy, he took a ship from Charleston, S. C., and landed in La Guaira in December.

Chapter IV

THE POWDER KEG EXPLODES

✤

WHILE Bolívar was walking about Italy and great
dreams were forming in his mind out of the ideas
implanted by his master, another man was already in action, inspired by the same dreams. In history he is known
as the Precursor of the Liberator. In many ways he was
better fitted to play the leading part than Bolívar himself;
but things worked out differently.

Francisco de Miranda was Spanish by blood, a Venezuelan by birth, a soldier and world-traveler by profession, apostle of human liberty by religion. From a world-
wide view he was at that time his country's most illustrious citizen, although his name was scarcely known
within it. He had been away many years and his beginnings in the colony were obscure. He was a general in the
Grand Army of France and his name was inscribed on the
Arc de l'Etoile. Napoleon had called him a visionary luna-
tic but with a spark of intelligence seldom found in the
type.

Miranda's first military experience was gained in the
army of Spain. He served in Morocco and then in Florida
and Louisiana under General Galvez and in Cuba under
Cagigal. When the American Revolution broke out he
made his first efforts in the interest of human liberty and
enlisted in a Spanish contingent under Rochambeau. In
the struggle of the North American colonies against England he had no opportunities to attain any great distinc-
tion; but he met Lafayette and Kosciuszko and established
for himself among that clique of international champions

35

of liberty a position which gave him prestige in Europe thereafter. After the victory in North America he busied himself with intrigue against Spain in Cuba, had to flee, and established himself in London. There, with two Jesuits, he evolved an elaborate scheme for the establishment in South America and Mexico of a vast Indian empire, democratic in nature, subject to the paternal guidance of hereditary "Incas." When President Adams was informed of the details of the scheme, he is said to have remarked that he didn't know whether to laugh or cry. Miranda pled with the British government for armed aid; but he got nowhere at all, of course. He left London and spent several years roaming about Europe, explaining his great plans to anyone who would listen. He went to Russia, became a friend of Potemkin and a short-time lover of Empress Catherine. In Prussia he mixed with the officers at Potsdam and studied the methods of the magnificent army built up by Frederick the Great. With the outbreak of the revolution in France he hurried there and offered his services; won rapid promotion and, in 1793, found himself a general at the siege of Maastrich. He was the hero of the retreat from Les Islettes and was the first to enter Antwerp. Under Dumouriez he was in command of the French left at Neerwinden. As a result of the disaster there, brought about by the treason of Dumouriez, he was court-martialed and imprisoned for eighteen months in La Force. He made a famous defense and, at the death of Robespierre, he was released and exonerated. After his return to England he resumed his efforts to interest the British government in his project, was rebuffed again and sailed for the United States.

In America, Miranda found Jefferson and Madison no more interested than the English had been. However, he did find a group of New York merchants who, in the hope of profit and trade benefits in the event of success, agreed to finance an armed expedition to South America. So the first movement from outside to liberate the Spanish colonies was organized in New York and most of its personnel were North Americans.

A merchant named Samuel Ogden recruited some two hundred young adventurers to man the filibuster. They were signed on under false pretenses and few of them had any idea of the real nature of the undertaking they were embarking upon. The 200-ton armed brig *Leander* was fitted out and, with two small vessels, the *Bacchus* and the *Bee,* as transports, the expedition sailed for Venezuela early in 1806—about the time that Simón Bolívar was in Italy, swearing to drive all the Spanish *carajos* from his native land. He didn't know that others were already setting out under arms to attempt the same thing.

The Spanish Minister in Washington had informed his government of the little armada's sailing, and when it arrived off Ocumare on the coast of Venezuela in March, several warships of Spain's Caribbean fleet were there to greet it. The *Bacchus* and the *Bee,* slow, and carrying only troops and having little armament, were taken at once. The *Leander,* with Miranda aboard, got away by jettisoning the ordnance.

Of the sixty-odd Americans who were taken prisoner, ten were immediately hanged, their heads severed and their bodies quartered in the accepted manner. The rest rotted away in the dungeons of Cartagena. They found out at last what they had signed on for. In Puerto Cabello on the Venezuelan coast a monument stands today in honor of those misguided and gallant young North Americans.

Miranda took the *Leander* to Trinidad, where the British authorities closed their eyes while he raised another force. A few months later he sailed again for the mainland. This time he succeeded in landing at La Vela and capturing the near-by town of Coro.

Miranda put his foot on his native land for the first time in more than thirty years—and he suffered a rude awakening. He had expected to be hailed as a hero, to be joined by all his countrymen in a great spontaneous uprising. Instead, the Corianos, always ardently pro-Spanish, rebuffed him, harried his little band with armed attacks. They had never even heard of this big, strange general who forced his way into their community and preached revolution with a foreign accent. When word of his presence reached the capital, the creole committee hastened to declare that he came with no authority, that no one had called him; and a price of 30,000 pesos was put on his head. That was the final blow for Miranda. He got aboard his vessel and sailed away to Trinidad. There he disbanded his troops and returned to England.

When Bolívar arrived in Caracas a few months later he found everyone talking about this man Miranda. All the young creole aristocrats were agog about the almost unknown Venezuelan who had suddenly appeared from out of nowhere and championed the cause of liberty. They probed into his history and revealed all the facts of his career and were impressed by his extraordinary military record and his prestige abroad. Bolívar particularly was impressed. This Francisco Miranda, ex-general of France, came to occupy a prominent place in his thoughts.

The story of Simón Bolívar during the next few years is so involved with the events occurring in the mother-land and their reverberations in the captain-generalcy of Venezuela that it is necessary to review them at least summarily.

During most of that period, superficially he was occupied with his private affairs in Venezuela. He was of age now and he relieved his brother of his share in the management of the estates. He made long journeys into the mountains and llanos to his hatos and haciendas, attended to legal matters in the courts, concerned himself with financial affairs and the marketing of crops. In these things he had always the help and counsel of María Antonia. She was very capable in money matters. She was even avaricious, some say—which Bolívar certainly never was in the least. There was a complete understanding between these two, even in the matter of their love affairs; and María Antonia was as notorious as Bolívar himself in that regard. In fact, in the sexual sense, there was little of moral virtue in any of the Bolívars. Even quiet, earnest Juan Vicente was living with a woman named Tinoco and had four illegitimate children.

Bolívar devoted himself as well to his military duties with the militia, and in 1810 he attained the grade of colonel.

All these activities were, as we have said, superficial. Secretly, his great purpose was always uppermost in his mind and he was working constantly in its interest. Nearly all the members of that group of young radicals who used to meet in Madrid were back home now and they were joined by their friends who held similar views. José Félix Ribas was there with his little red cap. There were also José's brothers, Juan José and Luis, Mariano and Tomás Montilla, the Salías, Pelgróns, Sojos, Ibarras, Palacios, Ustáritz, Pontes, Briceños, Vicente Tejera, Nicolás Anzola, Germán Roscio—all of them young aristocrats, some of them lawyers, some of them veterans of the Spanish wars with Portugal, some of them even of Spanish birth. They met nightly under the stars in the patios of their homes and the thick walls deadened their fiery, seditious words to the spying ears on the streets. Simón and Juan Vicente Bolívar were with this group heart and soul. At first, however, there wasn't much any of them could do beyond talk and engage in discreet proselytizing.

It was Napoleon Bonaparte who unwittingly set off the Spanish powder keg in South America. Early in 1808, under the pretext of invading Portugal, Murat led the French army into Madrid. There "incidents" were created which served as an excuse to seize the supreme power in Spain. At Bayonne, on June 23, a treaty was signed by which Carlos IV agreed to abdicate and Fernando, the crown prince, renounced his right of succession. In May, Napoleon proclaimed his brother Joseph King of Spain. There was a violent reaction to this among the Spanish people. A bloody uprising occurred in Madrid which resulted in the establishment of a Junta at Aranjuez, recognizing Fernando VII as king. It was an anomalous situation—the land in possession of foreign troops, the king and crown prince, bewildered, having forsworn their sovereignty, an outlaw government proclaiming allegiance to the legitimate successor to the throne. Amid the confusion that ensued, the Junta was forced to flee to Seville, then to Cádiz and then to the island of Leon; and at one time there were two different Juntas, each claiming authority over the loyal subjects of Fernando VII.

The news of the great political changes in Spain arrived in South America very slowly and at long intervals; and during those months the colonies were seething with excitement. In Caracas the clear mountain air was alive with rumors of every sort. With every rumor there was a wave of fear, hope, despair or elation, depending mostly upon the class to which one belonged.

Word of the Spanish king's abdication first reached Caracas in July when two deputies arrived on a French vessel and proclaimed the dominion of France over the colony. This was too much even for the conservative patriots. There was a spontaneous demonstration of all classes and the French deputies had to flee for their lives.

Our group of young radicals seized upon the situation with great glee. This was exactly the sort of thing they were waiting for. They threw themselves into it, egged the people on, exhorted them with their long pent-up oratory at every street corner. But they were very careful just then to confine their words to the current issue. The crowds marched the streets around the central plaza with torchlights by night, with banners by day; and the words they shouted were not "Liberty!" but "Long live Fernando VII! Death to the French!"

At this time there was no organized movement in favor of complete independence in the colony at all. Only the members of Bolívar's small group agitated for that—and they were pretty quiet about it. They had no authority whatever, no official status. The Ayuntamiento, or City Council, represented the people; and this body, made up of older aristocrats, the fathers and kinsmen, in some cases, of the young radicals, had never dared cast a glance in the direction of liberty. Only two years before, they had denounced Miranda and put a price on his head. They were appointed by the Spanish authorities and had scarcely any power beyond the right of petition to the captain-general.

Now, however, emboldened by the arrival of British gunboats under Admiral Cochrane, who encouraged resistance to France, and by the news that Juntas similar to that in Spain were being established in other colonies, the Council became considerably more self-assertive. They were urged on by the radical group and by the knowledge, too, that the captain-general, Don Juan de Casas, was a bit unsure of his authority because of the confusion existing in Spain. Casas, who had originally proposed the establishment of a Junta recognizing Fernando VII, began to see where things were heading and attempted to forestall the action he had initiated. But it was too late. The Council demanded the formation of a Junta and, sure enough, along with the proposal was a complete renunciation of the authority of any captain-general sent out by the Regency in Spain. What they proposed was a completely autonomous state under the crown of Spain. Not independence at all, but government of the colony by colonials. The Council had advanced a long way under the spur of the group in which Bolívar was now a leading spirit.

Juan de Casas answered the demand of the Council by ordering the arrest of all the members and sentencing them to banishment to their haciendas, away from the city. However, when the Central Junta in Spain had word of this, strangely, it declared that the Council was within its rights, removed Casas from office and named Don Vicente Emparán to replace him.

In all this the little group of radicals were playing their game, joining forces with the more conservative Council, seeing in this an opportunity for "boring from within," for agitating toward their real purpose of complete independence. They shouted as vehemently as the rest of them, "Viva Fernando VII, Rey!"

About this time the Regency in Spain issued a strange proclamation to the Indian colonies—possibly to win their help in the war against France, for there was no hint of living up to it later. Anyway, it served to bolster the drive for independence and to weaken the position of the Spanish representatives. The decree read, "From this moment, Spanish Americans, you are elevated to the dignity of free men. You are not now, as you were before, burdened under a yoke much more unbearable because of the great distance from the center of power, looked upon with indifference, harassed by greed, destroyed by ignorance. . . . Your destinies now do not depend upon Ministers nor Viceroys nor Governors; you are in your own hands."

When Don Vicente Emparán arrived in May, 1809, he found himself in a difficult spot. The people were clamoring for a Junta and for an autonomous state; and he had no idea how far he could let them go or to what extent his actions would be backed by the Central Junta. As Inspector General of the Army he brought with him Don Fernando del Toro, brother of the Marqués del Toro and uncle of Simón Bolívar's wife, Teresa. Don Fernando had been a companion of Bolívar in Madrid and he had also been a sympathetic friend to all that little group of malcontents which had gathered there. Now, because of his powerful position, he was a valuable recruit to the ranks of the radicals in Caracas.

In March, 1810, some of the more impatient of the radicals proclaimed publicly for the autonomy of the colony. Emparán ordered their arrest and, following the example of Casas, sentenced them to banishment from the city. Among them were the Bolívars. The sentence was no more severe, perhaps, because of Bolívar's connections with the Marqués del Toro and Don Fernando.

On the morning of Holy Thursday, April 19, 1810, the Council sent a deputy to the captain-general requesting his presence at an extraordinary session. Emparán acquiesced, went to the assembly hall, made a short, conciliatory address, excused himself and went on his way to Mass. On the cathedral steps Francisco Salías took the captain-general by the arm, threatened him with a dagger and led him back to the assembly hall. Emparán's guard refused him assistance, refused even to salute him.

Inside the hall the captain-general was confronted by a silent, determined group, among them some of the most outspoken advocates of independence. José Félix Ribas was there in his red cap. With him were his brother, a priest, Francisco Ribas, another priest, José Cortés de Madariaga, Germán Roscio and Félix Sosa. Roscio and Sosa, lawyers, began the discussion with a formal demand for the establishment of a Junta, recognizing the sovereignty of Spain but composed of colonials in full control of their own affairs. The priest, Cortés Madariaga, interrupted. He accused Emparán of perfidy, declared that they could have no confidence in him, that he would dissolve the Junta on any pretext. He demanded Emparán's immediate resignation in favor of the people. A great crowd had collected outside the hall. Emparán went to a balcony and asked the people if they were content with his government. Madariaga, behind him, made signs with his hands and the people, following their cue, took up the cry, "No! No!"

Emparán looked down upon the crowd and waited for silence. "Then," he said, "I do not wish to govern."

The powder keg went off with a roar. The South American Revolution was on.

Two days later Emparán and other representatives of Spain were conducted to La Guaira and put aboard a vessel. The colony of Venezuela was left to stand on its own feet—and to face fifteen years of war as ruthless as the world has ever seen.

Chapter V

THE PRECURSOR

✤

IN July, 1810, Lord Wellesley, the British Secretary for
Foreign Affairs, received the emissaries of the Junta of
Caracas in Apsley House, London. The head of the commission was Colonel Simón Bolívar and his two aides
were Don Luis López Méndez and Don Andrés Bello.
Bello was the famous Venezuelan poet who had been one
of Bolívar's tutors years before.

Wellesley carefully read the credentials and the instructions of the emissaries, and looked at the young man who
stood before him. Bolívar, in full regimentals and high
Wellington boots, was an impressive figure.

When the formalities of introduction were over, Bolívar
spoke. His dark eyes flashing in that odd, characteristic
way, his small hands moving in slight, graceful gestures,
speaking in French, the words flowed from his lips easily
—forceful and eloquent. He pleaded that the government
of His Majesty recognize the Junta which he represented
as the legitimate government of a sovereign people free
of obligation to any foreign power; that, as an independent nation, Venezuela be granted the privileges of diplomatic relations and of commerce; that the British government lend military aid to lift the blockade which Spain
had placed upon the coast and to protect the existence of
the new nation against the power which now threatened
it.

Wellesley, surprised, heard him through. Then he said,
"But your instructions say nothing of an independent

nation. They state clearly that the Junta recognizes Fernando VII as its sovereign."

If Bolívar was a bit taken aback he didn't show it. He went on to say yes, officially, the Junta recognized Fernando VII; but, he argued, complete independence was inevitable, only a matter of a short time. The attitude of the Regency in refusing to accept the good offices of the Junta, its resort to arms in blockading the Venezuelan coast and the determination of the Junta to stand upon its intentions, all indicated war—and war meant the necessity for independence. It would be best for all to accept the inevitable now, at once. It would save time and lives.

Wellesley made no comment. He bowed and said that the reply of His Majesty's government would be forwarded to the commissioners later.

Outside, Bolívar is said to have admitted to Méndez and Bello that he had never bothered to read his instructions. It is probably not true but it might have been, then. Bolívar still had a lot to learn. There was only one purpose burning inside him and he had no patience with any formalities standing in his way.

Wellesley sent his reply to the commissioners in a few days. Britain, cagey as always, anxious not to lose the cooperation of Spain against their common enemy, France, agreed to consider the just complaints and aspirations of Venezuela. She ignored the question of independence and dealt with the colony as being still loyal and subservient to Fernando VII; as, indeed, it was. She offered, graciously, to lend all military aid should the colony be invaded by the forces of France.

The Junta in Venezuela had not found the going easy. The provinces of Coro and Maracaibo regarded it with open hostility and continued to harbor and obey the representatives of Spain. A very generous and conciliatory letter had been sent off to the Regency in Cádiz immediately after the deportation of Emparán. The Junta de-

clared its loyalty to Fernando and offered to send aid in
the war against the French invaders. The Regency, acting
strangely again, replied by declaring the Venezuelans
rebels and traitors, and instituting a strict blockade of the
coast.

The Junta saw a fight on its hands. It dispatched envoys to foreign lands to get aid if possible and to buy
armaments. Bolívar was sent to London, perhaps only
because he agreed to pay his own way, for by now the
Junta was beginning to be a little worried by his impetuosity. His brother Juan Vicente was sent to the United
States, carrying with him sixty thousand pesos for the purchase of arms. Others were sent to the British West Indies
and to the other colonies of Spain in South America.
Following the lead of Caracas, Juntas were established
within a few months in Buenos Aires, Santa Fé de Bogotá
and Santiago de Chile.

After his fiasco on the coast of Coro in 1806, old General Miranda, discouraged but still not disillusioned, returned to London and established himself in a house on
Grafton Street. There he went on with his old plotting,
dreamed his old dreams of a great South American republic. He never tired in his efforts to interest influential
men in the project. He became a familiar figure about the
Foreign Office and the ministries in London.

Simón Bolívar had never forgotten Miranda. During
the four years since the expedition from New York, he
had been thinking about that distinguished old warrior
with the love of liberty deep in his soul. Accordingly, as
soon as he reached London on his mission—though he had
been warned against that very thing by the apprehensive
Junta—he hurried to Grafton Street and introduced himself to Miranda. That was the beginning of a relationship
which had great consequences for both. It set one upon
the path of glory and the other upon the way of tragic

disgrace. It was the first meeting of the Precursor and the Liberator.

After the failure of his commission to get any tangible declaration from the British government, Bolívar stayed on in London to confer further with Miranda. The general, nearing sixty now and a bit worn down by his many disappointments, gained stimulation and renewed energy from the enthusiasm of his young compatriot. Together they plotted and argued. They composed long letters addressed to the people of England and published them in the *Morning Chronicle* and the *Edinburgh Review*. In them they set forth the problems, needs and aims of their country.

There were two principal convictions which Bolívar gained from this association with Miranda. The first was that the aid and sympathy of at least one great foreign power was absolutely necessary to the establishment of a permanent republic in the homeland. He never abandoned this conviction, and he worked always to gain that sympathy and aid. The second became an essential part of his political philosophy—which was singularly consistent throughout his whole career. It was an idea derived from Miranda's old scheme for an empire governed by "Incas" and born of the conviction that South America, because of the ignorance of its people and of their racial weaknesses, was not ready for pure democracy.[1] That idea was the necessity for an hereditary senate—a distinct class of people who should be raised and educated by the State

---

[1] Democracy, as used in this book, conforms to the meaning of the word as interpreted by the South Americans of the time. It had no "party" implications as it had in the United States and was used to designate the political philosophy of self-government by the masses in unrestricted form. It stood at the far end of the picture from "autocracy," and any limitations placed upon the expression of the free-will of the people—such as hereditary senates or wide powers for the executive—were regarded as deviations from it. Republics, on the other hand, were governments under an elected executive, whether or not their natures were "democratic" in the above sense. Thus a "republican" could also be a "democrat," though he need not be.

solely to govern. Political virtue as well as great political knowledge should be inculcated in them from early youth by methods of training similar to those used by the Church to instill moral virtue. The idea also included a plan for a distinct branch of government, a sort of third House, consisting of a group of hereditary "censors" somewhat in the nature of the censors of Rome or the Areopagites of Greece. These censors would be the high priests of government. Austerely righteous, they would have in their hands the training of the youth destined to sit in the upper House. With no voice in legislation, they would be purely arbiters of political virtue, observing closely the political conduct of all State officials and having the power to sit in judgment upon individuals of both Houses as well as of their own group who were suspected of self-interest or incapacity.

These details were Bolívar's own as he worked them out later; but the foundation for them was laid in those early discussions with Francisco Miranda.

Bolívar, with his usual great enthusiasm and vigor, urged upon Miranda the proposition of returning to his native land once more in an effort to break the Spanish yoke for good. In the light of future happenings it is certain that he pictured the chances for success and the solidarity of the Venezuelan people in too-glowing terms; but he convinced the old warrior, and that was the main thing. Facts didn't matter much.

The British government, during the whole course of revolutionary action in South America, looked, unofficially, with favor upon the struggling colonies. Officially, she gave them no aid; but she closed her eyes always to their doings in London and in her West Indian possessions. Now, in spite of the protests of the Spanish Minister, she permitted Miranda and his aides to sail for Venezuela aboard a British ship, the *Avon*. Bolívar, as a representative of the Junta, was sent home aboard a warship, the corvette *Sapphire*. Méndez and Bello established themselves in Miranda's house on Grafton Street, where they remained during the whole course of the revolutionary wars, working in the interests of their country.

Bolívar arrived in La Guaira on December 5, 1810. He was greeted by the news that his brother Juan, returning from his mission to the United States, had been lost in a storm at sea. It was undoubtedly a severe blow to him, for he always had a strong clan spirit and a deep affection for all the members of his family; but he hid his grief this time in his preoccupation with the political affairs of the country. There are no sentimental outbursts recorded anywhere over the loss of his only brother. By Juan's death, he inherited the full management of the estates left by his father and mother. He adopted Juan's bastard children and placed them in the care of María Antonia, and all his life he provided for them as his own.

Bolívar learned, too, that there had been bloodshed in the colony. The Spanish blockading fleet had its headquarters on the island of Puerto Rico and had established bases on the mainland at those two centers of royalist sentiment, Coro and Maracaibo. The citizens of those towns had greeted the arrival of Spanish war vessels with Te Deums in the cathedrals and torchlight parades on the streets, and had furnished them with every aid. In November the Marqués del Toro, that easy-going, pleasure-loving old uncle-in-law of Bolívar's, rode out of Caracas at the head of 3000 men with the object of putting an end to such doings. His expedition was badly organized, badly officered and lacked even a full round of ammunition per man. At Coro, faced by a force of 1800 Spaniards and Coriano royalists, they were routed completely at one charge, and the Marqués fled back to Caracas without even his personal belongings. That was the first military action of the revolution—not a very glorious one, surely.

Chapter VI

THE RED CAP

❖

NINE days after Bolívar landed at La Guaira, the
Avon dropped anchor in the harbor. A rowboat put
out from the crowded quay, crossed the dancing, sunlit
water and pulled alongside the British vessel. Shortly
after, the rowboat headed shoreward once more, with the
Precursor and the future Liberator of five nations standing together in the bow.

Miranda, burly and erect, was an imposing military
figure wearing the uniform of a general of the Grand Army
of France. The tropic sun gleamed upon his brilliant coloring—upon the sky-blue of his coat and his tight white
breeches, upon the red, white and blue of his sash. It
glinted from his great polished boots, from the massive
gold epaulets, from the hilt of his sword, and danced
from the gold fringe and tassels that moved with the
gentle breeze. His cold gray eyes squinted under the great
half-moon hat that was worn at an angle across his head,
and his curly hair was powdered and drawn to a queue
behind. In one ear he wore a gold ring.

Beside him, dressed in the uniform of a colonel of
Venezuelan militia, Bolívar appeared very young and
slight—eager, restless. His fingers played with the hilt of
his untried sword, and his face was alight with animation
as he talked constantly, moving his head and shoulders
in quick gestures. His eyes, glancing over the familiar
shore ahead, turned upward to the towering green mountains that were the northern edge of that vast land he
had sworn to deliver into the hands of a free people.

Ashore, Miranda was greeted by cheering crowds and by Padre Cortés Madariaga, the radical priest, the man who had forced the resignation of the Spanish captain-general, Emparán. He had been sent by the Junta as its official representative.

Mounted on horses, the party climbed the long twisting mountain trail to the city of Caracas. There were twenty-odd miles of that trail. Paved in places with cobbles, it was still mostly a "natural" highway, worn into the rock and clay by the hooves of pack-animals over three centuries. Mounting always, it was narrow and difficult in places, winding between sheer rises of rock. Climbing it, sweating under the fierce heat that burned from above, that struck from the earth below and from the glinting surfaces around, Miranda must have had his first qualms. He must have had the beginning, at least, of a realization of the difficulties ahead of him, of the problems of waging war in this land. It had been nearly forty years since he had climbed that trail before. Certainly he had forgotten a little how difficult it was. And this was the principal highway of the whole colony—the only road between the sea and the capital city. It was unsuitable for any sort of wheeled vehicle. What, he must have thought, would other routes through the country be like? How would one transport troops and cannon and munitions of war, one who was trained in the methods of European warfare, who understood only the movements of deep phalanxes, the maneuvering of rigid formations?

At the end of this trail lay a large city whose wealthy inhabitants enjoyed a. life of luxury comparable to that of people of their class in Europe. Up this difficult trail, on the backs of mules and sometimes on the backs of a hundred slaves, came huge casks of Spanish wines, cases of fine china, bales of silk, great crystal chandeliers, massive pieces of furniture—pianos, even. At that time, the city of Caracas had five orchestras of thirty pieces each and a theater where opera was performed. The natives would

know how to wage war in this country. Miranda might
have considered that; but apparently he didn't—or perhaps he was too old to learn.

The party crossed the saddle-back just as the dying sun
was painting the mountain-tops with bronze and the long
purple shadows were falling across the tiled roofs of the
city that lay in the high valley like a bowl of many-colored
berries. Bolívar took the veteran general of Napoleon's
army to his house on the Plaza San Jacinto.

Bolívar had had quite a time with the Junta over the
coming of Miranda. They were still straddling the fence,
still supporting the fiction of a loyalty to Fernando; and
to welcome this sworn champion of liberty, this unequivo-
cating, lifelong warrior in the cause of the independence
of nations, would give the lie to their feeble pretense and
would be almost a direct challenge to Spain. And too,
there was still the matter of that price put upon Miranda's
head by the Junta five years before. It was an embarrass-
ing situation, surely. Nevertheless, Bolívar, with the aid
of Cortés Madariaga and other radical members of the
Junta, succeeded in getting permission for Miranda to
land and in organizing an official welcome of a sort. He
worked hard, against the opposition of the conservatives
in the Junta, to stir up some enthusiasm among the people; and when Miranda arrived there was a demonstration
of greeting which was notable less for numbers than for
the enthusiasm of a few ardent souls. Miranda was left to
cool his heels about the city for a time while the Junta
pondered.

Bolívar was not a member of the Junta. The champion
of Miranda in that body was Padre Cortés Madariaga.
This priest, a Chileño by birth and a bitter enemy of
Spanish domination in any form, was a handsome, gallant
figure of a man, capable and eloquent. In the matter of
Miranda he had to fight the opposition of the clergy as
well as of the Junta, for his man had been excommunicated by the church. Nevertheless, he forced the Junta to

grant Miranda a commission and salary as lieutenant-general. When the Junta decided to dissolve and place its power in the hands of a Congress composed of representatives of all the Venezuelan provinces, Miranda's few but ardent backers had him elected as a deputy from Pao de Barcelona. The first Congress of the new nation met on March 2, 1811. Miranda, in June, became one of the 44 members. He swore along with the rest of them to "defend the rights of Don Fernando VII"; but he hadn't the slightest intention of keeping that oath.

Bolívar, with those young radicals of the old group who were not abroad on foreign missions, formed an organization called the Patriotic Society of Agriculture and Economy. They rented a large house in the center of the city and there, the windows open to the outside now and crowds of people gathered to hear their words, they met nightly and proclaimed their radical sentiments. They began to publish a newspaper to further their ideas among the people. The Society became a thorn in the sides of the mantuano members of Congress. It harried Congress constantly with petitions backed by pressure of public opinion and gathered a following so powerful that it became in effect a second Congress. Miranda, almost completely blocked in Congress by the conservatives, devoted his efforts to the Society. He was the great hero to the young radicals and presided at their tumultuous meetings.

It is difficult to determine just when the breach began in the friendship between Bolívar and Miranda—a breach that ever widened until it ended in tragedy. It is almost certain, however, that it began almost immediately Miranda set foot in the country and saw how he had been misled by the glowing picture which Bolívar had painted for him in London. He was surprised and disappointed at the coldness of the Junta and its lack of unanimity in sentiment for independence. He was bitterly disappointed, too, at the miserable condition of the native troops he found under his command. "Where," he cried petulantly, "are the armies worthy of the dignity and reputation of a general of my position?"

Then, too, the distinct personalities of the two men were bound to result in dislike sooner or later. The very qualities of the youthful Bolívar—his optimism and impetuosity, the qualities which had attracted the aging general in the beginning and inspired new vigor in him—began to sour and gave rise to irritation and intense dislike. Coldly practical (except in the matter of his Quixotic political dreams), completely self-disciplined, he came to resent strongly the uncontrolled vitality and puerile theatricalism of Bolívar.

There was another matter, too, which contributed to the growing mutual dislike. Curiously, and in spite of his democratic idealism, Miranda had a tremendous class and race pride. He was unable to curb or hide his distaste for the pardo, or colored, class. This class, numerically great, had, since the formation of the Junta, become increasingly self-assertive, had agitated for the right to hold minor offices and had succeeded in getting representation in the Congress. Our old friend Ribas, he of the red cap, the kinsman of Bolívar, had been named to uphold their interests. Bolívar himself—and in this he showed himself to be more truly liberal and much more far-sighted than Miranda—worked constantly to gain sympathy and backing among the pardos. He looked upon them as the backbone of the nation, the national racial type of the future and the most important element in waging a successful war against Spain.

Miranda lived with Bolívar in his house for some time, but the champion of human liberty and his principal sponsor drew constantly further apart.

On July 3, the Patriotic Society held a meeting which is famous in Venezuelan history. It marked Bolívar's début as an orator, for he made his first formal and recorded speech that day. He began by answering the complaints of the mantuanos that the Society was assuming

the rôle of another Congress. "It is not," he said, "that
there are two Congresses. The Patriotic Society respects,
as it should, the National Congress, but the Congress
should heed the Society which is the focus of revolutionary intelligence and interest." Then he went on to lay the
question of independence squarely on the table. "Why,"
he thundered, "will those who best know the necessity for
union foment schism about it? What we want is an effective union to unite us in the glorious enterprise of our
liberty. To unite merely to repose, to sleep in the arms
of apathy, was a disgrace yesterday; today it is treason.
The National Congress discusses what ought to be decided. And what do they say? That we ought to begin
with a Confederation—just as though we have not been
confederated against a foreign tyranny. That we should
wait for the results of the conflict in Spain. Why should
it matter to us whether Spain sells her slaves to Bonaparte
or keeps them herself, when we are resolved to be free?
These quibblings are the sad results of our old chains.
They say that great resolves should be arrived at in calmness. Are three hundred years of calm not enough? Does
the Congress wish for three hundred years more? Let us
lay the cornerstone of South American liberty without
fear! To hesitate is to be lost! I propose that a commission
of this body carry these sentiments to the sovereign Congress."

Bolívar's proposition was voted upon and approved,
and a text in favor of absolute independence was written
by Dr. Miguel Peña.

All the following day, July 4, debate raged in the National Congress over the action proposed by the Patriotic
Society. Miranda delivered a forceful speech in which he
pointed out that the United States, with a mere 3,000,000
inhabitants scattered over an area twice that of Venezuela
and divided into many small states, had been successful
in waging a war of independence against the greatest
European power. Nearly all the deputies had something

to say and the session closed without reaching a decision.

Congress reconvened on the morning of the fifth. Discussion began again, but it was apparent to President Rodríguez Domínguez that the sentiment was almost unanimously in favor of independence. Only one member, a priest, Manuel Vicente Maya, held out forcefully against it on the grounds that they had all taken an oath of allegiance to Fernando VII and that he had been specifically instructed by the community he represented. A vote was taken and then the President "solemnly declared the Absolute Independence of Venezuela." Germán Roscio and Francisco Isnardy were commissioned to draw up the formal act.

That night the city of Caracas went wild with jubilation. The people danced around bonfires in the streets and paraded with torches behind bands of native instruments—reed pipes and drums and rattles. What they shouted was now, at last, "Viva la libertad!" The royalists hid in their houses behind barred doors and windows. There were still many of them.

On the fourteenth, the anniversary of the Fall of the Bastille, there was a formal celebration in the Plaza Mayor. Two sons of José España, the patriot who had been beheaded and quartered in that same plaza twelve years before, presented the new flag to the troops. With horizontal bars of yellow, blue and red, it was the same flag that Miranda had used for his expedition from New York on the *Leander* in 1806.

Chapter VII

"EVEN NATURE OPPOSES"

❖

THE new-born republic was not long in finding trouble on its hands. Only six days after the Declaration of Independence, some seventy Canary Islanders and creole royalists, armed and mounted, gathered in Los Teques, a mountain village twenty miles west of Caracas. Carrying a flag with the picture of Fernando and shouting "Viva El Rey! Death to the traitors!" they began a march toward the capital. Within a few hours, however, they were all prisoners of the patriot troops. They were tried quickly and sentenced. Many were exiled, sixteen were shot in the Plaza Mayor. It is claimed that Miranda insisted upon the old Spanish custom of quartering the bodies by way of warning to others, but he was overruled. These were the first castigations of the republic and were used by the Spaniards later as an excuse for their horrible cruelties, which they termed "reprisals."

On the same day, July 11, a more serious uprising occurred in the city of Valencia, the second city of the colony, eighty-five miles back in the Andes. Word reached the capital on the thirteenth and the patriot army, again under the Marqués del Toro, was sent out to subdue the city. Miranda still had not the confidence of the government and, though he had the rank of lieutenant-general, was not given a command. The gouty, easy-going old Marqués was regarded by the youthful element as "wearing better the title of marquis than that of general." He certainly proved the opinion to be true. He foolishly attacked the royalists at the Pass of La Cabrera near Lake

Valencia, where they had taken a strong position. The patriots were routed and forced to retire to Caracas in disorder. Bolívar, because of the circumstances of the battle, saw no action in it.

The Congress was now forced, at last, to fall back upon General Miranda. Reluctantly it named him commander-in-chief of the army.

The old warrior's position was bitterly distasteful to him and extremely difficult. He had been trying nobly to instill some discipline into the troops and to train them in the European manner. In this he was handicapped by the fact that the creole officers, whose military rank in most cases was more a social honor than a result of training, and who were spoiled, indolent youths and all friends from childhood, gave him little aid. The troops, largely recruited by the individual officers from among their own peons, were inclined to recognize the authority of those officers before that of the commanding general. Pardos mostly, they felt the disdain which Miranda displayed for them; and they hated him for it.

Besides, there was the question of supplies and finances. The government was in a bad way financially. The Spanish blockade had almost entirely shut off the national income from commerce. A year before, the Junta had had a cash surplus of 2,000,000 pesos; but when the first Congress met in March, 1811, there wasn't a real in the treasury. Paper money was issued which circulated at a great discount throughout the colony, when it was accepted at all.

Meanwhile, the breach between Miranda and Bolívar had widened still further. At a review of troops before the commander-in-chief, Bolívar is said to have pirouetted his horse in a thoroughly unmilitary manner—an exhibitionistic flourish which is quite believable in him—and to have shouted unauthorized commands to his battalion. That was the last straw for Miranda. When he was ready, at last, to march out against the royalists in Valencia, he

went before the Executive Committee and declared that
Bolívar was a "dangerous youth," in no way qualified to
march at the head of his battalion. He demanded that he
be ordered to remain behind. Bolívar, thoroughly aroused,
blasted out to the Committee that Miranda was "a tired-
out old military who did not know Venezuela as a nation
nor a social center." He cried, "He is a pretentious person
of insatiable vanity. Dangerous youth, indeed! He calls
me that because I dare to oppose his erroneous policies!"
The Marqués del Toro stepped into the conflict and
agreed to take Bolívar on the expedition as his aide.

Meanwhile, the royalist sympathizers in Valencia had
been greatly reinforced by slaves and mestizos who had
been stirred up by Franciscan friars and agents sent out
by the Spanish commander, Cortabarría, in Puerto Rico.
When Miranda's columns approached the city along the
shores of Lake Valencia, they were met by a burst of fire
from gunboats hidden among the tall reeds and from
royalists stationed among the rocks in the narrow defiles.

This was Bolívar's first military action. His behavior
was gallant and effective. The patriot troops, demoralized,
were routed at first, and fell back upon the rear. Bolívar,
coming up, re-formed the cavalry and, shouting like a
madman, led a charge which encouraged the army to a
new assault. The royalists broke from their positions and
retreated into the streets of Valencia with the patriots on
their heels.

When Miranda marched into the city at the head of his
troops there wasn't a shot fired or scarcely a sound of any
kind. He should have been suspicious, but apparently he
wasn't. He had almost reached the central plaza when
gunfire suddenly poured out upon his men from windows
and roof-tops and from barricades in the streets. The
slaughter was terrible, the confusion complete. Bolívar
was everywhere, trying to rally his men, hurling himself
at the barricades. Miranda, seeing the situation was hopeless, ordered the retreat sounded; and the remains of his

army withdrew from the city. Outside, he re-formed them and laid siege, awaiting the arrival of cannon which were on their way from Caracas by pack-mule. Eight hundred patriot soldiers had been killed and 1500 wounded. Among these was Fernando del Toro, Bolívar's old companion in Madrid, who lost a leg and took no active part in the revolution from then on.

On August 13 the besieged royalists, starving, surrendered the city of Valencia. It is clear that Miranda's opinion of Bolívar as a leader of troops had been sincere, for now, after seeing him in battle, he altered it. He sent Bolívar to Caracas with prisoners to carry news of the victory, and in his dispatch to the Committee he cited Bolívar for bravery and withdrew his objection to his commission as colonel.

The Congress of the new nation, magnanimous in its first military triumph, pardoned all the Valencians involved in the uprising and allowed them to return to their homes. Miranda heartily disapproved.

Miranda was all for advancing at once against the cities of Maracaibo and Coro but the Congress, antagonizing him as usual, ordered him to return to Caracas. Had they permitted him to carry out his plans at that time, the history of the nation might have been vastly different. The old warrior was becoming more and more exasperated, and with good cause.

During the summer and fall the Congress busied itself with the writing of a Constitution for the nation. Its collective head full of the political philosophy of the French Revolution and of the North American Union, of the teachings of Voltaire, Montesquieu and Rousseau, of the declaration of Lafayette that all a nation needed to be free was to will it, the Congress leaned heavily toward complete equality of individuals and a federation of sovereign states with a weak central government. Its members ignored the facts of the great differences between their country and the States of the North. Their own provinces, separated by vast distances and difficult routes of communication, had never enjoyed any sort of self-government before; while the British colonies in the North had always exercised a degree of autonomy. Ignoring, too, the fact that of their seven hundred thousand inhabitants only an infinitesimal part was literate, the Constitution which they proposed was modeled after the Constitution of the United States of America and included universal suffrage. It proposed a limited executive power invested in an elected triumvirate.

Altogether it was a clear, logical, idealistic piece of work—not suited at all to the conditions of the country. The product of landed aristocrats, it was an amazing testimony of disinterestedness—abolishing titles and prohibiting the importation of slaves.

Miranda and Bolívar both saw the weakness of this Constitution. Holding to their old beliefs in a strong central government and an hereditary senate as against federation, they devoted their efforts to defeating it. They were, in a sense, upholding the views of Washington as against those of Thomas Jefferson—and with far more reason. Bolívar, not a member of Congress, had no voice in affairs at all, of course, while Miranda, though a member, had no influence in the governing body. On December 21, 1811, the Constitution was voted upon and adopted. Miranda, signing it, could not refrain from adding his protest under his signature. "It is not," he wrote, "adapted to the population, habits and customs of the states, and may result, not in uniting us in one consolidated group or social body, but in dividing us, jeopardizing our common security and our independence. I enter these observations in fulfillment of my duty."

The republic, composed of seven sovereign states, was named The United States of Venezuela, and the seat of the central government was designated to be the city of Valencia because of its location. That was the city which had just risen in an armed revolt that had taken 800 republican lives.

On March 10, 1812, a Spanish frigate captain named Monteverde, with 320 men—sailors from his ship and royalists from Maracaibo—marched inland from Coro. He was under orders of Miyares, the Spanish commander at Maracaibo, to capture the republican outpost at Siquisique. He was a brutal and ignorant man. Arrived at the town, he met no resistance and was joined by nearly the whole garrison, some 300 men, under the persuasion of a priest who was a sworn enemy of independence. With this sizable force under his command, Monteverde began to feel the stirring of ambition and to look about him for possible loot. A short distance up the valley of the Tocuyo lay the town of Carora with a large store of republican supplies. So, disobeying his orders to return to the coast, he marched up the river and fell upon the unsuspecting village. The people put up a valiant resistance but were overwhelmed. Monteverde turned his men loose to pillage and murder. No one who could not escape was spared —neither woman nor child. The corpses were stripped of their clothes and rings were torn from women's bleeding ears. Rifles, ammunition and seven pieces of artillery fell into Monteverde's hands. Jubilant now, he began to look about for more towns to conquer. Not far away was Barquisimeto, a still richer prize.

Word of these events reached Caracas a few days later; but the effect was lost in the appalling thing that happened there.

On Holy Thursday two years before, the patriots of Caracas had forced the Spanish captain-general to resign and had set up an independent government. Now it was another Holy Thursday.

At four o'clock in the afternoon the city lay quiet in its mountain bowl under a cloudless, brassy sky. The streets were deserted and silent except for the voices of the priests that droned from the open doorways of the churches. A short while before the bells had been clamoring and people swarmed the streets on their way to vespers. Barefooted peons and Indians from the hills padded along beside mounted officers and handsome, slave-borne litters, carrying women in black lace and high mantillas. But it was all very quiet now.

Suddenly, from the earth below came a great shuddering, a thundering, rolling roar. A cloud of yellow dust rose slowly from the city, blanketing it, rolling lazily upward along the mountainsides. Underneath, upon smashed and mangled bodies, lay the ruins of the city. The thin, high wail of stricken thousands rose to startle the vultures among the surrounding peaks.

The Chapel of San Jacinto was a pile of debris. From under the blocks of shattered masonry red trickles came like water from a sponge, formed little rivulets that ran into the clogged gutters and lay there in pools. Bolívar, in his shirt sleeves, choking with the dust, worked frantically at the heavy slabs of stone. Raging, almost sobbing, he paused to shout into the agonized clamor, "If even Nature must oppose us, we will battle with her, too, and compel her to obey!"

In Caracas alone there were ten thousand dead. The earthquake struck in other places too and there were nearly twenty thousand dead in all. La Guaira, Barquisimeto, Mérida and San Felipe were in ruins—and they were all strongly republican towns.

The clergy, ardently royalist in the main, was quick to seize upon this circumstance. They had plenty of evidence to work with. The royalist cities had been singularly spared. Valencia, Coro, Maracaibo, Guayana and all the pro-Spanish villages in the east were unharmed. The advancing force under Monteverde hadn't lost a man. San Felipe was swallowed up almost entire, along with a patriot force of six hundred men which had just arrived there. In Barquisimeto, a regiment of fifteen hundred patriot troops was passing in review when a fissure opened in the earth and engulfed them all. There were other signs of divine displeasure, too. As in all such occurrences there were many seemingly miraculous preservations—a crucifix left intact in the niche of a doorway, an image of the Virgin, untouched, with a little devout flame still burning beneath it, the Arms of Spain left intact upon a column in a church. Besides, there was that circumstance of the dates. The disaster fell on the anniversary of the day that the people had risen against the power of Spain. That was a potent sign of God's anger, surely.

Armed with these powerful weapons of propaganda, the priests swarmed out among the afflicted. Kneeling in the ruins, administering to the dying, they raised their voices in prayers for forgiveness for the great sin of the people. At night, beside the flaming pyres where bodies burned, they called upon the weeping, bereaved survivors to recognize God's sign and repent. And repent they did, by the thousands. Kneeling on the streets, they struck their breasts and implored divine forgiveness, shouting, "Viva España! Viva la Inquisición!"

Bolívar, distraught and angry, tried to stem the wave. Coming upon a priest who was exhorting a crowd, he seized him, drew his sword and threatened to run him through if he continued. He rallied a group of soldiers, and went about silencing the priests by force.

The Congress had moved to Valencia under the decree of the new Constitution. Practical men, devoted to their cause, they were not stampeded in the general wave of contrition. They demanded of the archbishop, Coll y Pratt, that he issue a pastoral denying the hand of God in the disaster. At first, the head of the Church in the colony refused. Finally, under pressure, he did issue a statement; but what he said was that, while rain, hail, lightning and earthquakes proceeded from natural causes, God used them to His purposes to punish the wicked and turn the hearts of sinners. He compared Caracas and the other republican cities to Sodom and Gomorrah. The Congress prohibited the circulation of the prelate's pastoral.

The Congress exerted its right under the Constitution to confer dictatorial powers in the emergency. They turned first to the Marqués del Toro, who wisely refused. Then, a last resort as always, they named General Miranda.

Monteverde, meanwhile, came on in triumph almost unopposed. The earthquake had made things easy for him. It had swallowed up the whole patriot force in Barquisimeto; he marched in to help himself to their supplies. From there he advanced along that ridge of the Andes, the principal highway of the nation, and took Trujillo; and then, along the edge of the llanos, he took Araure, San Carlos and San Juan de Los Morros. Looting, murdering, raping, with the village priests preceding him and proclaiming the divine sanctity of the Spanish cause, he met little resistance. Whole garrisons of patriot soldiers went over to him voluntarily. His army became a mad, murdering horde, jubilant in the happy combination of license and righteousness. On May 3, with fifteen hundred men, he advanced upon Valencia. The Congress left the city and fled to La Victoria, a town nearer to Caracas, and Monteverde moved in unopposed. He ignored the orders of Ceballos, who had replaced Miyares as captain-general in Maracaibo, and declared himself in supreme command.

In the east, too, the republicans suffered disaster. Far down on the Orinoco, across the llanos, a patriot expedition had been defeated at Angostura and the river flotilla had been destroyed by a Spanish squadron. All that was really left now of the independent nation which had risen so hopefully less than a year before was Caracas, a short stretch of the Andean Cordillera back to the valley of Aragua and a few widely separated cities in the east.

II: PALADIN

Chapter VIII

"BLESSÉ AU CŒUR"

✤

MIRANDA left the army opposing Monteverde in the command of Colonel Ustáritz and went to Caracas to raise more troops and funds. He was in supreme authority at last, with no Congress to harass or hinder him. The Secretary of War had ordered, in conferring the dictatorial powers, "Do not consult any but the supreme law of saving the nation." But it came too late. Something had gone out of the ex-general of France. The many disappointments and failures had undermined his faith in the Venezuelan people and shaken his self-confidence—though not his ego.

Colonel Bolívar was ordered to take command at the coast town of Puerto Cabello. Though far removed from the scene of hostilities, this was really an important post, for it was the best harbor on the coast and was dominated by a fortress in which a large number of wealthy and influential royalist sympathizers were imprisoned; but Bolívar accepted with ill grace, feeling that it was a deliberate move on the part of Miranda to get him out of the way—which it may have been.

With a draggle-tail and undisciplined army of 2300 men and ten pieces of artillery, Miranda marched out of Caracas on the first of May. He followed the Andean Cordillera southwestward, joined forces with the main army and took a position in the city of Maracay. Ustáritz had been defeated by Monteverde in several battles, during which his whole cavalry had gone over to the enemy. Nevertheless, Miranda now found himself commanding

69

more than five thousand men, as against the three thousand who opposed him under Monteverde. And now there is evidence that Miranda was indeed, as Bolívar had charged, "a tired-out military."

The Generalísimo remained inactive in Maracay, trying to teach his motley soldiers the parade steps of Prussians and his officers the unsuitable tactics of European armies—while Monteverde made a flank movement by a mountain path and occupied the heights of Cabrera, dominating the patriot position. Miranda had to retire to La Victoria and Monteverde, following quickly, again threatened him from San Mateo. Miranda had lost the offensive—and with superior forces. In fact, he had openly announced a policy of defensive tactics. The native officers were astounded at this and objected vigorously; but Miranda wasn't taking any advice now from native officers. He wasn't even speaking to them any more than he could help, and had so alienated them that prominent patriots, such as the Marqués del Toro and his brother Fernando, refused to participate in the campaign under him. He surrounded himself with foreign officers—French and Italian soldiers-of-fortune mostly—and associated with them entirely, speaking in French so that the creole officers couldn't understand. He told his aide, Carlos Soublette, who was half French, that he had only one fault— that of being half Venezuelan. The Great Patriot had traveled far along the road of disillusion since the days of London and New York.

The man seems to have been almost completely uninterested in the military task before him. Convinced more than ever that the aid of a foreign power was necessary, he spent all his time writing letters to governments abroad, planning to send envoys. Some envoys were even dispatched. A Frenchman, Louis Delpech, was to go to the French West Indies and then to Louisiana; the Italian, Molini, was to replace Méndez in London; Du Cayla, another Frenchman, was to return to France. Miranda in-

structed Orea, the representative in Washington, to approach the envoy of Napoleon there. His eyes were still
seeing only his old dream of an Incan Empire. And all
this in the very face of the enemy.

Monteverde was in action all the time, raiding and
looting villages, harassing Miranda with guerilla tactics—
tactics which Miranda refused to adopt himself. Monteverde attacked La Victoria itself twice and was driven
back; but Miranda refused to follow up, and the royalists
fell back safely to their position in San Mateo. The native
officers, raging, held themselves in check with difficulty.
Monteverde, the ignorant minor naval officer, with a
much smaller force and operating 240 miles away from
his base in Coro, was out-fighting, out-marching and
out-maneuvering the great veteran general of Napoleon's
army.

That was the situation when Miranda received a note
from Bolívar in Puerto Cabello. It was the first anniversary of Independence, July 5, and Miranda was giving a
dinner for a hundred officers. When he read the short
note, he said, in French, "Gentlemen, Venezuela is
wounded to the heart."

Bolívar had been killing time in the sleepy, steaming
town of Puerto Cabello for eight weeks. The rains fell
every day, turning the streets into mudholes, making
marshy lakes of the tidal flats in the outskirts. Even riding
was unpleasant. Bolívar lolled in his hammock in the inn
and played chess with his fellow-officers.

The fortress of San Felipe was on a rock in the harbor,
connected with the town by a drawbridge, and had a garrison of two hundred soldiers under the command of
Colonel Aymerich, guarding the prisoners. There were
provisions for a long siege and quantities of ammunition,
and the cannon on the ramparts dominated the city. Bolívar, in command only of the city itself, had a small force
of soldiers and little artillery.

On the afternoon of June 30, Colonel Aymerich was absent from the fortress and Lieutenant Fernández Vinoni, a subordinate of Bolívar's in his own battalion of Aragua Militia, was in command. Bolívar was startled from his hammock by the sound of cannon fire. He ran to the street to find the flag of Spain flying over San Felipe, the drawbridge raised and the cannon hurling balls into the town. He knew at once what had happened. The wealthy royalist prisoners had "gotten to" Vinoni, and seduced him and the troops under him.

Bolívar was in a bad spot. He went into action at once, ranged his small force on the higher parts of the town, trained what pieces of artillery he had upon the fortress and opened fire. Then he sent off a runner with a note to Miranda. The note said, "My general: a Venezuelan officer, unworthy of the name, with the prisoners, has taken possession of the Fortress of San Felipe and is at this moment firing heavily upon the city. If your Excellency does not attack the enemy immediately in the rear, this position is lost. Meanwhile I shall hold it as long as possible."

All afternoon Bolívar fired upon the fortress and sent demands for its surrender. The replies were more round shot and cries of derision. During the night one hundred and twenty men of Bolívar's meager force, with their officers, deserted their posts and went inland toward Valencia, where they joined Monteverde. The next day the civilians of the town began to evacuate the city, heedless of Bolívar's demands that they stay and defend it. To a request that he capitulate, Bolívar replied that he'd see the town in ashes first and that he had just had word of a great patriot victory over Monteverde. He ordered a parade through the town with fifes and drums in celebration to lend support to the fiction.

To add to the difficulties of his position, a royalist force from Coro appeared at the outskirts of the town and drove in the outposts. Bolívar immediately ordered nearly all his remaining force, two hundred men under Colonels Míres, Montilla and Jalón, out to meet them. This force was reduced, in less than an hour of battle, to seven men; and when word came back to Bolívar, it was the final blow. But he refused to surrender, even then. It was the city itself which surrendered, the civil authorities. Bolívar, with only eight officers remaining loyal and no troops at all, was through. He had held out for seven days against impossible conditions.

That night Bolívar and his companions waded along the swampy shore, in water to their armpits, under the dark walls of the fortress. A rowboat lay hidden among the mangroves. With muffled oars they rowed out to the schooner *Zeloso,* anchored behind an island. They bribed the Spanish crew and sail was set to tack against the light east breeze. Dejected, almost weeping, Bolívar carried away with him a burning hatred for the traitor Vinoni.

Six days later, in the depths of moral anguish, exhausted from lack of sleep for thirteen nights, Bolívar landed in La Guaira. He rode the twenty miles to Caracas the same day and there, in the quiet of his house across from the ruins of the Chapel of San Jacinto, he wrote to Miranda.

He wrote a detailed account of the events of the loss of Puerto Cabello, and then he went on to say:

. . . How can I summon the courage to write you after having lost the stronghold confided to my hands? . . . I was not to blame and I saved my honor; a pity that I saved my life also and did not leave it under the debris of the city. . . . My spirit is so dejected that I have not the courage to command a single man. Vanity made me believe that my desire to succeed and my ardent zeal for our country's cause would supply the talent for commanding which I lack. I beg you to place me under the most lowly officer. . . .

. . . I performed my duty, my general. If one soldier had remained with me, I should have fought the enemy. But they abandoned me and there was nothing I could do to hold them.

   . . . How is it, my general, that I have not lost my mind, having lost the most important stronghold in the country?

   In pity, do not oblige me to see your face. . . . I am disgraced.

   With the greatest regard and respect, I am the devoted subordinate and friend who kisses your hand.

BOLÍVAR.

   He hadn't much time to indulge his despair, for the next night word reached the city that slaves, stirred up and armed by those wealthy royalists whom the magnanimous Congress had permitted to remain free upon their estates, were only a short distance away, advancing without any force to oppose them.

   On top of this, the word fell like another earthquake that Miranda had surrendered to Monteverde in La Victoria. The First Republic of Venezuela was dead, after one short year of life.

   That steep, tortuous trail down the mountains to La Guaira was clogged with crawling humanity like an army of migrating ants. Day and night, packed close, moving a few steps at a time, the patriots made their way down to the seacoast from the capital. Monteverde was advancing upon Caracas with his victorious horde. Men, women and children, sick, aged and blind, with a few of their most precious belongings packed on burros, stumbled and slipped down the shaly slopes. The few streets of the coast town were jammed with people, lying upon their bundles in the rain and heat. There was no egress from that village. The open sea lay before it. There were ships at anchor there, but Miranda, acting on orders of the victorious Spaniard, had closed the port and forbade sailing. One vessel, loaded with refugees, tried to get away. A shot from the fortress on the headland crossed her bow.

Bolívar was staying in the house of Manuel Las Casas, the military governor of the port. With bitter, smoldering heart, he watched the refugees pouring into town. All his abject humility and self-condemnation over the loss of Puerto Cabello were converted now into violent hatred for Miranda, the man he considered to have betrayed his country. All his resentment against the man he had sponsored, the insults and criticism he had suffered at his hands, revived now in his memory to blind him to any consideration of possible justifications. Reason was no longer in him.

When Miranda himself suddenly appeared in La Guaira on the night of July 30, there was consternation and added fury. Miranda had slipped out of Caracas secretly. In the eyes of all, he had sold out the patriot cause; and now he was deserting them in the face of the savage Monteverde.

Miranda's first acts in La Guaira were such as to lend support to these suspicions. A British vessel, the *Sapphire,* under Captain Haynes, the same vessel that had brought Bolívar from England, had appeared in port only a few days before and now lay at anchor in the harbor. Miranda immediately sent all his effects aboard and ordered Las Casas to clear her for sailing—lifting, for that one ship alone, his own embargo. However, there was no breeze just then and sailing was deferred until the following morning. Miranda remained ashore and went to spend the night in Las Casas' house. He retired to his room immediately after dinner.

Las Casas, Bolívar, the civil governor, Miguel Peña, Juan Paz del Castillo, José Míres, Manuel Cortés, Tomás Montilla, Rafael Chatillón, Miguel Carabaño, Rafael Castillo, José Landaeta and Juan José Valdés—all patriot civil and military officers—got together the moment he left, and the dams of vituperation burst.

Bolívar undoubtedly was the most violent of the accusers against Miranda. He had plenty of evidence to work with. The first and most damning facts were Miranda's weeks of vacillation at Maracay and La Victoria, his resolve upon defensive tactics and his inexplicable surrender to Monteverde when he still commanded a superior force. They didn't know then that the surrender had been made only after conferences with members of the federal Executive, Roscio and Espejo, the Secretary of War, Sata y Bussy, the Secretary of the Treasury, the Marqués de Casa León, and the Minister of Federal Justice, Francisco Paúl, who had all concurred in it. They ignored the fact, too, that Miranda was threatened in the rear and his communications with Caracas jeopardized by the fall of Puerto Cabello. They could see only the things which spelled guilt.

The terms of Miranda's surrender were that there should be no reprisals on the part of Monteverde; that no one should be arrested or tried; that no property should be confiscated; that all who wished to leave the country should be given passports; that all political prisoners should be released. But Miranda, for some strange reason, had kept these terms secret. So the patriot army, the 5000 of them, with full field equipment, resentful, bewildered, drifted back along the Cordillera to Caracas. They burned supplies and spiked guns as they went. These acts were seized upon by Monteverde as nullifying the terms of surrender, and as an excuse for violating them. Coming along behind the patriots, he permitted his men to indulge in their favorite practices. The haciendas along the way to Caracas were sacked and burned, the helpless people slaughtered. There was no reason to believe the same fate would not befall the capital city. And now Miranda was getting away, abandoning them in the face of this grave danger. Surely, with the army still largely intact, he should at least remain to see that the terms of surrender were respected.

There was another matter, too, which further enraged the group of men whispering there, huddled about the sputtering lamp. It was a matter of money. There was a rumor abroad that the Secretary of the Treasury, Casa León, a Spaniard and therefore suspect, had promised Miranda seven hundred and fifty ounces of gold when he left the country; that he had given the Dictator an order for twelve thousand pesos on the fiscal agent, Patrullo, in Caracas; that the money had been paid over to the agent in La Guaira with instructions that it be forwarded to George Robertson, Miranda's agent in Curaçao, and that no receipt be taken. No definite proof of these doings has ever appeared. Some historians have admitted the transmission of funds to Robertson in Miranda's favor, but claim that they were intended to be used by Miranda in an effort to reconquer Venezuela from a base in the Antilles. Certainly there is nothing in the hard, bare life which Miranda had chosen for himself to suggest any motives of monetary gain. He had had little of that in his sixty years, surely. His great fault now was that, for a long time, he had lost confidence in the native officers, had wiped his hands clean of them and had failed to inform them of any of his intentions. There was no inclination now, among these bitter inquisitors, to guess about possible good intentions. Mere suspicion was enough for them.

By three o'clock in the morning they had decided. Las Casas wrote out the order for Miranda's arrest. He, Bolívar and several others roused Soublette, the general's aide, and told him to waken his chief. Behind him they marched to Miranda's room, weapons bared.

The general sat up on his bed in his nightshirt, blinking, while Las Casas read the order for his arrest on the charge of treason. The lantern, held aloft in the darkness, cast its yellow light on the deep-lined, tired old face. When the voice of Las Casas ceased there was a moment of silence. Then Miranda muttered, "Hubbub. Stupid hubbub. All these people know is stupid hubbub." He dressed slowly and followed them along the dark streets to prison without another word.

That same night Monteverde had entered Caracas. The next day he sent an order to Las Casas to close the port and to relinquish his authority to his own officer, Cervériz, who took over the custody of Miranda at once.

Later Miranda was taken to the prison at Puerto Cabello, then to Puerto Rico and then to Cádiz, where he was confined in the fearful prison, La Carraca. He died there four years later, chained to the wall by a collar around his neck like a dog, and his body was thrown on a dump heap. He had suffered in six prisons during his life in the cause of human liberty; and his reward was a grave on a dump heap. But he had had his glories, too, in his younger days. He was a sensualist and among his archives there is preserved a collection of the pubic hairs of the famous and highborn women of Europe who had loved him. And today in Caracas, in the Pantheon, near the tomb of the Liberator, is an empty marble sarcophagus. The lid is held open by the claws of a great eagle.

Never after did Bolívar express any remorse over his part in the tragic end of the Precursor. In fact, he often expressed the belief that he was absolutely justified. However, he did regret that Miranda fell into the hands of the Spaniards. That had not been his intention. He accuses Las Casas of perfidy in that, in yielding to the demands of the agent of Monteverde. His purpose, which he insisted upon against the will of his companions, was to court-martial Miranda at once and execute him. That, at least, would have spared the old warrior four long years of suffering.

The fears of the Caraqueños had been well founded. Monteverde ignored the terms of the surrender and loosed his men on the populace. All the prominent patriots who could be found, some 1500 in all, were dragged by mules through the streets and over the long, rough trails to the prisons in La Guaira and Puerto Cabello. Germán Roscio, the co-author of the Declaration of Independence, was exhibited in the stocks in the Plaza and then he, with his colleague Isnardy, the patriot priest Cortés Madariaga, and five others, were shipped from La Guaira to the prison in Cádiz. Miranda, from his cell in Puerto Cabello, wrote a protest to the Audencia which had been set up in Caracas. "I have seen," he wrote, "old age, youth, rich and poor, the laborer and the priest, in chains, breathing air so foul that it extinguishes a flame, poisons the blood and brings inevitable death. I have seen distinguished citizens, sacrificed to this cruelty, expire in these dungeons, deprived of bodily necessities, of the consolation of their families and of the spiritual rites of our religion—men who would have preferred to die a thousand deaths with the weapons, which they so generously surrendered, in their hands." But the protest was ignored, of course. Still worse was to come, in that same prison, after Miranda was gone. Five casks of quicklime were dumped over the walls of a small court on to a group of patriot prisoners and all of them were burned to death.

Bolívar, in La Guaira, had no hope of escape. All the refugees were trapped there under the embargo order. At the first opportunity he disguised himself, stole through the Spanish pickets and made his way, in darkness, back to Caracas. There he went to the house of the Marqués de Casa León, the Spaniard, the former Secretary of the Treasury. León had escaped trial at the hands of Monteverde, along with a few others of Spanish birth. Bolívar remained hidden there in the house while the Marqués made efforts in his behalf. Don Francisco Iturbe, another Spaniard and a close friend of Bolívar's, went before the Spanish commander and offered his own life as guarantee for the young patriot colonel. Monteverde ordered that Bolívar be brought before him.

"In recompense for the service you have rendered the

King," he said, "in arresting Francisco Miranda, I shall grant you a passport."

Bolívar blew up. "I?" he said. "A service to the King? I arrested Miranda because he was a traitor to his country!"

There it was again—the foolish, dramatic gesture. But it was the last one Bolívar was to make. From then on all his talent for the theatrical was to be used wisely and to good purpose.

He got away with it, anyhow. Iturbe hastened to explain that Bolívar was just a youthful hot-head, carried away by the stress of anxiety. Monteverde obviously considered him a very unimportant figure, anyway. He turned to his secretary and said, "Pay no attention to the fool. Give him his passport and get him out of here."

Monteverde had no idea what he was letting slip through his fingers. He lived to learn that it was the power of Spain in northern South America.

Bolívar, with José Félix Ribas, that old compañero of Madrid and of the Patriotic Society, sailed for the near-by island of Curaçao on August 27. Watching the green ranges above La Guaira drop down into the blue swells of the Caribbean, he knew that the Revolution was over in his native land. From then on he was the Revolution. It would move only as he moved, flame as he flamed, sleep when he slept.

Chapter IX

GLORY IS BORN

✣

OUT of the ruins rose a new Simón Bolívar. The paladin that now suddenly appears was born of sheer adversity.

Venezuela had never been in a worse state at any time during her whole history. In the hands of a ruthless conqueror, her agriculture and commerce destroyed, her leaders in prison or exile, her people homeless and starving through earthquake and pillage, there was not one little gleam of hope for her. Bolívar himself was in a strange land, penniless. The twelve thousand pesos he had brought away with him were taken by the authorities in Curaçao as a fine against the vessel for irregularities in her papers. His estates had been confiscated by Monteverde and his sisters were in hiding somewhere in the stricken land.

But there isn't one word of despair now, nor of self-pity. None of the groveling humility which he expressed in his letter to Miranda after Puerto Cabello—not now, nor ever again in his whole career. From now on he only thinks, plans and acts. His talents disciplined, he uses them wisely, coldly, to his purpose. Indiscretion falls from him like the first coat of a lion, leaving audacity in its place.

From Curaçao he looked southward and scanned, in his mind, that whole northern coast of the continent, looking for a likely spot to start again. In New Granada, the neighboring colony to Venezuela, there was one port held by patriot forces—Cartagena. That was the place, he decided at once. That the Spaniards held nearly all the rest of the country, and that the capital city, Santa Fé de Bogotá, had set up its own independent government and recognized that of Tunja—to which Cartagena adhered—not at all, didn't bother him. Cartagena it was. With no hesitation whatever, he sailed westward and southward to a land he had never seen, where his name had never been heard.

He presented himself to the authorities in Cartagena, was given a commission as colonel and assigned the command of the near-by village of Barranca, under the orders of General Labatut, a Frenchman. In the new post, a quiet place, removed from any chance of hostilities with the Spanish, he sat down to write a manifesto to the people of New Granada. What he produced there, and published, is one of the three greatest documents of his career.

He began with a clear, masterly analysis of the causes, political and military, of the downfall of the First Venezuelan Republic. He pointed out the fundamental error of the leaders in failing to subdue, at the very beginning, the royalist cities of Coro and Maracaibo—thus permitting a base for the Spanish blockading fleet and an ingress into the country by the capital's rear. Then he decried the weak policy of the Congress in dealing with rebellious conspirators, permitting them to remain as festering sores in the very bosom of the Republic. "We had," he said, "philosophers for statesmen, philanthropy for legislation, dialectics for tactics and sophists for soldiers. . . . Our division, and not the Spanish Army, brought us back to slavery. . . . Internal dissensions were, in fact, the poison which carried the country to its doom." He expressed forcefully his old opposition to the federal system and to pure democracy, acknowledging the latter as the ideal; but, "as yet our fellow citizens are not in a condition to exercise their rights, for they lack the political virtues which characterize a true republic and which can never be acquired under an absolute government. . . ."

"It is necessary," he wrote, "that a government identify

itself, so to speak, with the circumstances, times and men surrounding it. If they are prosperous and calm, the government can be mild and protective; but if they are calamitous and turbulent, the government must show itself terrible and must arm itself with a firmness equal to the dangers, *without paying heed to laws or constitutions until peace is re-established."*

There we have, in the very beginning of his career, a direct statement of the political philosophy which he held to firmly all his life. He had no power at all now and no reason, really, to hope that he would ever have any. Certainly a consideration of this declaration should confound those who claim that "ambition grew in him with his power," and who characterize his later assumption of dictatorship on various occasions as a result of that power. It was no such thing. It was a fundamental part of his political philosophy, based upon his deep understanding of the weaknesses of his people. "I am convinced," he wrote, "that, until we centralize our American governments, the enemy will have every advantage—we shall always be surrounded by the horrors of civil war and conquered by the handful of bandits who infest our borders. . . . If Caracas, in place of a hesitant and unstable federation, had established the simple government which its political and military situation demanded, you would still exist, O Venezuela, and you would still enjoy your liberty today!"

Then he went on to point out to the New Granadans that their own hopes for independence were vain so long as Spain held Venezuela. ". . . Making a proportion, we find that Coro is to Caracas as Caracas is to entire America [South]; consequently the danger which menaces this country is the ratio of the above progression; because, with Spain in possession of Venezuela, she can easily dispatch men, food and munitions of war under the direction of chiefs trained against those masters of warfare, the French, and penetrate from the provinces of Barinas and

Maracaibo to the uttermost confines of South America."
The fate of New Granada was, then, inextricably involved
with that of Venezuela. He speaks for the first time of the
two colonies together as "Colombia." The term had been
used before in his old discussions with Miranda; but now
he introduced it publicly, implying a union between the
neighboring colonies.

The cause of independence in New Granada, then, im-
periously demanded the immediate reconquest of Venezuela. Bolívar proposed and outlined an audacious plan
for a campaign to that end. "New Granada's glory depends upon her assumption of the task of liberating the
cradle of *Colombian* independence, its martyrs and those
meritorious people of Caracas whose outcries can only be
directed to their beloved compatriots, the New Granadans, whom they await with mortal impatience as their
saviors. Let us hasten to break the chains of those victims
who groan in their dungeons, awaiting salvation at your
hands! Do not abuse their confidence! Do not turn a deaf
ear to the lamentations of your brothers! Let us fly
quickly to avenge the dead, to give life to the dying, freedom to the oppressed and liberty to all!"

The Manifesto of Cartagena had a profound effect upon
the people of New Granada. It won Bolívar the immediate attention and high regard of Toríces, the Governor
of Cartagena, and of Camilo Torres, the President of the
Congress in Tunja. "It began," says Parra-Pérez, "a flow
of eloquence which was to continue for eighteen years."

Cartagena lies near the mouth of that great, turbulent
river, the Magdalena, which rises among the Andes five
hundred miles back and flows northward to the sea, following the valleys, falling in great rapids and pooling
over shifting sand bars amid towering jungle. It is the
principal route of ingress to the capital city, Santa Fé de
Bogotá, four hundred miles inland. It is the lifeline of
the province. In December, 1812, it was held almost
throughout its length by the Spanish forces.

Bolívar, in command of a small garrison of a few hundred men in Barrancas, was in no mood to remain there in idleness among the thatched mud huts. Just up the river at Teneriffe lay a Spanish force, strongly entrenched, and dominating the navigation of the whole stream. Bolívar was spoiling to get at it. His superior, Labatut, had been one of those foreign officers who surrounded Miranda, and he shared the sentiments which the Precursor had held regarding the "dangerous youth." When Bolívar applied to him for permission to advance against Teneriffe, Labatut refused bluntly. But who was Labatut now, or any other *carajo*, to oppose him? Bolívar went over the Frenchman's head and applied directly to Toríces in Cartagena. And while he was waiting for a reply, he found a bit of romance to amuse himself with.

He was riding through the narrow, sun-baked streets of the village of Salamina. His roving eye caught a pretty, blue-eyed girl standing in the doorway of a hut. He smiled at her and touched the visor of his shako.

"Bon jour, monsieur," the girl said.

Bolívar reined up beside her and dismounted. "You are French, then?" he asked.

"Yes, sir. Anita Lenoit, to serve you."

Bolívar, smiling, bent over the shy young thing and turned on all his famous charm full force. He spent the night there in her room and her French peasant father and mother whispered outside the door, in awe of the handsome young officer of whom everyone was saying such great things.

The historian, Gil Fortoul, says that Bolívar never lived alone, that women accompanied him everywhere, throughout his whole life. On the other hand, women never meant anything to him. They never possessed him. They were to him a pastime, a relaxation like wine or music, a necessity for his nervous temperament and his ego. He was the dominant male, always; and he must win, whether it was in love or war. But glory was his only real love and he never forgot it, in battle or in the arms of women.

So it was now with Anita Lenoit. Only a few days of passion with her and then word came from Toríces, giving him authority to advance upon Teneriffe. He forgot Anita at once. He didn't even say good-by to her. Jubilantly, his mind soaring ahead into wild dreams of glory, his eyes shining with their peculiar dark brilliance, he flung himself into the enterprise of which the German, Gervinus, says, in *A History of the Nineteenth Century,* "This campaign is not inferior to any we know of as among the most audacious in Europe."

It was the night of December 21. Bolívar loaded his two hundred men on ten small rafts. All night the little flotilla poled its way upstream, hugging the darkness under the low-hanging jungle of the shore. When the rafts grounded on shoals, the men went overboard and worked them off. They showed no lights and the only sounds were the gurgling of the current against the blunt bows, the occasional thump of a pole on the gunwale and a whispered command, stealing from raft to raft. Before daylight came they brought the rafts against the bank, made them fast and swarmed ashore. They followed the guides along the jungle trail. Out of the darkness suddenly a challenge came, *"Quién vive?"*

The men fell upon the Spanish sentinel quickly and cut his throat and then, when the outpost came running up, there was a brief, fierce struggle with muskets flaring in the gray light and royalist soldiers sinking to the ground. The alarm had been given. Bolívar shouted an order and his men ran forward, yelling, firing their pieces, driving the bewildered royalists before them to the very ramparts at the entrance to the village. It was dawn now. Bolívar formed his men in a concealed position and called upon the Spanish commander to surrender. He said that if the answer was no, his artillery—of which he had none—would blow the town to bits. The Spaniard believed that

he was besieged by the whole army of Labatut. He hastily
fled with his five hundred men, abandoning the town and
his whole arsenal to the patriot force. Bolívar had won his
first battle. He hadn't lost a man.

That afternoon he was resting in his hammock in the
old quarters of the Spanish commander. He couldn't sleep
for the jubilation that he felt and the great plans that
were surging through his mind. A small figure appeared
in the brilliant light of the open doorway. Bolívar jumped
from the hammock and ran forward, crying her name,
"Anita!"

Laughing, he took her hands and dragged the tired
little girl to a place beside him on the hammock. She had
followed him on foot from Salamina. He stroked her
golden hair and raised her chin with his hand. "What?"
he said. "Crying at a time like this, chiquita? Come, come,
little daughter, nothing of that today! This is the day for
rejoicing only. Nothing else is permitted here!"

Talking happily, he petted the girl, cajoled her; and
soon her eyes were dry and her head was against his breast.
In his exalted spirit, he forgot all about his resolve never
to marry again. "We will be married, little one," he declared, "when my task is done and my country is free.
I'll come back to you in triumph and you shall be queen
of a great celebration and ride to the cathedral in Cartagena in a golden litter. How will you like that, eh?" Anita
admitted that she'd like that very much.

After a while, Bolívar led the girl to the doorway. He
kissed her and sent her away, out into the bright sunlight. He waved to her, calling, "Remember, querida, wait
for me!"

Anita Lenoit waited for him there in her little village
for seventeen years; but she never saw him again, in life.

That same night Bolívar moved up the river once more.
In the morning he appeared before the town of Mompox,
a place of strong republican sympathies, and found that

the Spaniards had fled from there, too, at word of his approach. At the head of his unkempt and mud-spattered
troops he marched into the town in the midst of great
enthusiasm. He addressed the people in the plaza and recruits poured into his ranks. "I was born," he said afterwards, "in Caracas; my glory, in Mompox."

He didn't stay long to taste the delights of his glory.
The next day, with five hundred men and fifteen armed
boats besides his ten rafts, he continued up the river after
the Spaniards. He drove them from the fortified towns of
Guamal and Banco and then, following fast, his oarsmen
working furiously, he turned up a branch river, the César,
caught them in force at Chiriguaná and beat them badly
in a short, furious battle. Many prisoners, four gunboats,
cannon and large quantities of guns and ammunition fell
into his hands. But there was no time for rest now. He
returned to the Magdalena immediately, occupied Tama-
lameque, and continued upstream to the important town
of Ocaña. He was greeted there with wild rejoicing. He
had fought six battles in six days and won them all. Meanwhile, Labatut had captured the port city of Santa Marta
and the whole province of Cartagena was free of royalist
forces.

Bolívar wrote to the Congress in Tunja, ". . . I have
succeeded in opening the navigation of the Magdalena,
in reconquering all the territory held by the enemy, completely destroying its troops and taking one hundred prisoners, many officers, ammunition and provisions. . . . All
these operations have been executed within two weeks'
time."

Labatut wasn't at all pleased with the success of the
young Venezuelan upstart. Bolívar's orders had been only
to advance against the Spaniards at Teneriffe; but he had
gone on from there without any authority from anyone.
Labatut sent an order for Bolívar's arrest and court-martial for insubordination. The Congress refused to back up
the order. Victories, nothing else, were important now.

Before Bolívar now lay his project of crossing over into Venezuela and marching toward Caracas. Five thousand of Monteverde's men stood between him and his goal, besides nearly five hundred miles of the worst terrain which nature has produced on earth. One thousand royalists, under Ramón Correa, occupied the border city of Cúcuta, and a New Granadan republican force of only three hundred opposed them at Pamplona under Colonel Manuel Castillo.

Under the eloquent ardor of Bolívar, the reconquest of Venezuela by the benevolent action of her neighbor was taking on the aspects of a holy crusade. Around his youthful, shining, conquering figure came rallying all the young aristocratic patriots of the near-by territory. Prominent among these were Anastasio Giradot and Antonio Ricuarte—romantic young men of Bolívar's own cut. In New Granada, as in Venezuela, there was practically no revolutionary sentiment among the lower classes. The movement was purely of the upper-class creoles against the Spaniards and their sympathizers. The slaves and peons, when active at all, were largely in the ranks of the Spaniards, for there lay the opportunity for loot. Monteverde's army, except for the officers, was almost entirely made up of Venezuelan zambos, blacks, mestizos and mulattoes. What few of the lower classes in Cartagena Bolívar could urge into his ranks usually deserted at the next town, after garnering enough loot to satisfy their modest desires. So the army of five hundred which Bolívar commanded at Ocaña was composed mostly of ardent white aristocrats.

Bolívar harangued these men on every occasion. He was never too tired and he always found time, whether it was on the march or struggling in the river currents or resting for a moment at mealtime. His words were eloquent, exaggerated, inspiring always.

When permission came from the Congress, Bolívar set out eastward upon a march which was the first of many that have made him famous in the annals of military his-

tory. It was early in February, 1813, only a month and a
half since he left Barranca and only two months since he
had landed in Cartagena, penniless and unknown.

The route lay over the towering heights of one of the
main Andean ranges. It was a trackless waste of thick
jungle, frigid plateaux and deep gorges, inhabited only by
savage Indians. It is much the same even today. There was
no shelter, no means of subsistence; and besides carrying
its arms and equipment, an army must drive its meat on
the hoof, its ordnance on the backs of mules. Bolívar had
never made such a march before nor moved an army at
all, except within the last few months on the Magdalena.
But his self-confidence was boundless. He was not rash.
He considered the obstacles before him and made his
plans carefully, quickly.

For ten days and nights the little army struggled eastward. Sweating in the steaming low places, bleeding from
the thorny bush and ravenous insects, they scrambled up
the sheer rock faces, clinging with knees and fingers.
Lightning played about them and thunder rolled and
echoed among the dark gorges. Men and animals slipped
from narrow ledges and fell away to crash far down
among the diminutive tree-tops, and their faint cries were
lost in the wind that screamed between the peaks. At
night the living lay exhausted on the bleak páramos,
soaked by the sleet and numbed by the bitter cold. Bolívar
was everywhere among them, driving them, inspiring
them with his words. He did the work of a dozen men.
He was tireless. He tugged at foundering animals, hoisted
the fallen loads upon their backs, supported his bruised
and injured comrades. The worn-out men could only look
upon the slight body of their leader with stupid wonderment. His eyes flashed fire and his lips spoke jests and
at night he sang ribald songs in French.

On the Alto de la Aguada, Correa waited with a hundred men to defend the pass. Bolívar's scouts brought

word and he immediately sent a runner forward, bearing a false message from Castillo that he was coming from Pamplona to fall upon Correa from the rear. Correa captured the runner, fell for the ruse and abandoned his position and hurried back to Pamplona to catch Castillo unaware. Bolívar whipped up his exhausted men, drove them pell-mell after Correa, took him from behind and routed his force so completely that it was never able to re-form.

Joined by the force of Castillo, he pushed on to Pamplona and then, with only a few days of rest for his men, he followed after Correa toward Cúcuta. He crossed the Zúlia River and confronted the town in the valley on February 28, only three weeks from the day he left Ocaña. Bolívar kept his main force in reserve and attacked with his vanguard, which immediately fell back and drew Correa out from the fortifications with his whole army. That was what Bolívar planned. Now was the chance. With fixed bayonets, shouting, Bolívar's main column poured out from the woods and fell upon the surprised royalists. They broke and fled, leaving their dead and wounded. The patriots drove them through the town and to the border of Venezuela. The royalists crossed the Táchira and kept going, unpursued, to the town of La Grita. In San José de Cúcuta, Bolívar found all their supplies and ammunition and, unexpectedly, a million pesos in specie which had been sent there for safe-keeping. He was on the border of his native land at last.

He addressed his men in the plaza. He called them heroes and spoke of "Cúcuta, liberated," saying, "In less than two months you have carried out two campaigns and have begun a third, which commences here and must end in the land that gave me life. . . . All America expects its liberty and salvation from you, brave soldiers of Cartagena and of the Union." Bolívar had studied the ways of Napoleon with troops and had learned what could be done with words.

Chapter X

WAR TO THE DEATH

✤

BOLÍVAR had not received from the Congress at
Tunja outright permission to lead the troops of New
Granada into Venezuela. Anxious as he was to follow Correa and consummate his plan for liberation of his country, he dared not advance until that permission was
granted. From Cúcuta he dispatched a letter to the Congress, describing the victories of his army thus far, and
begging not that he be allowed to continue on to Caracas
—for he knew the Congress would never agree to any such
mad scheme—but merely that he might advance to the
cities of Mérida and Trujillo in order to complete the
demolition of Correa's force. But Tunja was a long way
off. He would have more than two months of waiting before he could hope for a reply.

He used that time to advantage. He sent José Félix
Ribas, his kinsman and old friend, who had come from
Curaçao to join him, to Santa Fé de Bogotá to win sym-
pathy and help from the republican government there.

That city, the oldest and most cultured of the northern
Andean capitals, had been the seat of the viceroyalty of
New Granada and was now the capital of the Republic
of Cundinamarca, independent of the Congress of Tunja.
Its president was Antonio Nariño. This was that intellectual patriot Nariño who had been imprisoned in Cádiz
for printing and distributing *The Rights of Man* in Santa
Fé. He had escaped from the Spanish prison, returned
to Bogotá, was imprisoned again and released during the
successful revolution of Cartagena in 1810. Then he had

established the Republic of Cundinamarca and was elected president by popular vote.

As Miranda is regarded as Bolívar's Precursor in Venezuela, Nariño may, in some respects, be considered his Precursor in New Granada. However, there are great differences in the viewpoints of the two men. Nariño was strictly a regionalist, while Bolívar, from the beginning, harbored the dream of a Union. For Nariño there existed only his Bogotá. For Bolívar there was only the whole of Spanish South America. In spite of this regionalist attitude of Nariño, Ribas won his sympathy and he returned to Cúcuta with the remnants of one hundred and fifty men from the garrison of Santa Fé.

Bolívar reorganized his army and garnered recruits and supplies from the surrounding valley of Cúcuta. He was joined, too, by some of his old friends and loyal adherents, among them the Venezuelan officers Rafael Urdaneta and Pedro Briceño Méndez.

Nevertheless, all was not going well in Cúcuta. The New Granadan Colonel Castillo and his subordinate, Major Francisco de Paula Santander, were restive under the command of the Venezuelan. Strictly regionalists also, they had no interest whatever in Bolívar's plan to reconquer Venezuela. They disagreed violently over the project and were loath to lead their troops into what they considered a foreign country. The dispute became so violent, at last, that Bolívar sent his resignation to Tunja. The Congress, as Bolívar had foreseen, refused to accept it and reaffirmed his authority over the New Granadan troops. He was promoted to the grade of brigadier general and made an honorary citizen of New Granada.

When word came from Tunja on April 27 giving him permission to advance, Bolívar, who had already crossed the border himself, ordered Castillo to march to La Grita and drive Correa from his position there. Castillo accepted the order with ill grace but Santander flatly refused to comply.

"You will give the order to march," Bolívar said to him. "Otherwise you will shoot me or I most certainly will shoot you."

Santander gave the order. This incident marks the beginning of many years of antagonism between the two men. In many ways it is analogous to those first dissensions between Bolívar and Miranda; and the final results were much the same—the downfall of one and triumph for the other. But in this case it was Bolívar who suffered ignominy; and many years intervened before the culmination.

Castillo and Santander attacked Correa at La Grita, defeated him and drove him eastward. Then they both resigned their commands, returned to Tunja, and Bolívar placed their troops in the command of Colonel Urdaneta.

Bolívar himself had been too impatient to wait for permission to arrive. With a small force he had crossed the Táchira into Venezuelan territory on the first of March and waited there while the main army remained in Cúcuta. He dispatched a message to Tunja which ended with the statement, "I ask Your Excellency to send the reply to this communication to Trujillo; I shall receive it there." He addressed the people of the village of San Antonia, saying, "Today the Republic of Venezuela is reborn." When he was ready to march he said to his troops, "Loyal Republicans, you go to redeem the cradle of Colombian independence as the Crusaders liberated Jerusalem, the cradle of Christianity!" The word "Colombian" is now a fixture in his thought and speech.

Bolívar moved eastward to San Cristóbal and then advanced along the Venezuelan Andes, following that great Cordillera which leads to Caracas, and arrived at Mérida on May 23. As he came on, the main Spanish army of 1000 men, driven from La Grita, had fallen back to Bailadores, then to Estanques and then to Mérida. There Bolívar's fame had preceded him; the people rose up at his approach and the royalists fled once more. Bolívar entered the city in a tumult of acclaim. His name, shouted into

the thin mountain air by Indians in the plaza and by
creole señoritas from their balconies, echoed among the
steep narrow streets and old Spanish buildings and rose
toward the army of mighty peaks that stood in review,
glistening white in the sunlight. There are sixty-seven of
those peaks over thirteen thousand feet high, and ten of
them are clothed in perpetual snow. The highest of all,
rising to sixteen thousand four hundred feet, now bears
the name that was shouted that day in the streets of
Mérida.

At the celebration in the plaza the mountain people
listened for the first time to a new concept of national
liberty and to the promise of a new order of human relations such as they had never dreamed of. A company of
Mérida militia under Major Vicente Campo Elías offered
its services to Bolívar's cause. Campo Elías was a character
worthy of comment. He was a Spaniard, but fanatical in
his hatred of those of his own blood. He had sworn that
after he had killed every Spaniard he would kill his own
family and then himself, so that there would be no more
of the race alive.

Dr. Vicente Tejera, one of the members of the old
Caracas Junta, joined Bolívar there, too, among other
patriots of the First Republic.

He had quite an army now, properly organized, even to
a medical staff. There was an advance guard under Giradot and Urdaneta composed of 560 men, and a rear guard
under Ribas with two pieces of artillery and 883 men.

On May 25, two days after entering Mérida, Bolívar
sent out detachments of the vanguard to dislodge the
Spaniards from their position. Captains D'Elhuyar and
Maza engaged Correa's force at Escuque and defeated it.
Correa retired westward down into the lowlands of Lake
Maracaibo and Giradot, following close behind, marched
into the city of Trujillo without resistance. Bolívar's way
was cleared. With the rear guard, he proceeded along that
difficult, mountainous Cordillera, following the old path

of the Spanish Conquistadores, and entered Trujillo on the fourteenth of June. That same evening he had word of a general order which the Spanish commander, Tizcar, had issued to his troops—an order that no quarter be given to those who surrendered.

Bolívar didn't sleep that night at all. He spent the long hours alone in his room, pacing back and forth. By morning he had arrived at a grave decision.

The proclamation of "War to the Death" which Bolívar issued at Trujillo on June 15, 1813, is, in the eyes of many historians, the blackest stain upon his character and the most ignoble act of his career. He submitted it to his officers and received their unqualified approval before he signed it. Before, in Mérida, he had stated, "The victims [of Spanish cruelty] will be avenged, their executioners exterminated. Our charity is exhausted now and, since our oppressors have forced us to a mortal war, they shall disappear in America and our country will be purged of the monsters who infest it. Our hatred shall be implacable and war shall be to the death." The decree of Trujillo said, in part:

The Spaniards have served us with rapine and death. They have violated the sacred rights of human beings, violated capitulations and the most solemn treaties; committed, in fact, every crime. They have reduced the Republic of Venezuela to the most frightful desolation. Thus, then, justice demands vengeance and necessity obliges us to take it. . . .

Every Spaniard who does not conspire with the most active and effective means possible against the tyranny in favor of our just cause will be held as an enemy and a traitor to the fatherland; and in consequence will be inexorably put to the knife. On the other hand, an absolute and general indulgence will be granted to those who pass to our army with or without their arms. . . . Spaniards who render conspicuous service to the State will be treated as Americans. . . .

Spaniards and Canary Islanders, count on death, even if you are neutral, if you do not work actively for the liberation of Venezuela!

Americans, count upon life, even if you are unworthy!

Bolívar was not personally a cruel man. There is no instance recorded of a single cruel act which he himself perpetrated; scarcely, indeed, of a cruel word. There are many occasions during the years to come when he failed to carry out the terms of his drastic edict; but there are occasions, too, when he ordered them adhered to ruthlessly. And there is evidence that he viewed the execution of his decree with repugnance. A week after, from San Carlos he issued another statement to the Spaniards which was almost pleading. "For the last time, Spaniards and Canary Islanders, listen to the voice of justice and clemency! If you prefer our cause to that of tyrants, you will be pardoned and will share in our well-being, our lives and honor; and if you persist in being our enemies, you must leave our country or prepare to die!"

There are many reasons for the policy of "War to the Death." There is no excuse, ethically, of course. There cannot possibly be anything noble in revenge nor justifiable in the doctrine that two wrongs make a right. Bolívar has defended himself many times; but his defenses are little more than a recital of acts which would excuse a desire for revenge. There were plenty of those. The Spaniards were cruel beyond the limits of normal imaginations. They offered a price for republican ears and decorated their homes with them. They peeled the feet of patriot prisoners and forced them to run over hot coals. After raping women they tied them in their hammocks and set a fire under them. O'Leary cites these things; but even he, wholehearted admirer of Bolívar, cannot propose them as justifying reprisals.

Yet even Henry Clay, speaking before the Congress of the United States, upheld this policy of vengeance. Always

an ardent supporter of the cause of independence in South
America, Clay, in 1818, speaking in behalf of recognition
of the new Republic of Colombia, defended Bolívar's action thus:

The gentleman from Georgia cannot see any parallel between our revolution and that of the South American provinces and contends that their revolution was stained by scenes
which had not occurred in ours. If so, it was because execrable
outrages had been committed upon them by the troops of the
mother country which were not upon us. Can it be believed,
if the slaves had been let loose upon us in the South as they
have been let loose in Venezuela, if quarter had been refused, capitulations violated, that George Washington would
not have resorted to retribution? Retaliation is sometimes
mercy, mercy to both parties. The only means by which the
coward's soul that indulges in such enormities can be reached
is to show him that he will be visited by severe but just retribution.

These are the arguments, of course, which are used now
and which always have been used by dictatorial leaders to
justify their ruthlessness. "The good of the State demands
it" is an age-old cry.

Bolívar believed sincerely in the necessity for the step
he took; there can be no doubt of that. He didn't like it
but he considered it a hateful necessity. He never hated
anybody with a personal hatred, not even Santander and
probably not even Miranda. He held his project of liberation above all personal feelings and was prepared to take
any measures which he considered necessary to it, however distasteful. The great dreams which drove him so
hard were his only consideration; and when anything
stood in the way of them, he could be implacable. In this,
too, he was in accord with those dictators who are on the
march today and with all those who subscribe to the doctrine that the end always justifies the means, that expediency comes before ethics.

The purpose behind Bolívar's decision was quite definite and logical. It goes back to that old fact that the war was not a clear-cut issue between the Spaniards and Americans; that only the creole aristocrats were fighting the Spaniards and that most of the lower classes were actually on the side of the royalists. The cruelties which Bolívar harped upon and which were being visited upon the patriots were the acts, mostly, of their own countrymen. The Spanish officers encouraged and ordered these barbarities, to be sure, but the native troops, because of their greater numbers, were most often the perpetrators. It was necessary, then, to create a psychological separation along racial lines. By assuring the creole royalists that retribution would not fall upon them but upon their Spanish officers, Bolívar hoped to win them over to the republican ranks. He placed the blame entirely upon the Spaniards. By constant repetition of the words, "Spaniards and Canary Islanders," by constantly heaping opprobrium upon them, he hoped to foster a race consciousness among the Americans, to unite them in sympathy. He had always believed that such solidarity among his countrymen was absolutely necessary to the winning of independence and he had always, almost single-handed, worked to bring it about. He hoped now, by a policy of utter ruthlessness against Spaniards only, to create between them and Americans a gulf of hatred "greater than the Atlantic Ocean." His policy was partially successful, but it took a long time to have effect; and meanwhile the results of it were monstrous.

Bolívar had not been the first patriot to proclaim "War to the Death" nor the first to put it into execution. Dr. Antonio Nicolás Briceño, a member of the First Venezuelan Congress and a signer of the Declaration of Independence, had escaped from Caracas after the downfall of the republic. He had been an eminent lawyer, a cultured gentleman "of gentle and peaceful character." The atrocious acts of Monteverde so affected him that he was seized with a violent hatred of the Spaniards and a pas-

sionate desire for revenge. He went into New Granada
and stirred up a sort of free-lance revolution. He urged
his few men to ruthlessness and earned the name, "The
Devil," throughout the colony. He proclaimed a policy
for advancement in his army thus: a soldier who presented
20 Spanish heads would be promoted to alférez; 30 heads,
to lieutenant; 50 heads, to captain; and so on. Bolívar,
who was then operating near by, condemned Briceño's
policy and even ordered his arrest. However, only a short
time later in Trujillo, when he learned that Briceño had
been captured and executed at Barinas by Tizcar, he himself issued a similar proclamation of "War to the Death."

In Trujillo, Bolívar had advanced into Venezuela as far
as the Congress of Tunja had permitted him to go. But
Caracas was his goal, whether or no. Correa had been
cleared from the path ahead but in Barinas, on the eastern slope of the Andes, on the edge of the llanos, was
Tizcar with 1500 royalists. Bolívar's left was threatened
by the forces in Coro and Maracaibo; and Tizcar, on his
right, could block his advance or strike at his rear by
Táchira, cutting his lines into New Granada and shutting
off his path of retreat. He had to decide quickly. He wrote
to the Congress, "My resolution is made. I shall act with
the utmost vigor and rapidity."

With Giradot and Ribas from Mérida and Trujillo advancing to protect his rear, he dropped quickly down the
steep mountainsides, defeated a force of royalists and occupied Guanare, a town beyond Barinas, in Tizcar's main
line of communication with Caracas. Tizcar, at Barinas,
didn't even know he had moved. An admirable maneuver,
surely. On the same day, July 1, Ribas and Urdaneta, advancing with 400 men, engaged a royalist column of 800
under Martí at Niquitao. The battle began at nine in the
morning and lasted throughout the day. When sunset
threw its long mountain shadows over the bloody field,
Ribas led a bayonet charge and the royalists broke, leav-

ing behind many dead and wounded, 45 prisoners, 450 rifles and one cannon.

Bolívar immediately hurried southwest toward Barinas. It was the first time he had forsaken the direct route to Caracas. But he hadn't far to go. Tizcar fled in the night, leaving behind 13 cannon and all his equipment. A detachment under Giradot followed him and drove him far down into the llanos to Nutrias. Tizcar was out of the way for good. Bolívar turned about and headed toward his goal once more. He had 1300 men now, including a squadron of llanos cavalry. Ahead of him were 2800 royalists divided into three forces under Oberto, González and Izquierdo, occupying three towns, Barquisimeto, Tocuyo and San Carlos, which formed a triangle with its base toward his position. He must move quickly and destroy them one at a time before they could close in.

He made a forced march of a hundred miles along the edge of the plains to Araure and advanced against the main Spanish force of Izquierdo at San Carlos. Ribas had been ordered to march against González at Tocuyo and then against Oberto at Barquisimeto. However, Oberto had perceived the move and called in González to join him in defense of the city. Ribas was a little too late to prevent the union. At Los Horcones, outside of Barquisimeto, he came upon the royalists, 1500 strong, well entrenched and supported by four cannon. Ribas had little more than one-third the number of men and no artillery at all. That didn't bother him. On the morning of July 22, his red French Revolutionary cap perched jauntily on his head, he led a mad charge against the Spanish center. His columns broke before a withering fire. He re-formed them and launched another assault upon the enemy's flank. Again the patriots were driven back. Re-forming again, Ribas flung his men against the other flank, turned it, drove on with bayonet and machete, captured the artillery and turned it on the fleeing royalists. His victory was complete. He marched into Barquisimeto and took possession of the enemy's supplies. Then he turned eastward and marched down toward the plains to join Bolívar at San Carlos, following his orders.

Ribas had won the two greatest victories of the campaign—Niquitao and Los Horcones; but Bolívar had planned the maneuvers.

The remnants of Oberto's army joined Izquierdo at San Carlos, but they abandoned the town in the face of Bolívar's advance and fell back toward Valencia where Monteverde had come with his troops from Caracas. Bolívar concentrated his army in San Carlos. He had 2500 men now, with cavalry and artillery. After only a few days' rest, he began a swift march after Izquierdo in order to destroy him before he reached Valencia.

At daybreak of July 31, the advance guard of Bolívar's troops caught up with Izquierdo, who had taken a position among the rocky heights at Tinaquillo. Urdaneta concentrated the advance guard and launched an attack. Bolívar, with the main body behind, heard the firing, spurred his horse and came up with the attacking force. Urdaneta had dislodged the royalists and they were retiring slowly and in order. It was obvious that they only hoped to hold off the patriots until they could join with Monteverde at Valencia. Bolívar ordered the cavalry to skirt the enemy's right flank and attempt to head off the column while Urdaneta followed, keeping constant contact with the enemy's rear guard. Thus, all day, the royalists retired slowly, the patriot cavalry harassing their right, attempting to overtake the main column along the rough terrain on the flank. Twenty kilometers were covered in this manner.

As evening approached, Bolívar realized that, with nightfall, the royalists could reach the cover of the range of mountains—very near now—and escape to Valencia. What he wished to do was block them on the plain of Taguanes, just ahead. He selected a hundred of the best horses of his cavalry, mounted an infantryman behind the

rider of each, and ordered them to dash forward in all
haste and place themselves across the enemy's advance.
Spurring their tired horses, shouting, scrambling among
the bush along the stony slopes by the right flank, the
little squadron hurried forward. They dashed through the
enemy's fire and reached their position just as the royalist
advance came out upon the plain. Quickly Bolívar charged
from the rear with his whole column—advance, main and
rear. The two hundred men ahead held firm, stopped the
Spaniards with their fire. In a few minutes of furious
fighting the royalists were completely demoralized. Every
officer but one was dead, wounded or a prisoner. Izquierdo himself was taken prisoner and died shortly after
from his wounds. There was only Monteverde ahead of
Bolívar now, on his way to Caracas.

All this time Monteverde had not been loafing idly in
the capital. He was having his hands full with trouble
from another direction. In the east, several groups of
young patriots, all of the same class and background and
sentiments as Bolívar and his associates, had instituted
revolutionary movements which had met with considerable success. Juan Bautista Arismendi had taken possession of the island of Margarita, his place of birth. From
the British island of Trinidad, forty-five men under young
Santiago Mariño had landed on the eastern extremity of
Venezuela and marched westward, defeating the Spanish
forces in several battles and capturing the towns of Maturín, Cumaná and Barcelona. Among them were the
Bermúdez brothers, Manuel Piar and Antonio José Sucre
—all able warriors who later figured prominently in the
career of Simón Bolívar.

Monteverde himself was obliged to leave Caracas with
his main army of 3000 and march against the rebels in
the east. He attacked Piar at Maturín on May 25 and was
defeated so badly that he had to fall back upon the capital. There he learned of that astounding advance of

Bolívar's from the Andes. The obscure young Venezuelan, whom he had considered so unimportant less than a year before, had marched rapidly forward the whole length of the Cordillera with never a halt, defeating all the Spanish armies one after another, and was now approaching the capital itself like some invincible juggernaut. After the retreat of Tizcar from Barinas there was nothing for Monteverde to do but go out to Valencia himself to defend that city. He left Manuel del Fierro behind him as acting captain-general.

Bolívar was in a particular hurry to get to Caracas after he had word of the victories of Mariño in the east. He didn't want any competition in his business of liberating. He was somewhat justified in that attitude by the fact that he had made promises to the government in New Granada, had gone on without authority and would be in a bad spot if he failed to make good. Then, too, his own achievements were the more formidable by far. Besides, he wasn't at all sure of this man Mariño who had established a government in Barcelona and declared himself Supreme Chief and Dictator of the East.

After his victory over Izquierdo at Taguanes, Bolívar marched at once against Valencia. But Monteverde, with only a few hundred troops left now, had seen enough. During the night he fled down to the coast, to Puerto Cabello, and Bolívar entered the city unopposed.

Fierro, in the capital, realized that the end had come. He sent out a commission to treat with the victorious general and, to insure the best terms possible, he was careful to include among its members Francisco de Iturbe and Casa León, the two men who had protected Bolívar and helped him get a passport after Monteverde's occupation of Caracas.

Bolívar met the commission in La Victoria, the same place where, only a year before, Miranda had signed the death warrant of the First Republic. His terms for the surrender of Caracas were magnanimous in the extreme

and ignored completely his decree of "War to the Death."
There were to be no penalties whatever, no arrests or
confiscations or reprisals, and everything was to be done
to promote reconciliation among the various political elements and to smooth over past differences. The commission hastened to sign. Nevertheless some six thousand
royalists, Fierro among them, who had guilty consciences,
perhaps, fled from the capital to La Guaira.

In his first campaign as a general, Bolívar had marched
1200 kilometers over primitive mountain country, fought
six battles, destroyed five armies and reconquered the
whole western part of Venezuela—all in the space of
ninety days.

Chapter XI

A GILDED CHARIOT

✦

NEARING the city, Bolívar halted to change his clothes. Many people had already come out miles along the road to greet him. He took off his worn, sun-bleached uniform and put on a new one, gleaming white and blue, heavy with gold. Then he remounted—not upon the tough mule that had served him in mountain marches, but on a white Arab stallion. He rode toward the city of his birth and behind him marched the wan and tattered young veterans of New Granada with the battle flags of Spanish battalions fluttering from their bayonets.

At the little bridge over the Guaire there was an arch of flowers and under the arch was a great press of people. A committee of citizens stood waiting; with them were twelve girls dressed in white and garlanded with flowers. There was a small two-wheeled cart, a sort of chariot, hung with laurel and palm and decorated with eagles painted in gilt. When Bolívar reached the bridge a spokesman for the committee addressed him in extravagant words and bade him step into the chariot. Then, at a signal, the twelve maidens took up a silken rope and drew the hero into the city. Simultaneously the whole valley burst into an uproar. Cannon thundered from the forts, the church bells clamored, the bands struck up, the people screamed in wild acclaim.

The procession moved along the narrow climbing streets toward the plaza, the chariot at the head, the long column of troops, on foot and mounted, behind. People crowded the roof-tops and balconies. Roses, hibiscus, oleanders, camellias and bougainvillea showered down under the feet of the deliverers and smothered the bare head of Bolívar. The guards could not hold back the surging crowds on the narrow sidewalks; they broke out and swarmed among the troopers, embracing them, shouting hoarse vivas. Barefoot peon boys, men and women followed along beside the chariot of Bolívar, dancing and singing in a delirium of joy, their words lost in the general tumult. Old crones grasped his hands and kissed them, weeping. Here and there were the crumpled walls of buildings which had been the tombs of many thousands a year before; but all that was forgotten now. Forgotten, too, were the words of the priests that the cause of liberty was the cause of heretics. The priests themselves joined in the acclaim and even the archbishop, who had stood solidly behind Monteverde during his reign of terror, now hastened to do honor to Bolívar.

The dungeons had all been emptied of their political prisoners; patriots had come swarming out of long hiding and back from exile in near-by islands. Among the crowds that greeted Bolívar now were many of his old friends—companions of the Patriotic Society, of Madrid and Paris. They looked at him, bareheaded in his chariot, with curiosity and wonderment. It didn't seem possible. Only a year. He had been just one of them—not even an important one. He had always been a hot-head, a great talker—had loved to boss. But this—por dios, it wasn't possible. Still, there had always been something about him, something about his eyes.

In appearance Bolívar had changed greatly. Even now, smiling, bowing to the cheering crowds, his face alight with triumph, it was apparent. He looked older than his thirty years. The hardships he had suffered and the weight of responsibility had left their marks upon him. The youthful roundness was gone from his face. His high white forehead seemed even more prominent, his face longer still, his cheeks more sunken. The constant change of expression that played over his mobile features seemed somehow the studied efforts of a finished actor.

He dined that evening in his old home with María Antonia and Juana and their children about him. Hipólita and Matea hovered over him, their black faces shining with pride. He had to leave the table frequently to speak to the crowds that pressed against the barred windows.

The celebration in the city continued all night. There were fireworks in the plaza and dancing in the streets. Bolívar danced till dawn at a great ball given in his honor and there was one girl there, Josefina Madrid, with whom he danced most. He found her very pleasing. Thereafter, with her sister and her mother, she went everywhere with him for a number of years, even on long marches into wild and dangerous places. The soldiers called her Señorita Pepa.

Interlude

A CONTRADICTION—LIBERATOR
AND DICTATOR

✢

TEN days of incredible activity. How he found time
for all he accomplished during those first days in the
capital is a mystery, especially considering the fact that he
danced every night and pursued his new-found romance
on the side. He wrote letters by the hundreds, pacing the
floor in the early morning hours, dictating to three secretaries. To the Congress of New Granada he sent grandiloquent messages of gratitude and assurances of submission to its authority. He wrote to Torres in Tunja and to
Nariño in Santa Fé and dictated innumerable proclamations to the people and to the troops, urging them to continued labors in the cause of liberty.

Peace had been signed, but there was no peace. Fierro
had fled the country without signing the pact his commissioners had accepted and Monteverde, secure in Puerto
Cabello, declared that he had no intention of dealing
with rebels. Spanish sympathizers were flocking into his
ranks and the unguarded seacoast afforded him access to
supplies from Puerto Rico.

So the war was still on. The country had been bled dry
during the Spanish occupation, the patriot troops were in
rags and starving. They had received no pay since crossing the Venezuelan border. Bolívar, in desperation, imprisoned the Spaniards who had fled to La Guaira, confiscated their property, levied upon the merchants of
Caracas and disposed of some of his own estates to raise
funds. On August 6, only ten days after he entered the

capital, he left to command the forces before Puerto Cabello.

During that time he had named Cristóbal Mendoza, a New Granadan, civil governor and formed a government under the sovereignty of the Congress of Tunja. He acknowledged Mariño's supreme authority in the east and he proclaimed to the people, "Nothing shall turn me, Venezuelans, from my first and only intentions—your glory and liberty. An assembly of notable, wise and virtuous men must be solemnly convoked to discuss and approve the nature of the government and the functions it shall exercise in the critical and extraordinary circumstances that surround the republic."

Ustáritz and Sanz drew a plan for local governments, named secretaries of War, State, Marine and Justice and conferred on Bolívar "Supreme executive and legislative powers, without other restrictions than those imposed by the General Congress of New Granada." The General Congress was too far away to impose any restrictions at all.

A siege of Puerto Cabello was out of the question, with no vessels to blockade the harbor. Mariño had a small fleet of gunboats in Cumaná but he refused Bolívar's requests for co-operation. So, for nearly three months, the patriot action was confined to skirmishing about the environs of the town; and then what Bolívar had feared actually happened. Twelve hundred troops under Colonel Salomón arrived in war vessels from Puerto Rico to aid Monteverde.

The skirmishing went on—raids by Urdaneta and Giradot into the city streets, counter-sallies by the royalist troops—and nothing came of it all. The Spanish commander refused all proposals to exchange prisoners and, in reply, Bolívar hanged a Spanish officer in the plaza of the town, in full view of the royalist garrison. This worthy was one Zuazola, the Spaniard who had established the custom of paying bounty on patriot ears and noses. It was his quaint habit to wear a collection of those ears on his hat for decoration and he had invented, too, the little game of sewing the bare backs of two prisoners together with stitches through the flesh, so that every movement of either one was agony.

In a sharp battle on the heights of Barbula young Giradot, the valiant New Granadan who had crossed the Andes with Bolívar, took a musket ball between the eyes as he was planting the flag of the republic on the enemy breastworks. Bolívar immediately formed a single corps of all the New Granadans, named it the Batallón Giradot, and placed D'Elhuyar, the dead officer's childhood friend, in command. "Go now," he told them, "and avenge your brother." Three days later the battalion attacked Monteverde's main column at Las Trincheras, destroyed it and drove the remnants back behind the walls of Puerto Cabello. Monteverde himself was wounded and was replaced by Salomón shortly after, to disappear from the revolutionary scene.

Bolívar seized upon the death of Giradot as an opportunity for staging one of those masterly theatrical performances for which he had so much talent. The spirits of the people were at a low ebb and something must be done to renew their enthusiasm for the cause. Besides, the government of New Granada must be kept ingratiated and in a mood to permit their soldiers to remain so far away, fighting a war that dragged on and on.

In Valencia he wrote a stirring proclamation. September 30, the date of Giradot's death, was to be a day of mourning forever throughout Venezuela. All citizens of the republic were to wear mourning for a month, the bones of the hero would be conveyed to his native Antioquia and his heart would be carried in veneration to Caracas. His family and heirs would receive his full salary forever from the Venezuelan government.

So the heart was removed from the body of Giradot and placed in a gilded urn. Then, from Valencia, a great procession set out toward the capital. A corps of massed drummers rolling a slow beat marched at the head, and behind came the chief army chaplain bearing the hero's heart. Following, Bolívar marched with his staff and three companies of mounted dragoons in full regalia. The villages along the route were draped with mourning and the people crowded the streets; a halt was made at every village while the local poet read a doleful elegy. In the capital, a Requiem High Mass was sung in the cathedral, the urn was placed in a crypt beside the altar, and Bolívar, his face a drawn mask of grief, delivered a glowing and Romanesque oration.

A beautiful and touching spectacle. Long after, Bolívar spoke with enthusiasm about how effective it was for his purpose.

The next day, October 14, the city council named Bolívar Captain-General of the Armies and conferred upon him the title "Liberator of Venezuela." Sincerely moved by the honor, he used only that title thereafter— and there were occasions when he refused more lofty ones and even crowns. "I regard it," he said, "as more glorious and satisfying than the scepters of all the empires on earth." To share the honor among his officers he created the Order of Liberators and conferred it upon Ribas, Giradot, Urdaneta, Ricuarte, D'Elhuyar and Campo Elías. As a political move he sent the decorations also to Mariño and his officers, accompanied by a letter begging them to accept. "I wear it myself," he wrote, "even though, in the noble undertaking which our arms have brought to a glorious end, I am the last to merit it."

But "the glorious end" was far from accomplished. Within a few days Bolívar was back in the field again, fighting the Spanish forces that appeared from every quarter. In a little more than three months he had organized a government, raised troops, supplies and funds, fought in six battles himself and won them all but one. Following his movements on a map, it is amazing how he could even cover so much ground in that time. His officers, too, were fighting constantly with their individual commands—winning mostly, but unable to attain a decisive victory. Ceballos came out of Coro with 1300 royalists, Salomón advanced on Valencia with 1200, Boves threatened Caracas with 2000 llanero horsemen and Yañez commanded a force of 2500 on the plains of Apure. The patriots under García de Sena were defeated at Barquisimeto and then Bolívar, joined by Urdaneta, lost a battle at the same place because of a retreat call sounded, by some error, at the moment of victory. It was the Liberator's first defeat. Campo Elías attacked Boves at Mosquiteros, won a bloody victory, took nearly half the enemy prisoner and put them all to the knife, Spaniards and Venezuelans alike. With Ribas and a force from the garrison of Caracas, Bolívar defeated Salomón at Vigirima and D'Elhuyar drove the demoralized survivors all the way back to Puerto Cabello once more. Finally, Bolívar concentrated the forces of Urdaneta and Campo Elías on the plains at San Carlos and confronted the combined armies of Ceballos and Yañez. The patriots numbered 4800 men, the royalists, 5200, with infantry, cavalry and artillery units on both sides—the most formidable armies that had ever met on Venezuelan soil.

The battle was fought on the fifth of December, 1813, on the rolling plains of Araure, and we see Bolívar for the first time in action as commander of the complete elements of an army in open combat. He proved himself as able in formal maneuvers as he had in guerilla war- fare. Standing on a low knoll he observed the action, directed the movements of his four columns of infantry, his cavalry and his artillery with superb skill. All day the smoke covered the plain and the roar of battle rolled up the mountainsides until, toward sunset, the royalists broke and fled, leaving on the field over a thousand dead, all their artillery and equipment and 700 prisoners. The

patriots pursued the scattered segments for twenty kilometers, hacking away with bayonet and machete. Ceballos
retired again to Coro, and Yáñez far into the llanos once
more.

A breathing spell at last. Bolívar returned to Caracas,
anxious to establish a more legal foundation for his dictatorial powers. He knew well how to get what he wanted
without seeming to desire it. He wrote to the Congress:

The possession of supreme authority, so gratifying to the
despots of other countries, has been for me, lover of liberty,
painful and depressing. . . . Return, therefore, Venezuela, to
happiness under the protecting laws decreed by your representatives and under magistrates named by legal and popular
election. . . .

I repeat what I have always declared; that I will retain no
part of my authority unless the people themselves confer it
upon me. To fight for my country is my sole ambition; and
it will be satisfied with whatever position is assigned me in
the army that wages war against the enemy.

The political leaders took the hint and called for a
popular assembly under the guidance of the New Granadan, Mendoza, and the president of the municipality,
Rodríguez Domínguez. Addressing the meeting, Bolívar
said, "To save us from anarchy and to destroy the enemy
which still sought to oppress us, I accepted and exercised
the supreme power. I long for the moment of relinquish-
ing it to the representatives who should now be named.
I hope that you will release me from the position which
one of yourselves could fill with dignity. I aspire only to
the honor of continuing to combat our enemies. . . ."

Mendoza replied with a eulogy of the Liberator, declaring that to convoke a congress now would be to invite
ruin once more, and that the only security lay in the continuance of supreme power in the hands which now held
it. Domínguez spoke more frankly still and used the term
"dictator" for the first time. "Continue, Your Excellency,"

he said, "as Dictator; perfect the work of salvation for the patria." Then, as the firm believer in popular government that he was, he dropped a little hint by adding, "and when you have succeeded, restore the exercise of sovereignty to the people, creating a democratic government."

Bolívar still held out and, undoubtedly sure of his ground, threw a sop to that jealous rival in the east whose help he needed. "There are more illustrious citizens than I," he declared, "who merit the honor of your confidence. General Mariño, Liberator of the East! There is a leader worthy of directing your destinies!"

But the assembly thought otherwise. In a general uproar the members shouted their insistence; and Bolívar, with a final show of reluctance, gracefully yielded.

Perhaps he didn't realize the full weight of the responsibility he was assuming. Perhaps he didn't grasp the evil portent and the power of that great cloud of horsemen which had formed in the remote llanos and was growing, rolling ever nearer, leaving desolation behind. Still, he was gifted with perception far beyond that of other men. His faith in himself was supreme.

The center of that destroying cloud was a Spaniard named José Tomás Boves.

III: PROPHET IN HIS OWN LAND

Chapter XII

THE INFERNAL LEGION

❖

THE great llanos of Venezuela lie behind the wall of
the Andes that begins at the Colombian border and
swings in a long arc northeastward along the Caribbean
coast. Sloping south and east into the basin of the Orinoco
and its great tributaries, the Apure and Arauca, they comprise nearly half the total area of the country. They are
almost level plains, covered with tall coarse grass, boundless as the sea. Thin strips of tropic forest follow the banks
of the innumerable rivers that have cut deep gashes in
the sandy soil. In the long rainy season the rivers rise and
flood the plains, converting them into shallow trackless
oceans dotted with little islands of green moriche palm
like coral atolls. It is the cattle country of Venezuela.

In the days of Bolívar, the llanos were inhabited by
vast herds of wild cattle and wild horses and by semi-
savage men—pardos, mestizos, zambos, mulattoes, blacks
and Indians. Living their lives on horseback in a land that
was flooded half the year, the llaneros were "half centaur,
half alligator." Their diet was entirely meat, dried in the
sun and carried in strips under the saddle to be salted
by the horse's sweat.

Slaves, mostly, of the absentee owners of the land and
cattle, the llaneros were nevertheless singularly independent and self-sustaining. It was not an uncommon thing to
find white freemen under the despotic rule of a negro
slave who had risen to the position of overseer of an
"hato," sheerly through physical prowess. Their problems
of existence extremely simplified, they were ignorant of

affairs throughout the rest of the country, untouched by Spanish oppression and unconcerned with the political struggles and aspirations for liberty of the city-dwelling upper classes. It was of these llaneros that Boves formed the army that became known as the "Infernal Legion."

Boves was a pirate and smuggler who had been imprisoned by the Spanish and exiled to the town of Calabozo in the llanos. He was an Asturian by birth, red-haired, big-headed, with a sharp beak and evil blue eyes. Even today, in the remote places of the llanos, his malignant spirit is thought to dwell among the misty swamps and his name brings terror to children. Cunninghame Graham says of him, "He was of middle height, capable of enduring extraordinary fatigue; active, bold, fearless, impetuous, rash, astute, hungry for power, cruel and bloody."

When the war of independence broke out he was keeper of a small store in Calabozo in the llanos. At first he joined the patriots as a minor officer under Juan Escalona; and it is said that when Escalona struck him for some insubordination, he conceived his terrible hatred for the white creoles and deserted to the Spanish. He fought first under Monteverde, became a captain, and then, after Monteverde's defeat at the hands of Bolívar, he went into the llanos and recruited his band. His only appeal to the savage llaneros was the promise of plunder— the only appeal they would have understood or listened to. He moved east and joined the Spanish general, Cajigal, and was given charge over the military stores in Barcelona. With one Tomás Morales, a Canary Islander of even greater ferocity, if possible, he immediately appropriated these stores and marched back into the llanos, gaining recruits as sugar draws flies. Defeated by Campo Elías at Mosquitero in his first real battle, he returned to the llanos and raised a new army. Then he roamed the plains, marauding hatos and villages, slaughtering men, women and children by the hundreds, in high glee. Before long he commanded a force of 7000 men. He swept down upon his old village of Calabozo and murdered nearly everyone who hadn't fled in time. Some of them he left tied to stakes with their heads shaved, to die in the fierce heat of the sun. He ordered that no one be spared but musicians and surgeons. "I want a band to cheer my men," he said, "and surgeons to cure their wounds."

The value of Boves's service to the cause of Spain was recognized by General Cajigal, who sent word that he was promoted to the rank of colonel. Boves replied, *"La pinga!* I make plenty of colonels myself!"

A story is told that once an old man and a young boy were brought before him, prisoners. The boy pled for his father, begging that his life be taken and his father's spared.

"If you will stand without flinching," Boves said, "while we cut off your ears and nose, I'll spare your father."

The boy agreed and stood perfectly still as his ears and nose were hacked away.

Boves, furious, roared, "Kill them both, *carajo!* Men like these are too brave to have for enemies!" The machetes fell at once on the lad and his father.

Inspired by the success of Boves, the Spaniard Yañez came out from his hideaway on the Apure, recaptured Barinas, beheaded eighty soldiers of the garrison and burned the town of 10,000 to ashes. Another Spaniard, Rosete, at the head of a similar band of cutthroats, entered the town of Ocumare, not far from the capital itself, and murdered everyone. His men entered a church full of people and beheaded them at their prayers. Rosete liked to skin people alive and disembowel women and cut off the hands of children and tear out their eyes.

Bolívar, in Caracas, was distraught at these new horrors. He cast about him desperately for means to keep his army in the field. Time and again he appealed to Mariño for help; but to no avail. Mariño wasn't doing anything to contribute to the glory of his rival Liberator. He did, on one occasion, send some vessels for an attack against

Puerto Cabello; but he countermanded the order and had them return to Cumaná, leaving Bolívar in the lurch.

On the third of February, 1814, Boves came out of the llanos and defeated Campo Elías at La Puerta, the gateway into the Aragua Valley. He was then in a position to advance toward the capital. Bolívar hurried to Valencia with all available troops and it was there that he received a message from the commander of La Guaira, Leandro Palacio. Palacio was gravely worried about the large body of prisoners under his care, the remnants of those who had fled from Caracas when the Liberator entered the city. What could be done about them? The garrison had been so depleted to provide troops for the campaign in the interior that there were insufficient men left to form an adequate guard. Besides, the food supplies were scarcely enough for the soldiers themselves.

Bolívar, remembering what had happened to him in Puerto Cabello under somewhat similar circumstances, was faced with an urgent problem. He was almost without funds and the large body of prisoners had been a severe drain on his meager resources. He had found, too, that when he had provided royalist sympathizers with passports to leave the country, they had almost invariably broken their word and returned to the still open ports and joined the Spanish forces.

So far, Bolívar had not enforced his decree of Trujillo in any definite manner. The killing of prisoners by Campo Elías and others had been personal acts which had brought down the wrath of the generalísimo. Now, however, on February 8, Bolívar sent an order to Palacio in La Guaira and to Arismendi, commander in Caracas, that all their prisoners be executed. To the protest of Archbishop Coll y Pratt he replied, implacably, "One less of such monsters in existence is one less who has slaughtered or would slaughter hundreds of victims."

Daily thereafter, the results of his order reached Bolívar in Valencia in a relentless procession. On the thirteenth

a report comes from Palacio: "In obedience to the order
of the Most Excellent General Liberator for decapitation
of all the Spanish and Canary Island prisoners held in this
port, the executions have commenced this night with 100
of them." On February 14: "Yesterday afternoon 150 men
of the Spanish prisoners were decapitated and between
today and tomorrow the rest will be executed." On February 15: "Yesterday afternoon 247 Spanish and Canary
Island prisoners were decapitated." On February 16: "Today all the Spaniards and Canary Islanders who were sick
in the hospital were decapitated, constituting the last of
all those included in the order of Your Excellency." For
four days the slaughter had gone on by night and by day.
The total was 517. But there was more to come. Arismendi still had his bit to do in Caracas.

Bolívar's order to the commander in Caracas had stated,
"With the exception of those who have been naturalized";
and Arismendi, on reading it, said, "What an ass the Liberator has for a secretary! He has written 'with exception,'
instead of 'with inclusion.' " Arismendi fulfilled his duty
according to his own interpretation. On February 25 he
wrote to the Secretary of War, "Please convey to the Most
Excellent General-in-Chief that the order communicated
by you on the eighth of this month has been complied
with in the execution of all the Spanish and Canary
Island prisoners, numbering more than 800, counting
those who had been found in hiding."

It is certain that these executions caused the Liberator
considerable anguish—but it is certain, also, that he believed he was absolutely justified. He issued a manifesto
immediately to the people and later to foreign nations,
in which he defended his action; but, like his attempts to
defend his decree of "War to the Death," they contain little more than a recital of the crimes of the Spaniards, and
rest entirely on the plea of expediency. Over this matter,
as over his part in the arrest of Miranda, he never spoke
a word of regret as long as he lived. . . .

It would be a lengthy and unnecessary task here to trace the movements of the Liberator during the following six months and to describe in detail the numerous actions of arms. As always, Bolívar was incredibly active, moving with amazing swiftness, marching and counter-marching from Caracas to Valencia, to La Puerta, to San Mateo, to Puerto Cabello, to La Victoria, back to Caracas, back to the Cordillera or to the llanos once more. Though always vastly outnumbered, and with his men and supplies constantly diminishing, he was almost invariably victorious in his battles. He was adroit, audacious and resourceful; but he was waging a losing fight. He accomplished wonders but even wonders could not achieve the impossible. It was like trying to force back the waves of the sea. The patriot victories were never decisive. Boves, defeated time and again in his thrusts toward the capital, simply withdrew into those trackless llanos where a large army could subsist indefinitely. Ceballos and Salomón, defeated in their constant sorties from Coro and Puerto Cabello, had only to fall back into their coastal strongholds. Bolívar, harassed on all sides, could not concentrate his weary forces for a decisive blow. He had to use them in small mobile units under the command of subordinate officers and supply them from his impoverished base in the capital. Meanwhile, the royalist forces grew by leaps and bounds. Wave after wave of enemy columns came out from Maracaibo, Coro and Puerto Cabello on the coast. The clouds of horsemen came rolling out of the llanos. The army of Boves increased to 8000 men, the army of Ceballos to 4000, Cajigal came out of the east with 3000 and Rosete's army in the valley of the Tuy was constantly growing.

Mariño came to the aid of Bolívar at last; but he came too late. Victorious at first, he failed to follow up his advantage and his union with Bolívar was prevented by the superior forces of Boves.

During those hectic times the patriots performed countless deeds of valor. Ribas, Urdaneta, Campo Elías, Ricuarte—all won great victories by sheer valor alone; and Bolívar heaped praise upon them in extravagant terms in speech after speech and proclamation after proclamation. There was never a sign of jealousy in the Liberator for those who served him loyally.

When Campo Elías was defeated by Boves at La Puerta and the royalist forces were threatening the capital itself, Bolívar sent a message to Ribas, "Save Caracas at any cost!" and Ribas responded nobly. With only a small force at his command, he recruited a battalion of school boys from the colleges in the capital and hurried out. He met the enemy in La Victoria and there, leading his half-grown youngsters, singing, in charge upon charge, he held the hordes of savage lancers until Campo Elías arrived to seal the victory. Ribas had three horses killed under him. One boy, dying, said to his comrades, "Please tell Ribas that I never took a backward step."

Bolívar himself won a great victory at Carabobo and another at his own hacienda in San Mateo. In the latter battle there occurred a deed of heroism which is one of the most dramatic in all the War of Independence. The powder magazine and munitions of the patriot army were located in one of the small buildings of Bolívar's hacienda, a sugar mill on the hillside overlooking the valley. Antonio Ricuarte, one of those valiant youths who had joined Bolívar in New Granada and marched with him across the Andes, was in charge of the small force of defenders. The magazine proved to be the main objective of Boves's troops, and Ricuarte beat back every assault from the fields below. However, he perceived that the enemy had flanked him and were descending from the heights above. He ordered the evacuation of the building by his troops, with their wounded. When this was accomplished, he remained alone, inside; and when the enemy troops were at the door, he tossed a match into the powder and blew up the magazine, and himself and the Spaniards with it. Demoralized, the army of Boves was driven from the field.

Perú de Lacroix, in his *Diario de Bucaramanga*, says that Bolívar told him, long after: "The death of Ricuarte was not as it was made to appear. He did not blow up the magazine at San Mateo, which he had defended with valor; I am the author of that story. I invented it to enthuse my soldiers, to demoralize the enemy and to give them an exalted idea of the Granadan soldiers." However, evidence seems to confirm the truth of the account and to brand Lacroix as a fabricator; but, on the other hand, such an invention would be in line with Bolívar's talent for using dramatic methods to achieve a definite purpose.

Bolívar won a victory at San Mateo, and Ribas a stirring one over Rosete in the valley of the Tuy; but such victories were empty, all of them. They only served to postpone the inevitable. The patriot armies were doomed.

The Liberator himself refused to recognize it. Hoping against hope, supremely self-confident, he threw himself into the battle, turning from one recourse to another. At the head of his men, wielding his saber with his left hand when the right had tired, he shouted encouragement. "Here, among my valiants, I shall be the first to die!" His officers had to insist that he remain in positions of comparative safety. "The art of conquering is learned only through defeats!" he shouted to his flagging soldiers. He was everywhere among the scattered segments of his army, urging them on. Suffering from hemorrhoids—a common ailment among horsemen in the tropics because of perspiration in the saddle—his slight body constantly racked by fever, he rode day and night without rest, seeking to stem the tides that assailed his troops from every direction. His behavior was very different from the behavior of Miranda under circumstances far less discouraging.

The end was bound to come, as we can see it now. Mariño, left in command near San Carlos while Bolívar went to aid D'Elhuyar at Puerto Cabello, was taken by surprise and completely routed by Ceballos without having fired a shot. Then Bolívar, in Caracas, learning that Boves was threatening Mariño at La Puerta, hurried out to his aid and arrived to find that the battle had already begun under conditions very unfavorable to the patriot forces; and it was too late to do anything about it. The patriots fought desperately against the waves of horsemen that poured out from the wooded valleys; but it was hopeless. They suffered final and complete defeat. A thousand of them lay dead on the field and 300 more were taken prisoner and put to the lance. Among those killed were the Secretary of State, Muñoz Tébar, and some of Bolívar's best officers—Campo Elías, De Sena, Jalón and Aldao. General Freites shot himself rather than wait to be tortured. Bolívar and Ribas escaped and hurried to Valencia, where the Liberator instructed Escalona for the defense of the city. Then they continued on to the capital to raise more troops if possible and to arrange for defense there.

La Puerta was the strategic gateway to the capital; Boves was free now to advance against Victoria and Valencia—which he did at once. The final blow came with the news that D'Elhuyar, besieging Puerto Cabello, had been attacked from two flanks and forced to escape by sea. There were not enough troops left in Caracas to defend the city, much less to march out to aid Valencia, besieged by Boves. Bolívar, desperate, even demanded the silver vessels from the churches in order to purchase aid from outside; but the amount he could raise was pitiful. He was convinced at last that the Second Republic, his own handiwork, was doomed.

The llanos, the mountains, valleys and seacoast literally stank with the unburied bodies of the thousands who had been murdered. The country lay in ruins. It was far worse off than when Bolívar came to redeem it a year before.

Escalona, penned up in Valencia, resisted every assault by day and by night for ten days. It was a hopeless defense, of course, for food and ammunition were woefully scarce and there was no chance of help from any quarter; but the patriots hoped to bargain for lenient terms from Boves. On the eleventh day a demand for capitulation came from the Spaniard and the terms offered were, indeed, surprisingly lenient. There was to be no execution of patriots—soldiers or civilians. Escalona hastened to accept.

When the troops of Boves marched into the city, the people were so overjoyed at the mercy offered them that a Mass was held in celebration. Boves himself attended and swore by the Blessed Sacrament that not a drop of blood would be shed—but even as the Mass was being sung, the killings began. The civil governor, Espejo, was dragged out and shot.

That night Boves rounded up all the women of the city and forced them to attend a drunken fiesta. The royalist historian, Heredia, describes the affair thus: ". . . Meanwhile the men had all been taken into custody, led to the outskirts of the city and put to the lance like bulls, without spiritual consolation. . . . The women at the dance drank their tears and trembled to hear the hoofbeats of the cavalry outside, fearing what was taking place, while Boves, whip in hand, made them dance the piquirico and other figures of the country, to which he was greatly addicted. . . . The killings continued for several nights more."

The same night a servant-girl in the household of Escalona was tied in her hammock and raped by a squad of soldiers. Then her tongue was torn out, her breasts were cut off and a fire was built on the floor under her.

Of Boves, Bolívar said once, "He was not nurtured with the delicate milk of a woman but with the blood of tigers and the furies of hell. . . . He was the wrath of heaven which hurled its lightning against the patria . . . a demon in human flesh which drowned Venezuela in blood."

After the fall of Valencia the whole western and central parts of the nation were in the hands of the Spaniards once more and Boves marched upon the capital city with nothing to oppose him. Only in the far east was there a bit of territory still held by patriot forces.

On July 6, 1814, Bolívar entered upon one of the most tragic episodes of his life. He led 10,000 men, women and children out of his native city to find refuge from the vengeance of the monster that was almost upon them. Among them were María Antonia and Juana, their children and servants, and Señorita Pepa, the mistress of the Liberator.

The earthquake had taken ten thousand lives in the old handsome city that had slumbered in peace for three centuries; the war had taken from it ten thousand more; and now another ten thousand depart, most of them forever—all in two years' time. There remain only the priests and nuns and the few thousands who prefer to meet death in their homes rather than among the unknown perils of the forests.

The route lies through trackless jungle and broken mountain ranges—not over the towering peaks and frigid páramos of the Andean crossings, but cut by deep vine-tangled ravines, endless fever-ridden swamps and swollen rivers. It is full rainy season.

Bolívar, with the few soldiers remaining to him, leads the long straggling column slowly forward.

These are not young crusaders, to be spurred on by fiery words and visions of glory; they are old and sick men, helpless women and children, to be served with compassion and helped on with acts of kindness. The goal is Barcelona, two hundred long miles away.

Most of them have never before set foot beyond the streets of their city. Nearly all of them are aristocrats, whose knowledge of the hardships of the forests is only from tales that have come to them like legends from a

far-off land. Now aged señoras and delicate señoritas,
raised in the cool seclusion of their patios, their skins
white and tender as an infant's, their legs unaccustomed
to bearing their bodies even to the church on the corner,
struggle on foot through tropic wilderness, carrying their
babies and clinging to a few precious belongings. Their
clothes in shreds, their flesh torn by the thorny bush,
their bodies burning with fever and their feet bleeding,
they sink to the soft, consoling earth by the hundreds.
Great flocks of vultures follow above the tree-tops, dark-
ening the rain-gray sky. Day after day the torrents fall
and the insects swarm in singing, burning clouds. The
nights are hideous with the moans of the dying, the delirium of the insane and the scream of pumas in the
jungle. Women tear their babies from their breasts and
dash their heads against the rocks in madness.

Bolívar rides ahead, wrapped in his dark cape, his chin
deep in his chest. His body seems very frail now and very
weary. His cheeks are hollower still, and his eyes more
sunken. He closes them to shut out the misery that sur-
rounds him, so that he can see better the visions of glory
that are still there. . . .

After twenty such days and nights, the remnants entered the town of Barcelona. Bolívar sent a detachment
of troops to aid the stragglers who still lived; and then
he sat down and wrote to Pedro Gual in Barbados to send
a commission to London to treat with the British government in the name of the Republic. The revolution moves
while he moves, lives while he lives.

A royalist force of 8000 under Morales had been sent
out by Boves and had hurried after the refugees, following them by a parallel course to the south along the llanos.
Now Morales was advancing toward Aragua, whence he
could destroy even these pitiful remnants of the patriot
army in Barcelona.

Bolívar went south at once to Aragua. There he gathered a force of 3000, some of them troops of Mariño's sent

from Cumaná under Bermúdez. Morales attacked in full force with his llaneros, strong from the red meat of the steers they had slaughtered along the way. The tired and hungry patriots fought desperately, almost to the last man. Only Bolívar and a few others survived to fall back to Barcelona. Morales entered the town and slaughtered 3500 civilians who had taken refuge in the cathedral.

Bolívar saw that his position in Barcelona was hopeless. He led his little band of refugees to Cumaná, where many of them, including his own people, succeeded in embarking for the Antilles. Ribas, D'Elhuyar, Piar and Bermúdez joined Bolívar and decided to move east to Güiria on the extreme tip of Venezuela and establish with Mariño a last stronghold against the Spaniards. Bolívar had in his possession 28,000 ounces of silver—the ceremonial vessels he had obtained from the churches of Caracas—and it was the sole bit of wealth left to the patriots.

The Liberator was now in uncongenial company. The liberators of the east, all brave and able officers, had always looked upon him with suspicion and jealousy— and now he was in their country, with no troops of his own. Bermúdez, Piar and Mariño intrigued against Bolívar for many years thereafter; and the best proof of his innocence in it all is that they intrigued against one another as well.

Trouble began among the patriot leaders at once. The sordid cause of it was those silver vessels, reluctantly donated by the churches of Caracas.

The plan was to proceed to Güiria by sea; and accordingly the treasure, along with what military stores there were, was put aboard a vessel commanded by an Italian adventurer named Bianchi. The Italian, eyeing the twenty-four cases of silver, felt the rise of temptation. That night, without waiting for the Venezuelans to embark, he ordered the cables to be cut and put out to sea. Bolívar and Mariño were the first to hear the news. They rushed to the shore, boarded another vessel and set off in pursuit. They caught Bianchi in Margarita, recovered sixteen cases of the silver, and returned to the Venezuelan coast at Carúpano.

The blow fell immediately they stepped ashore. They were confronted by Piar and Ribas with the charge of treason and the accusation that the whole business had been a scheme for absconding with the funds of the Republic. Mariño was put into prison. The outcome was determined when Bianchi, suddenly and unaccountably, returned and absolved the two liberators of all blame.

Bolívar was sick. The accusation of Ribas—Ribas above all people, his kinsman and the companion of his childhood, of Madrid and the Patriotic Society, his comrade in the march from New Granada and in half a hundred battles, the hero of Niquitao and Los Horcones and La Victoria, upon whom he had heaped all the honors within his power—was the severest blow he had suffered. He turned over the paltry bit of silver to Piar, boarded a ship for Curaçao, and sailed away from his native land once more. He was thirty-one; but he looked forty.

Piar was a handsome figure of a man with a smooth and beguiling tongue. Ribas, brave and single-minded and a bit naïve, was taken in by him. He listened to the calumnies spoken against Bolívar during his absence—that is the only explanation. Surely no one had seen better than Ribas the sacrifices the Liberator had made in the interest of his cause. His wealth, his slaves, his lands were gone. He was homeless and penniless. To accuse Bolívar of personal ambition is one thing; to accuse him of avarice is quite another.

It is hoped that Ribas lived to repent. There wasn't much time left him for repentance.

Mariño also had embarked for Curaçao. Boves had marched eastward from Caracas and captured Cumaná, slaughtering over a thousand men, women and children.

He gave another dance, *à la* Valencia, and improved upon it this time by killing the musicians when he was tired of it. Having killed a woman, Carmen Mercie, who was pregnant, he was vastly amused and astonished to see the convulsions of the still living fœtus within her body. Roaring with laughter, he shouted to his men, "Come here, all of you, and look at this! Isn't that the damnedest thing you ever saw?"

Ribas, Piar and Bermúdez made a final effort to save the east. They marched from Maturín and engaged Boves in a bloody battle at Urica. Boves himself was killed by a lance thrust, but the patriots were defeated. Miguel Sanz, Bolívar's old teacher, and Ustáritz, the author of the Constitution and the Declaration of Independence, also were killed. Piar got away to Jamaica, Bermúdez to Margarita and Ribas hid out among the hills.

The death of Boves was of little solace to the patriots in the country, for the man who took his place was even worse. Authority among the members of the Infernal Legion was disputed briefly; Morales won it by killing seven of his officers.

The end came for Ribas soon after. They found him, killed him while he slept, and cut off his head. Morales had the head fried in oil to preserve it, and sent it to Caracas, where it was exhibited in an iron cage with the little red liberty cap perched jauntily over one eye. Twenty-five members of the Ribas family had met death in less than two years.

Chapter XIII

HUSSARS FROM SPAIN

✤

BACK to Cartagena once more; back to where he had started.

He had led an army of New Granadans away from their homeland and now he returns alone, without a single man; and yet the people receive him with acclaim. His great deeds in Venezuela had been watched with avid interest, his constant reports and proclamations to the Congress received with appreciation: the honors he had heaped upon their heroes, Giradot, Ricuarte and D'Elhuyar, had created the warm gratitude and confidence in him which had been their object. The people of Cartagena hear his words with enthusiasm and offer him quarters in a palace which had formerly been the residence of the bishop.

Also living in the palace is Isabel Soublette, her sister and mother—the sisters and mother of Carlos Soublette, Miranda's half-French aide, who had been chided for being half Venezuelan. Bolívar is separated for the time from his Señorita Pepa, who had fled to the Antilles with the refugees from Caracas. Isabel is lovely, with long red hair. Bolívar pays ardent court, with his usual success; and the Soublette family become regular members of his entourage. Carlos becomes Bolívar's aide and serves him for all the remaining years of his life.

It is an interesting study, affording insight into the psychology and morals of the times, to observe the attitude of the people toward the Liberator's love affairs. There is never a word of criticism written of him anywhere; and his mistresses were accepted with all respect

134

and honor in the best social circles—that is, those of them who were born to merit acceptance. He never expected it for the others, nor intruded them where they did not belong. Gil Fortoul says, "Some of his officers owed their grades as much to the complacency of their women with Bolívar as to their bravery in battle." That is not entirely true—for Bolívar was a superb judge of men, weighed their talents carefully and placed them in the positions where they would be of the utmost value. He was intolerant of incompetence; the success of his undertaking was everything to him. Beside that, individual women were of no importance whatever. But many of his officers did regard his intimacies with their kinswomen and even their wives with perfect complacency and followed him loyally, ignoring them.

He journeyed now to Tunja and presented himself before the Congress, with the demand that he be treated as a prisoner before the bar to defend his conduct. The Congress replied with an ovation. Camilo Torres, the president, insisted that the Liberator accept a seat beside him on the rostrum. "General," he said, "your country is not dead while your sword is still alive. With it you will return to rescue her again from her oppressors. The Congress of New Granada will give you its protection, for it is satisfied with your conduct. You have been an unfortunate soldier but you are a great man!"

The Liberator responded with a clear and detailed account of his actions and an accurate analysis of the causes for the downfall of the Second Republic. The Congress reconfirmed his title of general and placed him in command of the troops of the garrison.

New Granada was in a far happier state than her neighbor Venezuela. Only the port of Santa Marta remained in the hands of the Spaniards. However, there had been trouble in the province of Cundinamarca, where Nariño had established his government at Santa Fé de Bogotá. Pasto, far down in the Andes, was a hotbed of royalist sympathy. There had been an uprising there and Nariño had gone out in person to suppress it; but he had been defeated by troops from Perú, taken prisoner and sent back to Spain. For the third time in his life, he was lying in the dungeons of La Carraca in Cádiz. A fellow-prisoner there was Miranda, who had not yet died. During the absence of Nariño, a conspiracy had been formed in Bogotá, the government was overthrown and Manuel Alvarez had set himself up as dictator in defiance of the Congress of Tunja.

Bolívar was ordered by the Congress to proceed to Santa Fé (Bogotá) and bring the recalcitrant government into subjection. The task was distasteful to the Liberator; but he saw the necessity for it and accepted. He sent a statement ahead to Bogotá, saying:

Heaven has destined me to be the Liberator of oppressed people and I will never be the conqueror of a single village. The heroes of Venezuela, victors of hundreds of battles, always in the name of Liberty, would not have crossed deserts and páramos and mountains for the purpose of conquering their fellow-citizens of America. Our only object is to unite the masses under a single direction in order that all elements may be united for the sole end of re-establishing in the New World the rights of Liberty and Independence.

In speaking of Venezuelan troops, he was referring to a division under Urdaneta which had succeeded, with great suffering and resourcefulness, in escaping across the Andes into New Granada after the catastrophe at Barquisimeto. Bolívar had come upon these troops at Ocaña on his way to Tunja. At sight of the Liberator, the men had broken their ranks and fallen upon him with wild acclaim. He chided them gracefully for their breach of discipline, praised the officer who commanded them, and urged continued loyalty to him. Then, all together, they had gone on to Tunja and offered their services to the Congress.

When Bolívar neared the city of Bogotá, Alvarez invited the Spaniards to join him in the defense—so the Liberator was spared, after all, the ignominy of making war upon fellow patriots.

The siege and capture of Bogotá was a matter of only three days. On December 12, 1814, Bolívar led an assault that carried his men into the streets. The defenders resisted every foot of the way, firing from rooftops and barricades. This was Bolívar's first acquaintance with the beautiful old Spanish city which von Humboldt had called "The Athens of America"—and which was later to be the scene of great triumphs and great ignominy for the Liberator. The introduction was not propitious; perhaps there was something portentous in it.

The Congress came up from Tunja, established itself in Bogotá and, for the first time since the inception of revolution, the whole former viceroyalty was united under one government. Bolívar was awarded the title of Peacemaker and given command over all the troops of the nation.

Meanwhile, things had happened in Europe. Napoleon had been defeated in Spain by the Duke of Wellington, the brother of that Marquis of Wellesley before whom had appeared the young Colonel Bolívar as a representative of the Caracas Junta. Joseph Bonaparte was removed from the throne of Spain and Fernando VII came out of virtual imprisonment to occupy it. His first acts were to overthrow the Regency which had acted for him for four years, nullify all the concessions it had made to the unruly colonies and re-establish the Inquisition. His troops free at last from warring against Napoleon, he organized an expedition of 15,000 men, 76 vessels and formidable armaments for the pacification of the colonies. The orders were to begin at the northern coast of South America and proceed southward to Buenos Aires, pacifying all the colonies en route, and then to proceed against Mexico.

All of this was to be accomplished in the space of one hundred and sixty days!

This was the first real army which Spain had sent against the colonies. Heretofore the patriots had been faced only with small expeditions sent out from Puerto Rico, captained by renegades, privateers and free-lance raiders who had won success only because they had enlisted the support of the lower-class creoles. This force was a fully equipped army of Spaniards—all veterans of the Napoleonic Wars. The commander was Field Marshal Pablo Morillo, who had fought with Wellington and had won that officer's recommendation for this command.

The expedition, occupying the island of Margarita off the eastern coast of Venezuela, established a base there, and Morillo proceeded with his army to the mainland. There he met Morales with his victorious llaneros who held the land in the name of the King.

Morales had 5000 men lined up in careless array. Indolently they sat their small, bitless and unshod horses; and their fierce dark eyes peered at the marshal of Spain from beneath long, unkempt hair, under caps of jaguar skin. They were bare to the waist and some of them wore only a bit of hide for a breech clout. Spurs were lashed to their bare ankles with rawhide thongs. Their long bamboo lances drooped carelessly at all angles and they made sarcastic remarks in their odd patois between glittering teeth.

Morillo strode the line in his gold lace and Wellington boots.

"These are your conquerors, Colonel?" he said to Morales.

"Yes, Excellency, this is my army."

"All of these men could be wiped out by one of my companies."

"That is what Your Excellency thinks; but not I."

"This army must be disciplined immediately or disbanded."

"That is impossible, Excellency. If you try to do either one, these men will pass over to the revolutionists."

Morales was right. Before very long, these same men were fighting for the cause of liberty under another leader, then unknown; and Morillo found that not one of his companies nor his whole army could defeat them.

When the Congress of New Granada learned of the presence of the Spanish expedition in Venezuelan territory, they ordered Bolívar to the coast at once to drive the royalists from Santa Marta and form an eastern bulwark against the invasion that was sure to come.

We come now to the aftermath of that disaffection, which began in Cúcuta before the march into Venezuela, between Bolívar and the former commander of the New Granadan forces.

The Liberator's instructions were to proceed to Cartagena and there take under his command the patriot forces and munitions to aid in the attack on Santa Marta. The commander of those forces was Manuel del Castillo, the jealous officer of Cúcuta. When Bolívar approached with his army he learned that Castillo had overthrown the civil authority in the city and declared his intention to refuse the surrender of his command or any of his supplies. Bolívar appealed to the President of the Republic and the reply came promptly, confirming his authority over Castillo. Torres wrote:

I shall never doubt that Your Excellency is the Liberator whom Providence has chosen for Venezuela, nor think a more worthy chief could be placed at the head of this enterprise. My hopes have not been disappointed, nor have I regretted my opinion. . . . I admired nothing so much as the consideration and respect which you have always shown for the Congress of New Granada; how, even when vested with the supreme power in Venezuela, you never took a step without

informing us and giving an account of your means and operations, and asking for orders.

With Venezuela lost, the writer still believed that she continued to exist in General Bolívar—a belief which he will not
discard while he lives. . . .

But Castillo refused to yield. The situation was a bitter
impasse. Bolívar was loath to resort to arms against his
fellow patriots. With him now were some of his old comrades—Tomás Montilla, Rafael Revenga, Pedro Briceño
Méndez and Florencio Palacio; but within the fortress
of Cartagena, supporting Castillo, were others of them—
Pedro Gual and Mariano Montilla, brother of Tomás.

Bolívar acted in all generosity. He appealed repeatedly
to Castillo, promoted him to brigadier general, asked for
a commission to act as arbiter, naming Castillo's brother
and an uncle as members; but to no avail. Castillo refused to yield an inch. Bolívar sent his resignation to the
Congress but it was not accepted. He sent Tomás Montilla
inside the city to treat with Castillo as his agent, and
Montilla was driven out by a mob inspired by the jealous
commander. Then the Liberator moved his troops closer
and occupied the heights of La Popa, over the city; and
he was met with fire from the fortress and found the water
wells poisoned.

For five months the bickerings dragged on—five months
in which the enemy was gathering its forces and preparing
for its drive against New Granada. It was a longer time
than it had taken Bolívar to cross the Andes, reconquer
Venezuela and establish the Second Republic.

Cartagena was the most strongly fortified city on the
Spanish main. In the times of the pirate raids by Morgan
and Drake, the Spaniards had encircled it with a wall of
masonry thirty feet high and fifty feet wide. It is still
there today and hundreds of the city's poor live within its
gloomy chambers. Bolívar, with no artillery at all, had no
hope of taking that fortress by assault. He laid siege to it

for several weeks, meanwhile making every appeal to Castillo, urging him to think, as he did, only of the safety of the republic. Castillo's replies were only insults, using such phrases as "the gross ignorance of General Bolívar."

The Liberator's army was shrinking to nothing; his men were dying by the score from fever and smallpox. The Congress could do nothing to help him. At last he resigned, irrevocably, and sailed for Jamaica on a British vessel.

It is difficult to say, even now, what Bolívar should have done under the circumstances. He did resign his post in the face of enemy advance; but there is no reason for not believing his own explanation—that he hoped thereby to remove discord and permit those remaining to unite in common defense. However, there is one thing he could have done; and that he failed to do it is one of the few things for which he is ever known to have expressed regret afterward. He could have occupied the Magdalena Valley and remained there to hold it against the Spaniards as long as he could, leaving Castillo alone until, in desperation, he should call for Bolívar's aid. In 1828, Bolívar expressed to Perú de Lacroix regret for not having done that. He should never have occupied La Popa, he said; but he did so because he had been assured by friends inside the walls of Cartagena that a revolution there in his favor would occur spontaneously the moment he appeared. In the same conversations he said, "Victory in civil wars brings glory to no one. My true glory is in having defeated the Spanish, beaten their armies and torn from them half of South America."

Glory was his chief concern always—abstract glory—not the tangible rewards for it nor the acclaim it brought forth, but merely the relish of it in his mouth, the feel of it inside himself. It was a strange, rather mystic thing. Perhaps it explains his hold on his people that persists to this day. . . .

After Bolívar's departure from New Granada, the end came quickly for that republic, too.

Morillo came with his army by sea; Morales came along the coast by land and Cartagena was subjected to a siege which was the most horrible in all the history of the two Americas. For a hundred and six days the people huddled within those great walls, while the Spanish guns thundered from the sea and the creole troops of Morales poured roundshot from the hills. The walls held; but the city rotted inside with thirst, starvation and disease. Every living thing was eaten—every horse, burro, cat, dog and rat, every blade of grass, every bit of moss from the moldering walls; and the people dragged their skeletons over the sun-baked earth, searching for ants and grubs. Six thousand of them died.

In the inner harbor lay a small fleet of sailing vessels— fishing boats and small coastwise trading sloops. On December 6 some 2000 people, all who could find room, crowded aboard them; sail was set and the boats headed out to run the blockade of Spanish gunboats. The open sea struck them at the harbor mouth and many of the overloaded vessels foundered; but some of them got away to safety. The next day the Spaniards entered the city to find the houses empty and the gutters strewn with rotting corpses. The 300 emaciated souls whom they found cowering in dark places they led to the beach and beheaded. Among these was Manuel Castillo. During the siege, the people had come to see his unworthiness at last. They had overthrown him and left him behind when they took to the boats.

The Spanish army ascended the Magdalena—that great river which had been the scene of the Liberator's first triumphs—and arrived before the capital city, Bogotá. The republican government, with no means for defense, asked for amnesty as the price of surrender; and it was granted with the most glowing assurances. The Spaniards came in without resistance. They seized 600 of the leading citizens

at once and executed them in the principal plaza. Among
them was Camilo Torres, the great patriot, the loyal admirer and friend of Bolívar. Among them, too, was the
famous naturalist Francisco José Caldas. He was engaged
then on a scientific treatise which was to be the culmination of his life's work; and friends appealed to the Spanish commander to delay his execution until it could be
finished. The answer was, "Spain has no need of savants."

There was no independent government now in the
whole of northern South America. Morillo would have
been free to march southward in execution of his orders;
but among the forests and plains of eastern Venezuela
there were still a few guerillas—Monagas, Cedeño, Zaraza
and that unknown llanero, Páez—buzzing like hornets,
keeping the cause of liberty alive.

Chapter XIV

JAMAICA LETTER

✤

IN Jamaica, Bolívar has touched bottom. He is at the lowest point of his whole career. Fever and hunger and the hardships of nearly six years of constant struggle have reduced his slight body to skin and bones. His broad forehead is furrowed with deep lines, his long face is the face of a living corpse; but his sunken eyes are burning still. The Duke of Manchester, governor of the island, entertains him at dinner and says of him afterwards, "The flame has consumed the oil."

He is in a strange land, penniless, without even a change of clothes. He finds an English friend, Maxwell Hyslop, there, and writes him short notes, begging for loans—notes couched in words of ironic humor. "I haven't a single peso," he writes. "My laundress, patient soul, refuses to wash my only shirt." The loans are forthcoming—one hundred dollars one time, two hundred another.

He lives in a small hut with a floor of bare earth and a hammock for a bed. Night after night, sleepless with his streaming thoughts, he paces back and forth like a caged animal. By day he lies in his hammock, one foot dangling, swinging the hammock rapidly, rapidly. His eyes, fixed upon the eaves of the thatched ceiling, do not see the tiny lizards that scurry there. They still see only those great visions of glory.

There are other Venezuelan patriots in Kingston, too— Santiago Mariño, the Carabaño brothers, Briceño Méndez. The Liberator talks with them constantly—endless discussions, futile scheming. He joins them occasionally in games

144

of chess, in throwing darts, fencing, billiards; and he
bursts into loud, nervous laughter at his ability to beat
them all, using either hand. In the midst of a game he will
stop suddenly, say to his companions, "Excuse me, gentlemen, I can't go on," and throw himself into the hammock
to resume his rapid swinging.

Almost daily, little groups of refugees come drifting in
to the British haven from Venezuela and New Granada;
and the Liberator hurries to meet them and pump them
dry of the news they bring. He writes, writes, writes—
letters to Wellesley in London, to the representatives of
the defunct republic who are still hanging on in England,
in the United States, France and the Antilles, to Pepa and
María Antonia in St. Thomas.

Two commissioners from New Granada arrive, begging
him, in the name of the Congress, to return and take
command. Bolívar is pleased and tempted; but the commissioners can't assure him that the people are united in
their loyalty to him. The garrison at Cartagena is still at
odds with the Congress. Without anything to bring but
himself, the Liberator feels that his presence will serve
only to create more dissension; he sends the envoys away
with his refusal and his gratitude to the Congress.

To relieve the tension of his strained nerves, Bolívar
resorts to affairs with native women. His sensitive stomach
can't stand alcohol, except for a little wine at meals, and
he can't abide tobacco, even the smell of it. He loves fine
food and drink, but always with the delicate taste of the
gourmet, in moderate quantities and only when the spirit
is in accord.

One night, when his small room is dark, the single
door opens cautiously, a dark form enters and silently ap-
proaches the figure that lies in the hammock. A hand rises
and falls twice. There is a short gasp, a gurgling sound,
and then silence as the intruder steals away.

The dead man in the hammock is a friend of Bolívar's,
Félix Amestoy. A knife had pierced his throat and his

heart. Coming to visit the Liberator, and finding him absent, Amestoy had lain down on the hammock to wait; and he had fallen asleep. Bolívar's life was saved from assassins then, as it was to be again, by his addiction to women.

The murderer was found to be Bolívar's servant, a slave whom he had freed. The man confessed that he had been paid 2000 pesos by two Spaniards whom he couldn't identify. He was executed in the public square of Kingston and his head exhibited on a pike in Spring Lane.

On September 6, 1816, Bolívar completed a letter, supposedly written to Hyslop by an unknown South American, which was the second of the three most important documents of his life. It was of the length to fill a small volume, was published locally and abroad, and created world-wide interest. Clear, eloquent, not too verbose, considering the times, it was a masterpiece of political exposition and historic prophecy.

He began where he had left off in his Cartagena Letter, to review the events, with causes and effects, of the revolutionary movement in South America. He described with great perception the current status of the whole continent, from Mexico to Cape Horn. He analyzed the mistakes Spain had made, and criticized the attitude and actions of foreign powers.

"Europe itself," he said, "by policy, should have prepared and carried out plans for South American independence; not only because it is necessary for the proper balance of the world, but because it is a legitimate and safe means for obtaining commercial bases on this side of the ocean." With a little help from England, he promised, he himself would "free half the world and place the universe in a state of equilibrium." Knowing practical, cautious England, he made, with prophetic insight, an amazing suggestion. "The British can acquire (in return for aid) the provinces of Panamá and Nicaragua, forming with these countries the center of the world's commerce by means of canals, which, connecting the two great seas, would shorten the great distances and make England's control over world commerce permanent." Had a Disraeli been Prime Minister of England at that time, perhaps he would have come to terms with the Liberator, and the history of the world would have been different.

Bolívar continued with more prophesying. He predicted that the continent of South America would eventually be divided into fifteen or more independent republics; and he went on to envision the fate of the various colonies then existing. Mexico would have despots for presidents over long periods, supported by a collusion of the aristocracy and the military; and at times she would have monarchies. In this his accuracy was uncanny. Mexico has seen many despots and two monarchs—Iturbide and Maximilian. "In some large sections monarchies are inevitable," he said. Mexico and Brazil confirmed that.

Chile, he said, because of her geographical position and racial elements, would preserve her customs and maintain a stable government most consistently of all; and history has borne out that prediction.

Perú, he said, would suffer the greatest dissensions and political turbulence, because "she possesses two elements, enemies always of a just and liberal régime—gold and slaves. The first corrupts all; the second is corrupted by itself. The soul of a slave rarely rises to appreciate ordered liberty; it either rises in furious tumult or remains docile in chains." History has put her stamp of truth upon that prophecy, too.

Venezuela and New Granada, he predicted, would join as one nation in the Union of Colombia under a stable government; and there his vision failed him, as his own efforts to accomplish it failed.

Then Bolívar repeated his distrust of a federal form of government for the South American people and his belief in a modified democracy with a strong central authority. In Cartagena he had said, "We citizens have not yet learned the virtues which characterize true republicans. . . . The codes of laws which our magistrates consulted were not those which could teach us the practical science of government but those which were formed by well-meaning visionaries who, imagining fantastic republics, have sought to obtain political perfection, presupposing the perfection of the human race." Now, in Jamaica, he said:

We were in the position of slaves—not in the sense of mistreatment so much as of ignorance. We had no part in our own affairs, no knowledge of the science of government and the administration of state. We were, in effect, slaves, suddenly risen, without knowledge or experience, to play a part in the world as administrators, diplomats, magistrates and legislators. If we had even managed our domestic affairs before, we should have known something about the nature and operation of state.

Pure representative government is not suitable to our character, customs and present conditions. . . . So long as our compatriots do not develop the talents and political virtues which distinguish our brothers of the north [the United States] the entire popular system, far from being suitable to our conditions, may, I fear, be our ruin. Unfortunately, these qualities seemed not to be developed in us to the extent necessary; and, on the contrary, we are dominated by vices which, developed under the guidance of Spain, became weighted with ferocity, ambition, vengeance and cupidity.

As to the form of government he would advocate, he said, "New Granada will unite with Venezuela if they can co-operate in forming a centralized republic. The government will be based upon the English system with the difference that, in place of a king, there will be an elective executive power. And, what is most vital, a hereditary senate (never hereditary when a nation desires

to be republican) which, in political crises, can intervene
between popular whims and governmental expediency.
The legislative body, popularly elected, shall have no restrictions other than those imposed upon England's House
of Commons."

In these ideas Bolívar was supported, paradoxically, by
our own great champion of democracy, Thomas Jefferson,
who said, "Ignorance and fanaticism are incapable of self-
government. I believe it would have been better for the
South American colonies to have attained their liberty
gradually."

"I wish to see," Bolívar said, "the formation in America of the greatest nation in the world. . . . Though I
aspire to a perfect government in my native land, I cannot
believe that, under present conditions, South America can
be governed as a great republic; since I consider it impossible, I dare not aspire to it. But even less do I wish
for monarchy." Republics, he pointed out, being guided
by the will of the people, who never share in the fruits
of conquest, tend to become self-sufficient and to remain
within their legitimate bounds. Monarchies, on the other
hand, governed by an individual who would find personal
gain in conquest, usually become imperialistic. But a government acquires no right or advantage over a conquered
people, and they remain a dissatisfied and dangerous element within the state; therefore a monarchy, becoming
imperialistic, decays into despotism in order to hold its
new elements. Monarchy, then, is undesirable on purely
practical grounds. The characteristic of small republics
is permanency; of monarchies, evanescence.

Then he ventured to reveal his great dream—a dream
which he recognized as impractical now because of great
distances and lack of communications; but which someday
might be realized. It was a union of all the republics of
America, not governmental, but purely cameral in function, to form a united front and provide mutual assistance
against encroachment of the decadent political philoso-

phies of the Old World. He envisioned a great and permanent Congress of Panamá, "to treat and discuss in the high interests of peace or war with the nations of the other three parts of the world."

"How beautiful," he said, "if the Isthmus of Panamá should become for us as the Isthmus of Corinth was for the Greeks!"

This, in the year 1815.

The problems which Bolívar discussed in the Jamaica Letter, the political tendencies and racial characteristics which he analyzed, the destinies which he predicted, covered an area 10,000 miles in length and 4500 in breadth, and involved 16,000,000 American people who were facing the uncertainty of their future existence. He himself was an exile in a foreign land, penniless, without resources of any kind, almost without influence anywhere. He had been defeated by his own people, renounced by his own comrades-in-arms.

He spent six gloomy, nerve-racking months in Kingston; and during it all there was only one ray of hope. He received a letter from a wealthy Jewish merchant of Curaçao, Luis Brión, a young and ardent worker for South American independence. He had been captain of a frigate under Mariño and now he had just taken delivery from London of a 24-gun corvette, the *Dardo,* loaded with munitions, representing an investment of $100,000 of his own funds. He asked the Liberator how he and all his resources could be of benefit to the cause.

Bolívar answered Brión at once, addressing him as "My dear worthy friend." He described, without pretense, the tragic hopelessness of the situation; but he declared his willingness to co-operate in any effort, however desperate. Then he sat down to await a reply. The months passed; no answer came, and it appeared that the ray of hope had vanished.

As the month of December approached, word came to

Kingston of the siege of Cartagena. The Liberator could wait in idleness no longer. Without any military resources at all, he borrowed a final $200 from Hyslop, chartered a small vessel, the *Popa*, and sailed for New Granada.

On the high seas a few days later, the *Popa* spoke a privateer, the *Republicano*, which gave news of the fall of Cartagena and reported that the refugees were heading for Aux Cayes on the coast of Haiti. Bolívar ordered his vessel about at once to lay a course for the same port.

The revolution was on the move once more.

Interlude

HOMBRÍA

✤

IN Aux Cayes Bolívar met with a pleasant surprise. Luis Brión, that ray of hope, was there with his vessel and munitions of war, and the two men embraced on the wharf. Brión had sailed from Kingston before the answer to his letter had arrived. Also, there were hundreds of refugees from Cartagena at Aux Cayes; and more hundreds came sailing in daily in their tiny boats. Among them were Mariano Montilla (Bolívar's old friend, who had supported Castillo against him) and Bermúdez and Carlos Soublette. Soublette was accompanied by his mother and two sisters—one of them Isabel of the long red hair. There came, too, from Jamaica and the mainland, Mariño, Piar, Briceño Méndez, Francisco Zea and many other officers of the revolution.

The black republic, which had thrown off the yoke of France and defeated the armies of Napoleon, welcomed the starving thousands of South Americans, sheltered them and gave them daily rations of bread and meat. What pleased Bolívar most was that the President of Haiti, Alexandre Pétion, had been impressed by the Jamaica Letter and now offered to contribute funds and arms for a new expedition against the Spaniards on the mainland. Another benefactor came forward, too—a wealthy English merchant named Robert Southerland. The Liberator's spirit soared with new hope, and energy flowed back into his emaciated body.

But once more he was in uncongenial company. That contingent of conniving officers of the east, Piar, Mariño and Bermúdez, was there, as well as Montilla, who had turned against him at Cartagena. He had his own loyal supporters, Briceño and Soublette among them, and, most important, the backing of Brión, Southerland and President Pétion. Nevertheless, in the planning of the new expedition, the undercurrent of rivalry and personal ambitions which had begun at Carúpano the year before sprang into life again here. Bolívar was to be plagued for the rest of his days by this bitter struggle of personalities. He was never to be free for a moment from the terrible psychological war with his own officers—a war which caused him greater anguish and more defeats than those inflicted by the armies of Spain.

Now, however, a semblance of unity was achieved. An election was held and Bolívar was voted Supreme Chief of the expedition, Mariño second in command, and Brión admiral of the fleet. Only three officers cast dissenting votes—Montilla, Aury and Bermúdez. Montilla sailed away for the United States, Aury for New Orleans, and Bermúdez chose to remain behind in Haiti. Bolívar proved himself above these petty differences by writing to Pedro Gual, who had supported Castillo in Cartagena, and inviting him to join the expedition.

Here, also, two foreign officers join the cause—Gregory MacGregor, a Scottish adventurer, able but mercenary in motive, and Ducoudray-Holstein, a Frenchman who had once been on Napoleon's staff. The latter became a nuisance to Bolívar from the start, complaining, seeking special privileges and honors, demanding promotions in rank. After only two short months of his annoying company, Bolívar was forced to discharge him; and those two months of acquaintance with the Liberator supplied the Frenchman with material for a bookful of calumnies which was published in the United States, England, France and Germany.

The expedition of 250 men, seven vessels, arms to equip 4000 troops, and several small pieces of artillery, set sail on

March 31, 1816. It was a brave little sailing, the officers all in full dress, the guns on shore firing a salute, the officers' women crowding the rails and waving their silk mantillas. There were brave women among the creole South Americans of those days. They went with their men everywhere. Bolívar himself had two women on this occasion, for he had sent to St. Thomas for Señorita Pepa; and Isabel had come with her brother. There is no evidence anywhere of anything but the most pleasant harmony among all concerned—which fact, alone, should establish the Liberator's place among the world's great diplomats, since the mothers of the girls went along, too.

A few days later the patriot fleet anchored at Juan Griego on the Island of Margarita—Venezuelan territory. Arismendi, that Margariteño patriot who had carried out Bolívar's orders to execute the prisoners in Caracas, had returned to the island after Morillo's departure, raised a small force of fishermen and farmers armed only with machetes and clubs and farm implements, and wrested part of the island from the Spaniards. Bolívar set up a government at once, declaring the independence of Venezuela yet again on a tiny island not a thousandth part of the area of the country, which was held by ten thousand veteran troops of Spain and many more thousands of creole royalists! He declared the freedom of all slaves in the land, in accordance with the promise he had made Pétion. He also declared his willingness to abolish the "War to the Death," if the Spaniards would agree to abandon their ruthless practices. Morillo's answer, when it came, ignored the proposal and offered a reward of 10,000 pesos for the Liberator's head.

He hoped to strike at the capital by the back way while the armies of Morillo and Morales were still in New Granada. Landing at Carúpano on the mainland, he left Mariño and Piar to proceed to Maturín and, with new volunteers and most of the fleet, he sailed westward to Ocumare, beyond La Guaira. There his expedition met disaster. The very day he occupied the port, the army of Morales entered Valencia, returning from the victories in New Granada, and the main body of patriot troops under Soublette and MacGregor which proceeded inland was trapped. Learning of the situation, Bolívar was forced to cut his ships' cables and sail, leaving his precious munitions behind. He returned to Güiria in the east to rejoin Mariño.

Meanwhile Soublette and MacGregor escaped with 800 of their troops, executed a daring march through hundreds of miles of territory and joined with Piar and the guerilla bands operating in the east. At Juncal they won a brilliant victory over Morales, and then MacGregor, becoming involved in a dispute with the other leaders, sailed away to his native land.

No sooner had Bolívar left Mariño and Piar to their own devices than the plotting against him began again. Bermúdez, who had been sulking back in Haiti, came to join them and when Bolívar returned he was confronted by a full-fledged mutiny. His rival Liberators accused him of incompetence in the conduct of the campaign and of personal cowardice. There was a sordid display of temper and emotionalism, particularly unbecoming in men of proven bravery. Only Bolívar maintained his dignity. Bermúdez showered abuse upon him, threatened him with his sword and had to be subdued by his fellow officers. The Liberator turned his back upon them, boarded his vessel and sailed back to Haiti, with the shouts of his aroused countrymen ringing in his ears. He had heard, for the first time, his own people crying, "Down with Bolívar."

Thus it was to be during all the remaining years of the Liberator's struggle in the interests of the task he had put himself to. Only in his presence, under his own inspiring and dominating leadership, was there unity of purpose and harmony in action. Immediately his back was turned, the dissensions spread and all that had been achieved fell away into dust. No one knew that fact better than he. No

one saw better the disruptive tendencies in his comrades
and that fatal weakness of his people—the dependence
upon and the psychic need for a dominant, forceful personality to hold them together. That need is deep in the
character of the Spaniard and is augmented, in the Spanish
American, by a sense of weakness. The torero must dominate the bull, man must dominate woman, the leader
must dominate his men. Bolívar recognized that trait in
his people consistently in his political doctrines, and
sought to satisfy it in the strongly centralized form of
government which he always advocated.

He knew that he himself possessed those qualities of
dominance and leadership. He had always possessed them.
He felt his power over people and over the other leaders,
felt it in their presence, psychically, the way the torero
feels it over the bull in the arena. He was to feel it later
when he confronted the Marshal of Spain, Morillo, and
again still later when he was face to face with San Martín,
the Liberator of Argentina. The Spanish have a word for
that power to dominate by sheer strength of will. It is
hombría. Bolívar believed sincerely that he alone possessed it, as well as other mental qualities, to the degree
necessary to bind his people together in the struggle for
freedom and the establishment of a stable government.
And that explains, far more logically than the facile
charge of personal ambition, his manipulations always to
exercise the supreme command.

President Pétion of Haiti welcomed Bolívar once more
and, with Southerland, offered to equip a new expedition.
Soon, too, Brión appeared with his small fleet; and he
begged the Liberator to make another try, in spite of the
dissensions among the various officers still operating on
the mainland. Arismendi, who had succeeded in driving
all the Spaniards from Margarita, wrote to him, urging
that he return. Meanwhile, those guerilla chiefs, Monagas,
Anzoátegui, Cedeño and Zaraza, who had joined with

Soublette and Piar and MacGregor to win the victory at
Juncal, had come to realize the necessity for a leader to
guide their scattered efforts in effective action. They sent
Francisco Zea to Port-au-Prince to treat with the Liberator
in their name. Zea presented himself to President Pétion
and said, "In Venezuela there still survives a remnant of
good patriots. The country still lives in hopes; but the
one superior man, capable of converting these hopes into
reality, is no longer there. With this idea, the army and
the cities have turned their eyes upon General Bolívar as
the one chief in war."

In the face of these manifestations, Bolívar forgot the
humiliation that had been heaped upon him and agreed
to return. So, after only two months in the Haitian capital, he sailed for Venezuela once more—this time never
to leave South America again as long as he lived.

He landed at Margarita, proclaimed the re-establish-
ment of the republic, and again called for the formation
of a Congress. Then he proceeded to the mainland and
joined Arismendi at Barcelona. Their combined forces
numbered 700 men.

At the moment, conditions seemed propitious for a
quick dash overland in the direction of Caracas—a rash
and hazardous venture, but one of the kind in which the
Liberator had been fortunate in the past—and the results, in the faint chance of success, would be tremendous.
But this time Bolívar's luck failed him. He got as far
west as the Unare River, where an overwhelming force of
Spaniards defeated him and drove him back to Barcelona.

Now Mariño and Bermúdez, the two officers who had
denounced him at Güiria and had driven him from his
own land, came forward in repentance. The arrival of
Bermúdez with his army was most timely, for the pursu-
ing Spanish troops were approaching Barcelona. Bolívar
rode out to meet the officer who had threatened his life.
On the little stone bridge over the Neverí, they came
face to face. Both dismounted. They walked toward each

other and embraced, with tears in their eyes. Bolívar said, "I embrace the liberator of the Liberator"; and Bermúdez shouted, in quavering voice, "Viva, America Libre!" The two remorseful officers did not, however, offer to submit their 1700 troops to the Supreme Chief's command. Bolívar himself had only 600.

Meanwhile, in the Liberator's mind, an entirely new plan for the conduct of the war had evolved. He decided, finally, to take for himself the advantages of operating in those vast llanos, where troops could be moved quickly and maintained by the unlimited supply of beef cattle. He would establish his base in Guayana, far down on the banks of the Orinoco, where Brión's fleet could support him from the sea and maintain communications with the outside world, and he himself could campaign against the enemy from the rear—the way Boves and Morales had done against him. As always, his schemes soared far beyond the immediate problems. They included now not only the liberation of Venezuela but a movement against Bogotá from the interior, down the Andes to Quito and Perú; a distance of 2500 miles, every inch of it held by Spain; territory where there was not even a definite desire on the part of the inhabitants for liberation.

With this amazing man, the formation of a plan always meant immediate action; accordingly, with only fifteen officers and their orderlies, he set out from Barcelona southward toward the Orinoco. He left behind 400 men under General Freites to defend the town, and Mariño was instructed to follow to Guayana with his army.

With Bolívar out of the way, Mariño began his plotting once more. Ignoring his orders, he remained in his camp thirty miles from Barcelona and sought to influence his officers to join him in a scheme to set up a new government in opposition to Bolívar. Meanwhile the main eastern Spanish army under Aldama advanced against Barcelona and Mariño ignored the desperate pleas of Freites for help. The Spaniards attacked the town, reduced the fort with artillery and slaughtered the soldiers who defended it to the last man. Entering the plaza they beheaded 700 prisoners and 300 civilians, some of them on their cots in the hospital and some of them women and children who had taken refuge in the church. A general order to the Spanish troops had been issued a few months before to "burn cities, behead their inhabitants, ravage the country; to respect neither sex nor age, to replace the peaceful farmer with a ferocious warrior, the instrument of the vengeance of an angry king."

Mariño, oblivious of the tragedy at Barcelona, went blithely on his way north to Cumaná. Arismendi, Soublette, Zaraza, Valdez and Bermúdez refused to follow him and marched southward with their troops to join the Liberator. The conversion of Bermúdez was sincere this time, for he served under Bolívar with unswerving loyalty from then on.

Piar had preceded Bolívar into the Orinoco country. He was a brilliant and daring commander of great resourcefulness, a leader of Bolívar's own type. With no artillery and few troops, he had laid siege to Angostura, the principal city of the Orinoco; and then he had gone south into the wilderness of Guayana and recruited an army of 2000, among them naked Indians armed with bows and arrows. He commandeered every horse and burro and steer in the vicinity. Then he sent a detachment up the Caroní to take possession of the Indian missions of the Capuchín monks—valuable throughout the war as a source of food supplies and Indian recruits. This detachment—whether by order of Piar or not has never been established—put to death all the twenty-two monks of the convent. Then Piar established headquarters at San Félix, below Angostura, and succeeded in enticing the Spanish General La Torre out into the open for battle. Piar had only 500 muskets among his 2000 men. The majority were armed with bamboo lances and bows and arrows. He faced 1600 perfectly equipped Spanish veterans; and he defeated them in a bloody battle in which 700 royalists were killed, wounded or taken prisoner—among them 73 officers. La Torre himself barely escaped back to Angostura with his life. But Piar soiled the glory of his victory by slaughtering 300 of his prisoners—all of them who were Spanish-born.

When Bolívar arrived on the banks of the Orinoco with the troops that had deserted Mariño to join him, he found that most of the work of clearing the river had already been accomplished. He reprimanded Piar for slaughtering prisoners in disregard of the proclamation abolishing the policy of "War to the Death." But Piar and his troops declared their undying loyalty to the Liberator; and Bolívar was not one to stand too much upon principles when the good of his cause was involved.

About this time word came that Mariño had established his "United States of Venezuela" in Cariaco on the north coast, named civil and judicial heads, and proclaimed himself commander-in-chief of the army. His "assembly" had even sent letters to the governments of the United States and England, asking to be recognized and offering free commerce. He had caused a rumor to be circulated that Bolívar had been taken prisoner and killed on his journey to Guayana.

However, Mariño's little government was short-lived. A Spanish army threatened them in their headquarters at Pampatar, Margarita; the members of the assembly fled, and Mariño himself took to the mainland, where his army was destroyed by the forces of Morillo. From Maturín, he wrote to Bolívar, asking to be taken back into the fold. The Liberator agreed to give him one more chance—and only one. Mariño hastened to accept.

Now it was Piar's turn once more. He began to agitate against Bolívar and to insist upon an immediate assembly to depose the Liberator and place the supreme authority in him, where it rightfully belonged, he claimed, because of his successes in Guayana. Bolívar, sure of himself and his backing, gave him cold warning. "Never," he said, "has my position been so strong. The supreme power is in my hands. . . . Two thousand men obey me and are disposed to fulfill my commands. The ambitious ones and the intriguers must and will obey me. Shortly Piar will be no one to fear. He will not disturb our tranquillity for long."

Piar apparently was impressed. He asked for a passport to leave the country, got it promptly, and disappeared— for the time being.

All this outside the city of Angostura while the siege was in progress. One would expect the Liberator to be distracted beyond reason, tried beyond human endurance. But not at all. His thoughts are soaring with his new plans, his spirits overflowing with brightness and cheer. He laughs with his men, sings with them to the music of the guitars about the campfires at night. He sleeps in his hammock in the pouring rain or on the wet ground, wrapped in his cloak. Yet he is always meticulously clean, even elegant. He bathes and shaves daily, takes particular care of his hands and his excellent white teeth. He tends his own horse, spending hours over it, permitting no one else to feed or groom it. Long after all the men are asleep, when only the voices of the sentries disturb the quiet, he paces before the fire, dictating letters; and he is up before daylight, reconnoitering or inspecting the positions of his men.

A companion described him once in these words: "He is in constant agitation. Watching him, you would take him for a crazy man. Walking the forest trails, he goes fast—runs, jumps, tries to leave his companions behind and offers to outjump them. In his hammock he swings violently, singing, talking rapidly, reciting verses in French. He is sometimes loud and sometimes profane.

"That is when he is among his friends. When a stranger arrives, he shuts up like a clam. He shows no sign of anything. He dominates with his dignity, good manners and quiet amiability."

After two months of siege, the garrison within the city of Angostura began to feel the pinch of starvation. And then suddenly Brión, whom Bolívar had long been expecting, appeared from down the river with his fleet. La Torre was finished. He evacuated with all his troops and a large number of civilians and headed down river. Brión's squadron pursued them, caught them at Guayana Vieja and dispersed them, taking a thousand prisoners and most of their boats.

Bolívar entered the city that commanded the navigation of the Orinoco; and there his great and lasting glory began.

IV: PATH OF GLORY

Chapter XV

THE CENTAUR

✣

ANGOSTURA—now called Ciudad Bolívar—is located, as the old name indicates, at a pinched-in place on the south bank of the wide and deep Orinoco River. It was quite a city, even in those days. There were several cobble-paved streets along the waterfront and running up the hill, a plaza on a level spot on the hillside, an imposing cathedral and many fine buildings and homes of masonry built in the Spanish manner with roofs of colored tiles and patios with lovely gardens. It scarcely, however, merited its local appellation, "Queen of the Orinoco." Its outskirts touched the virgin wilderness and near-naked savages lolled about its sun-drenched streets. Isolated, its aspect, for all the visual touches of civilization and the European manners of many of its inhabitants, was crude and semi-primitive.

Though located nearly 250 miles inland, deep water carried to the sea and permitted the navigation of ocean-going vessels. Then there was one advantage—a great one in the days of sailing vessels—in a unique combination of winds and current. The river, flowing constantly, carried vessels seaward, while the almost constant easterly trade winds blowing upstream were strong enough to drive them, sailing free, against the current at a fair clip.

When Brión arrived with his fleet, he brought all the gay ladies who followed the patriot officers. They were quartered in the best houses of the departed royalists and, though their finery was worn and tarnished from their long wandering, they made a brave show in the frontier

165

city. There were nightly gatherings with singing, reciting of verses and dancing to the music of native instruments. There was much drinking of chicha, the native liquor, and the women as well as the men smoked small cheroots of native tobacco. A traveler of the times reported that they "smoked them very gracefully." Among them was Bolívar's sister Juana, a widow now and accompanied by her daughter Benigna, a beautiful girl and the Liberator's favorite niece. She was the belle of the little colony, courted by all the young unmarried officers of Bolívar's staff. Particularly ardent was Briceño Méndez, the Liberator's loyal companion and secretary.

The patriot soldiers had seen no money and very little food for many months. Bolívar confiscated all the property of the royalists, garnered what money he could and levied upon the citizens of the town. He made provisions for the royalist women and children who remained and divided the remaining supplies among his men, according to rank.

The day the patriots entered the town, Piar reappeared to make more trouble. Instead of leaving the country, he had been up the river, stirring up the mulattoes against the whites; and now he attempted to do the same thing among those mixed-bloods whom Bolívar, with great pains, had succeeded in drawing into his ranks. He also approached Bermúdez and those officers who had turned against the Liberator in the past; but he made a mistake there, for they reported him to the chief.

This Piar was an odd character. Like Brión, he had come from the Dutch island of Curaçao. Legend had it that he was the bastard son of a European prince and a high-born Venezuelan woman. Charming, handsome, he was rather dark-skinned but had brown hair and blue eyes. Nevertheless, he circulated the idea that he was a mulatto, in order to gain prestige among the pardos and blacks, with which element he had ambitions to found his own empire.

Bolívar ordered Piar to appear before him. Instead, he sneaked off, went north into the llanos and joined Mariño to take up his old schemes once more. Bolívar sent Cedeño after him with an order for his arrest. Cedeño caught up with Piar in Aragua, took him prisoner and brought him back to Angostura.

Bolívar wasn't fooling this time. He had meant what he said when he declared, "Piar will not disturb our tranquillity for long." Piar was charged with insubordination, sedition and desertion. Soublette was named attorney-general of the court-martial and Bolívar made an effort to insure fairness by appointing Brión, Piar's countryman, president, and some of the accused man's former officers as members. He himself took no part in the trial. He said, "If the Council applies the maximum penalty, I profoundly hope they will leave the road open to me for commutation."

The trial lasted for three days and nine witnesses were heard, all of whom testified against the defendant. The testimony, as it is recorded, leaves no doubt as to Piar's culpability. The finding was guilty; the sentence, death. After the court-martial a council of war sat, reviewed the whole case and reported the same finding and sentence. There was no provision made for executive clemency. Bolívar is said to have signed the death sentence with tears in his eyes. He struck out the clause calling for military degradation.

The next afternoon Piar was led to the little plaza on the side of the hill. All the townspeople were there and the troops were lined up at attention. Bolívar remained in his quarters. Piar faced the squad, refused a covering for his eyes, and, as the balls from twenty muskets tore into his chest, he cried, "Viva la Patria!" The cry was taken up by the soldiers and civilians. Then the troops were all marched past the body of Piar, slumped over in his chair there in the sun.

Bolívar has been criticized severely by many historians

for his execution of Piar, but he himself never expressed any regret, and insisted that it was a military necessity; that no one could deserve death more. He said to Perú de Lacroix years later, "It was necessary at that time, politically, to save the nation, to stop civil war and thus the triumph of Spain. Mariño deserved death, too, but he didn't present the same dangers and I could afford to indulge the sentiments of humanity and friendship for an old comrade. The execution of Piar destroyed sedition. It was the blow that disconcerted and subjugated all rebels, convinced Mariño, and put all under my authority, leaving me free to conceive and effect the expedition to New Granada and to create Colombia. Never has the death of one man been more useful, more politic, nor more deserved."

Just the same, it was Piar who prepared his way in Guayana and made possible the feat which was to bring him his greatest glory.

When Bolívar first came into the province of Guayana in May, 1817, he wrote to London to Luís López Méndez, his old-time associate on the commission from the Caracas Junta, who was still holding on there in Miranda's old house on Grafton Street in the name of the republic. Bolívar, exaggerating somewhat the happy state of his Third Republic, urged Méndez to exert every effort to recruit all the men he could, organize them and send them to his aid. He promised liberal bonuses and salaries and promotions in rank. Where the money was to come from, he failed to state. That was something to be dealt with when the time came.

From spring until late fall he was occupied with clearing the Spaniards from the river, and then with establishing a form of temporary government in Angostura and reorganizing his army. Retaining the supreme authority for himself, he formed three departments—State and Treasury, War and Navy, and Judiciary—to carry on affairs until such time as a more permanent government should be arranged. By this time the cruelties of the Spaniards and the constant efforts of Bolívar with speeches and proclamations had begun to have effect on the sentiments of the common people. The tide had begun to turn, at last, in favor of the patriots, and there were some 6200 men in arms throughout the country in the cause of independence. Unfortunately, however, they were in widely scattered groups, and the dispositions of the vastly superior Spanish forces made it impossible for Bolívar to concentrate the patriot forces into an effective body. Urdaneta, that veteran of the Cordillera campaign who had escaped into Colombia and met Bolívar there, had come back now and joined the patriots at Angostura. Bolívar gave him command of Piar's old forces, operating on the lower Orinoco and among the Guayana Missions. Bermúdez was placed in command in Cumaná, Monagas in Maturín, Zaraza in the eastern llanos, Mariño, who had been converted once more after the execution of Piar, in Cariaco. All these men were in constant action against the troops of Morillo and Morales, but their inability to join for concerted action prevented any decisive effects. From far up the Orinoco, in the western llanos, word was coming constantly of the daring operations of a patriot leader heretofore unknown—a man who held great prestige among the wild llaneros and who was fast winning the horsemen of Morales to his banner. His name was José Antonio Páez. Bolívar sent him a message, inviting him to serve under his orders and offering him full command in the western llanos.

At that time Páez was twenty-seven years old—seven years younger than the Liberator. He could neither read nor write and had never seen a city. Next to Bolívar he is the most important figure in Venezuelan history. He came to be president of the republic and ruled as dictator for sixteen years. He became enamored of "culture," educated

himself, became wealthy by none too honorable methods
and fell victim to the flattery of foreign diplomats. Guz-
mán Blanco said of him, "He was a murdering tiger in
the hills of Payara and a tame sheep in the salons of
adulation." He made a grand tour of Europe, was wined
and dined by royalty, was a favorite guest of the Empress
Eugénie. In the United States he was entertained by the
President, acclaimed by the public everywhere as only few
foreign rulers have been acclaimed, and was honored with
a huge parade on Broadway. He died in New York in 1873
at 83 years. At seventy he wrote a very creditable autobiography containing shrewd commentaries on the history
of his times.

He was almost the epitome of the llanero type. A horse
was as much a part of him as his eyes. Short of stature, he
was huge above, small below. His legs were short and
spindly, slightly bowed, his head big, his neck short and
thick, his shoulders, chest and torso powerful like a bull's.
He won his position of leadership among his wild, mixed-
blooded warriors through physical superiority, "sim-
patía" and "hombría." He spoke their terse dialect, ate
with them on the ground from the same kettle, competed
with them in their games of "coleando," capturing and
breaking wild horses, and tilting with the lance. They
followed him with a blind personal devotion. They called
him "uncle" and sang songs of his prowess as they rode
the limitless plains—the topical, monotonous and somehow
haunting couplets called "corridos" which are still the
lyrical expression of the Venezuelan llanero.

He was born in dire poverty in a daub-and-wattle hut
in the foothills of the Cordillera where it slopes to the
llanos. He was of almost pure white blood. His skin was
dark from the constant sun but his eyes were blue and his
hair light brown, fine and wavy. When he was just a
boy he was involved in a killing—self-defense, he claimed
—and fled to the great plains. He grew up on a cattle
ranch under the tyrannical rule of a negro slave who had

become an overseer. The negro lorded it over him ruthlessly, forcing him even to kneel and wash his feet. But the white boy developed fast and the negro came to admit, finally, that young Páez was a better man than he. In a few years he owned his own land and his own herds of cattle and horses.

When the revolution began, the Spaniards pressed him into their army under threat of death—a common practice on both sides—and made him a captain, probably to secure the services of his men and the benefit of his herds. Páez, however, unlike most men of his class, harbored patriotic sentiments. At the first opportunity he deserted alone, at the risk of his life, and gathered together a small band of llaneros. One of his first acts was to lead a raid against the town of Barinas and release over a hundred prisoners, many of them women and children, who were awaiting death.

That was in 1813, when Boves was beginning his fearful depredations in the plains. From then on Páez, working alone with his small band, unknown and almost unheard of by the other patriot leaders, kept up a guerilla warfare against the Spaniards. He established headquarters far down in the llanos at Achaguas on the Arauca River, and there he gathered great herds of cattle and horses to serve as a base of supplies. He maintained a constant contact with his base and vaqueros drove the animals north across the plains and swam them over the swollen streams to their chief as he hammered away at the Spaniards. For a time Páez served under regular patriot leaders—García de Sena, Antonio Rangel, Urdaneta and Olmedilla—but he left them, one after the other, to operate alone in his own way. He left them in disgust, mostly, at their incompetence; but he left Olmedilla, he claimed, because of the beheading of 200 prisoners over his protest.

Páez became a master of guerilla tactics in the llanos. He marched his men at night to avoid the fearful heat of the day, setting his course by the stars. Always close to the enemy, he learned that the cloud of dust which rose over horsemen on the plains was visible for miles. Beef could not be killed on the march for the clouds of buzzards that gathered over the carcasses revealed their position to the enemy. He knew the places where waterholes lay during the dry season and he could identify each of the myriads of identical-appearing streams, which are unmarked on maps even today, by the color and taste of their water. The sun was called, among his men, "the enemy." The llanero horses, small and wiry, descendants of the Arab stock brought over by the Conquistadores, were then, as they are now, trained to an easy, artificial gait, a kind of rack, that averaged six miles per hour. Sixty miles was a usual day's march in spite of swimming innumerable streams. Lassos then, as now, were made fast to the horse's tail—a cruel practice, though the tail became toughtened to it and there were numerous practical advantages. But there are many horses on the llanos whose tails have worn through and have torn away at the croup.

In battle, Páez was indeed a "murdering tiger." He was subject to epileptic fits. During an encounter he would thrust with his lance, slash with his machete, slaughtering right and left until he was spattered with blood and his arms were paralyzed with fatigue. His excitement rising with the heat of the combat to fever pitch, he would collapse suddenly, froth at the mouth and topple rigidly from his horse. His men learned to keep a constant watch on him during battle. Time and again he was saved from the lance of an enemy by the quick action of a comrade who would pick him up, toss him across the cruppers and carry him to safety.

He had an extraordinary power to win the affection of manly men. Early in his career as a guerilla he befriended a giant negro named Camejo. The negro followed him about like a devoted animal from then on. He became the leader's personal servant, cared for him hand and foot and never let him from his sight. In battle Camejo was awesome. Always at the front, he wielded an enormous machete, which he had hammered out himself and which was too heavy for an ordinary man. The men called him "El Negro Primero," The First Negro. He always kept a rolling white eye upon his chief; and many a time when Páez fell from his horse in a fit, he rushed to his side, picked him up like a child and rode off with him.

Páez himself relates an incident which reveals his hard humor and his almost innocent ferocity. In a lance duel with a Spanish officer, he struck the man from his horse, wounding him fatally. He dismounted and approached him. "Seeing him stretched upon the ground," he says in his autobiography, "I tried to remove a handsome cartridge belt which he wore about his waist and, as he broke out into a stream of blasphemy and ill-considered words not suited to the situation in which he found himself, I began to exhort him to make a Christian ending and recited the Creed to stimulate him to repeat it after me. Luckily, I looked down and saw that, instead of accompanying me in my prayers, he had half drawn a dagger from his belt. I confess my charity was completely chilled and, as my indignation did not allow me to waste more time on my adversary's future destiny, I freed him from the rage that was choking him more than the blood he was losing by a lance thrust."

After the death of Boves at Urica, the llaneros began more and more to join the ranks of Páez for the cause of the patriots. Morales, succeeding Boves, apparently had not the power of his predecessor to hold them. Then, too, Morillo arrived and tried to force regular military discipline upon them and sought to use them in formal maneuvers of battle. The llaneros had seen the superiority of their own methods and the effectiveness of a hundred tricks evolved from knowledge of the country and their own peculiar capabilities. They deserted the Spanish colors by scores and most of them eventually drifted into

service with Páez. His force came to number more than
10,000. Some of them were foot-soldiers, naked Cunaviche
Indians, armed with bows and arrows. The llaneros fought
as they had with Boves, raiding towns and haciendas, seizing everything of value they could lay their hands on,
carrying their loot away in rawhide "coracles" across their
saddles. Since the Spaniards had confiscated everything
belonging to the creoles, the wealth of the land belonged
to them now and looting, to be indulged in at all, had to
be done from the patriot side. The situation had been
directly reversed. Páez relates that he had eventually, at
his base in Achaguas, one million head of cattle and five
hundred thousand horses roaming the plains, 40,000 of
the latter broken and fit for service.

About this time the exploits of Páez began to attract
the attention of the government of New Granada. They
offered him the rank of colonel and urged him to become
a part of the army they were forming along the Andean
frontier and in the western llanos. The commander of
that army was Francisco de Paula Santander, the officer
who had refused Bolívar's order to march into Venezuela
and who had supported Castillo against him. Páez be-
haved with better grace than had Boves under the same
circumstances. He offered to put the proposal up to his
men; and they refused to recognize any authority but that
of Uncle Antonio. Páez continued to operate independently but he did act jointly with Santander whenever it
fitted in with his own plans.

His first battle with Spanish regulars in full array of
infantry, cavalry and artillery was at a place called Mata
de Miel, near the Apure River. The Spaniards, under La
Torre, numbered nearly 3000 and Páez at the moment
had with him only 500 horsemen. He located the position
of the enemy by that tell-tale cloud of dust rising over
their line of march and he held his own force where it
was encamped, waiting. He had never faced artillery before, and shrewdly decided to attack at night when cannon

fire would be ineffective in the darkness. His scouts watched while the Spaniards made their camp in a small moriche thicket and herded their 3000 horses into a rope corral.

When darkness came Páez executed a trick which had been used before in ancient times; but the illiterate llanero knew nothing of that. He took fifty of the wild horses he always carried in reserve and tied to their tails the big squares of rawhide which the llaneros used for their beds and for carrying their loot. Slapping the horses' rumps with lances and shouting like demons, his men sent the terrified animals flying among the Spanish horses, stampeding them in the darkness. Hannibal had used the same trick when he loosed his oxen in the camp of the Romans. On the heels of the flying horses, Páez charged into the confusion of the Spanish encampment. La Torre's veterans, routed at first, re-formed their ranks and retreated stubbornly to the thick woods along the banks of the Apure. They lost 900 men killed or taken prisoner, all their stores and all their horses. When daylight came the llaneros, many of whom wore nothing but Indian breech clouts, decked themselves out in oddly assorted garments of the brilliant uniforms of Spanish battalions.

About the time of Bolívar's occupation of the lower Orinoco, Páez won another great victory over La Torre at Murcuritas. This time he was faced by 1500 regular Spanish cavalry and 3000 infantrymen; he himself commanded 1100, all mounted. It was the height of the dry season and the tall grass of the plains stood in brittle yellow stalks, rustling in the breeze. During the night, Páez took a position to the windward of the Spaniards—a tactical advantage because of the dust that arose during cavalry charges. Rolling downwind, it would envelop the enemy like a smoke screen. On the morning of battle, he held his men until La Torre advanced within gunshot. Then he gave the order to charge "en barajuste." This was a favorite maneuver of the llaneros, one which would be disastrous for disciplined cavalry but which was very effective with guerillas who fought as individuals. It was nothing more than an open-order charge, a quick, scattered retreat, a re-forming to attack again. Its effectiveness lay in the fact that each horseman knew its operation and acted with definite, individual purpose, without commands. The Spanish right wing, held by cavalry, broke after several charges but the center, a battalion of hussars, veterans of the Peninsular Wars, held firm. They made a brilliant show in the sun on the open plain, coolly resisting the repeated charges of the wild, yelling horsemen. Their tall hussar caps were draped with yellow cord and from one shoulder hung yellow Hungarian pelisses. Behind them the main body of infantry retreated in good order to the protection of a thick wood surrounding a waterhole, and there it stood. But Páez had another trick ready—possible because of his windward position. Fifty men were detailed to set fire to the grass in a wide circle about the Spanish forces. The grass, dry as tinder, caught with a roar and bore down upon the brave hussars. Behind it came the llaneros of Páez, plunging through the smoke and thin line of flame, cutting down the Spaniards, circling, falling back to re-form and strike once more. The hussars fell back doggedly a "mortal league," fighting still, blinded by smoke and seared by flames. Only the waterhole saved the entire Spanish army from death by fire.

This was the first defeat suffered by Morillo since he had landed on South American soil. In his report to the King of Spain, he said, "Fourteen consecutive charges on my wearied battalions showed me that those men were not a scanty band of cowards as I had been informed, but organized troops, able to compete with the best in Your Majesty's service."

As Bolívar had been watching Páez, Páez had also been watching Bolívar. Word traveled over those vast distances then, as it does now, with mysterious rapidity. When the envoys of the Liberator arrived at the headquarters of Páez with the suggestion that he recognize the authority of Angostura, they were well received. Páez, as was his custom, put the proposition to his men. This time, however, he undertook to persuade them. With admirable fairness, he set forth his own limited field of experience, extolled Bolívar's achievements and explained that his abilities had been demonstrated in more varied phases of warfare and that his many talents entitled him to authority. His men were convinced and the envoys were sent back to report that Páez and his llaneros would co-operate with the Liberator. In this the illiterate master of the plains, in spite of his own personal ambitions, showed remarkable disinterestedness and insight into his own limitations. He recognized the truth of the judgment which Cunninghame Graham was to make of him more than a century later in his biography: "In spite of all the qualities of leadership which Páez displayed, they never rose above the talents of a chief of irregular cavalry. . . . The continuance of the republic at that time depended upon Bolívar and upon him alone."

This was in the last month of 1817. The Liberator set out from Angostura with 1500 men to join Zaraza for an attack against the Spaniards in the center of the country. His instructions to Zaraza were to avoid action with the enemy at all costs until the union could be effected. Zaraza, however, either from misunderstanding or over-eagerness, found himself forced into battle with La Torre at La Hogaza. He suffered a terrible defeat in which more than a thousand of his men were left dead on the field and all his stores captured. One of the dead was a nephew of the Liberator, a son of his sister Juana. Bolívar, learning of this disaster, returned to Angostura. There he conscripted every able-bodied male between the ages of fourteen and sixty, and set off up the Orinoco with 5000 men to join Páez. Transporting his army against the current in "flecheras"—long, narrow dugouts—he arrived at the llanero headquarters near San Fernando de Apure. He had traveled 900 miles in one month.

They met for the first time on January 31, 1818. Both men dismounted and embraced, in the manner customary among South Americans today. Cunninghame Graham describes it: ". . . Holding each other in their arms, their heads over one another's shoulder, in the same way the patriarchs embraced in the Old Testament." Páez, with a countryman's wariness toward one of city breeding, was cautious in his first judgment of the Liberator. From habit, he eyed Bolívar's horse and was pleased to observe its fine condition. He also found the Liberator's manner easy and courteous, his body full of health and of amazing vigor, charged with nervous energy. After an exchange of polite and flattering words, the two patriot leaders stood side by side to review their armies.

The ragged old men and boys of Bolívar's troops, worn out by their long journey, compared poorly with the vigorous, well-fed horsemen of Páez. The personnel of his army was now as heterogeneous in blood as the llaneros. Few were left of those young white aristocrats who had formed his first armies. Their bones lay scattered from the Andes to the delta of the Orinoco. In their place he had Indians, mulattoes, mestizos and blacks whom he had won over by his eloquence and personality or by threats. Even his officers now were largely illiterate men from these classes. Years afterward, commenting upon the predominance of ignorant men of low birth and mixed blood among the high-ranking officers in his army, he explained that it had been a necessity in those days to elevate men on the strength of valor in battle alone. With no money, it was impossible to reward them, or to enthuse the ranks to courageous action, except with the honor of promotion. "That explains," he said, "why there are so many generals in my command without other merit than brutal valor."

The troops of Páez, since their victories over the Spaniards, had come to present a far different picture. They were garbed in a bizarre assortment of the trappings of famous European regiments—shakos with scarlet brushes, dragoon helmets bound with gleaming brass, tall gold-braided caps of royal hussars. Richly embroidered capes hung from bare brown shoulders and medals won at Salamanca and Talavera dangled from shirts of jaguar skin. In place of the bamboo lances with their points charred by the fires that sharpened them, the llaneros proudly wielded long Spanish sabers with silver hilts. Their horses shied at the unaccustomed gleam of silver-studded and plumed bridles and ornamented saddles.

As Bolívar passed along the ill-formed lines, the llaneros shouted in wild acclaim.

Chapter XVI

RED COATS IN GUAYANA

✤

THE two men marched northward together at the head of their troops: the high-strung and intellectual aristocrat who had been the darling of the Spanish court and the salons of Paris, and who had chosen for himself a life of hardship, bloodshed and peril; and the stolid, illiterate vaquero who was to become enamored of and to enjoy, in his later years, those things which his companion had voluntarily foresworn. Both keen judges of men, they watched each other carefully. There was a third man marching with them, too, leading a detachment of troops from New Granada. He was Francisco Santander. These three, with strong individual qualities and diverging ambitions, were to determine, by their relations with each other and their future actions, the course of the life of each and the political destiny of millions of South Americans then living and of generations to come.

The columns arrived on the banks of the Apure at Paso El Diamante, the only spot along the jungle-lined river where there was a landing place on the opposite shore. Bolívar called his officers to solve the problem of crossing the river. The patriot boats had not arrived, and the river was a quarter of a mile wide, with a current that ran four miles an hour. Anchored in the middle of the stream was a squadron of small Spanish armed launches.

"I'll get boats for you, General," Páez said.

"Where?" asked Bolívar.

Páez pointed with his saber to the Spanish gunboats. "There, General," he said; "with your permission."

180

Bolívar nodded, reserving his opinion that Páez had gone crazy. He watched, with curiosity and suppressed amusement, the preparations that were made calmly and with complete assurance. Páez said only a few words to the fifty men he selected. Mounted upon white horses which it was the general belief among the llaneros were always the best swimmers, with girths and cruppers loosed, the fifty men, with Páez at their head, dashed at full gallop for the river. At the water's edge they slid their saddles off from under their rumps without dismounting and plunged their horses into the swift brown stream. Reins in their teeth, lances in their hands, they guided the swimming animals toward the Spanish boats by splashing water against their heads. Their comrades on shore kept up a constant frightful yelling. The Spaniards on the boats, taken completely unaware, gazed with astonishment at the men and animals splashing toward them. There was a frantic dashing about for firearms but before more than a few scattered shots could be fired the llaneros were swarming over the gunwales, thrusting with their lances. In panic the Spaniards jumped into the canoes alongside, or plunged into the water and swam madly for the other shore. Páez took all the boats without losing a man.

Cunninghame Graham remarks that this was probably the only time in history where cavalry skirmished against armed vessels.

The patriot army crossed the river in the captured boats and march was resumed northward. Bolívar regarded his new ally with increased respect.

The first battle in which the Liberator and Páez fought together took place near the town of Calabozo, well up into the llanos and not far from the mountains where nestled those cities which Bolívar longed to possess. Morillo himself commanded the Spanish forces. The march from the Apure had been so rapid that he had no idea the enemy was near.

The patriots had encamped in a deep wood at the edge

of the open plain. At sunrise a movement of Spanish troops was seen. It was a detachment of cavalry and infantry—a regiment of each—leaving for duty at another point. Páez, with his horsemen, immediately dashed from the woods in pursuit. He dispersed and destroyed the cavalry regiment first and then, wheeling, encircled the infantry battalions that had not reached shelter in the woods. Riding about them at full gallop in the manner of the Indians of the North American West, the llaneros cut them down with their lances and sabers. The Spanish veterans fought coolly among the fallen bodies of their comrades. They fought, as Páez put it, "culo con culo"— arse to arse—until the last man was slain.

Meanwhile, Bolívar, with the main army, attacked Morillo's regiments. His maneuvers were astute and rapid and the Spaniards fell back, fighting doggedly, retreating northward. Páez and Bolívar struck them repeatedly by the rear guard and by the flanks during three successive days and forced them slowly into the foothills.

Calabozo was a great victory for the patriots; but it failed in decisive results because Bolívar was unable to follow up. The fault was not his; he wanted desperately to continue in pursuit toward Caracas. Páez was the one to blame.

The llanero leader had not conceived for the Liberator the admiration and unquestioning confidence which he was to feel for him later. Beyond that, he and his men were loath to leave their beloved llanos. Unaccustomed to mountain country, they distrusted and feared it for themselves and their horses. Páez refused to follow Bolívar into it. He made the weak excuse that he felt he should return to the Apure and drive the Spaniards from San Fernando.

Bolívar knew that in spite of the assurance of complete obedience Páez had given him at their first meeting, he was not yet entirely submissive. He knew, too, that Páez's men gave full loyalty to their chief alone; that his own authority over them was only recognized so long as Páez willed it. Therefore, anxious to avoid causing, by an outright command, a breach with an element which was most valuable to the patriot cause, he observed the formality of granting permission for Páez to withdraw. Others of the llanero elements deserted him also—the entire brigade of Vásquez, large bodies of the troops of Cedeño and Monagas. His army was reduced almost to the remnants of those old men and boys he had conscripted in Angostura.

Undoubtedly he should have given up his drive against the north and consolidated his position on the plains. But Caracas was close over the mountains and his own hacienda, his beloved San Mateo, lay along the route. The temptation was too great.

Morillo had retired to Valencia and La Torre covered the approach to Caracas. Bolívar marched north and occupied, without resistance, Maracay, La Victoria and San Mateo. He had a brief visit in his old hacienda, where his slaves, who had remained there waiting through all the Spanish occupation, fell to their knees and kissed his hands. But his happiness was short-lived. The troops of La Torre advanced to the west to join Morillo, and Bolívar's army was caught between two fires.

The word came to Maracay when the patriot officers were dancing at a ball given in their honor. In the darkness and in the midst of a raging storm, they ran out to gather their men together. When daylight came they were formed and began the retreat southward once more. Morillo followed close on their heels and Bolívar halted to make a stand on the banks of a small stream called El Semen. He arranged his forces calmly, carefully, spoke to his men with animation. He laid aside his great cloak, removed his heavy helmet and replaced it with a cap of jaguar skin, and took up the short lance he always carried now. The lance flew a black streamer bearing a skull and crossbones and the words, "Liberty or Death." He waited for the enemy attack eagerly, almost with gaiety.

Morillo hurled his regiments—veterans bearing the names of famous Spanish victories in the war with Napoleon: Valencey, Burgos, Barbastro—against the weary patriots.

For six hours the battle raged back and forth across the ford of the narrow stream. The patriots resisted every thrust of the Spaniards and rushed out in counter-attack with bayonets. Morillo himself fell wounded and hopes were bright for a patriot victory; but in the afternoon the fresh battalions of La Torre appeared to reinforce the flagging royalist troops. The patriot army yielded and retired in disorder toward the rocky pass of La Puerta where Bolívar had suffered his first defeat at the hands of Boves. The Spanish army, following closely, cut them to pieces, destroyed them completely. Bolívar got away, leaving his personal belongings behind. A thousand of his men and most of his officers were dead and the valuable Urdaneta was wounded. Morillo received the title of Marqués de La Puerta from his king for this victory.

Bolívar found himself back in the plains once more with only a handful of men. But he wasn't through yet. The goal, Caracas, was still too much for him to resist. He raised another small army and marched northward again.

For the next few months Bolívar led one small army after another against the Spaniards in brave but rash attempts. Losing one army, he went back to the llanos for another—200 men one time, 300 another. He won some skirmishes but he lost more. He was always outnumbered, always lacking in arms and munitions. He hadn't the kind of men now that he had had in his early victories. He hadn't those brave crusading youths and those intelligent and intrepid officers who could accomplish miracles in the face of terrible odds. He hadn't a Ribas or a Ricuarte, a Giradot or a D'Elhuyar.

At first judgment Bolívar would seem to be open to criticism for continuing in this costly and futile effort to recapture the capital city. In fact, Páez did criticize him, declaring that "Bolívar was overfond of fighting"; but that was far from the real explanation. Actually, Bolívar had a logical purpose. He had a definite plan for another campaign in an entirely different direction—a march up the Orinoco and across the Andes, no less, into New Granada. His actions now were all by way of preparation. The time wasn't yet ripe for that great project. The rainy season, which would not come again for almost a year, was an essential element in the plan and the need for complete surprise was also imperative. These constant drives would create in the minds of the enemy the idea that he was obsessed only with the purpose of taking Caracas, that the capital city was his paramount objective. Then, too, he was keeping the Spanish forces confined to the north, permitting a patriot army to consolidate and train at his base in Angostura; and constantly, now, foreign troops were arriving there from England. Besides, there was always the slim chance that one of his audacious drives would win through to Caracas; such luck had fallen to him in the past.

Morillo said of Bolívar at this time, "Twelve consecutive pitched battles, in which his best troops and officers have been left killed on the field, have not been sufficient to break his self-confidence nor the tenacity with which he makes war against us."

These battles of the early years of the war, in view of the small numbers of men engaged in them—numbers which seldom reached beyond a thousand or two—seem trivial in the light of world history; but the principles involved and the vast areas at stake, often half the size of Europe, give them an importance far beyond appearances. And the total number of deaths over the years reached well into the hundreds of thousands.

During those months Bolívar was always close to the enemy, always close to death. Without shelter of any kind, he slept on the ground, wrapped in his cloak. He wore no uniform or signs of rank, only an old blue jacket, blue trousers, a llanero's wide-brimmed hat or cap of tiger skin and sometimes only alpargatas—homemade sandals—on his feet. His short lance was always at his side. He was always hungry like his men, and always racked with fever.

There are many stories told of him, of attempts on his life and narrow escapes from the enemy. Once, having escaped from the Spaniards by swimming a stream, he hid in the bushes with a few companions. As they huddled there in the dense thicket, the searching Spaniards passed so close they could hear their words. Bolívar's orderly had drawn his knife and held it in his hand. When asked what it was for, he replied that it was to kill the Liberator before the Spaniards should get him. Bolívar laughed and went on to speak in a low voice of his plans for creating the Republic of Colombia and a great union of all the nations of South America. The poor orderly shook his head and said, "At last the Liberator has lost his mind."

Another time he was sleeping and a few enemy soldiers who had scouted his position got through the sentry lines and approached him. He was wakened by the restlessness of his horse, tethered close by, and rose to investigate. Shots flared out in the darkness so near him that they singed his face. He leaped on his horse and fled, alone, thinking the enemy had attacked. It is claimed by some that Santander, who was with Bolívar at the time, had given the password to the Spaniards and planned the assassination; but evidence of it is lacking.

Bolívar at last gave up his futile warfare in the north, principally because he was anxious to establish a more permanent government in Angostura. With only forty men left, he went south to join Páez at San Fernando, where he lay ill with fever for a month.

Nothing at all had been accomplished since he left Angostura. He had performed great deeds in battle, made tremendous marches and lost thousands of men; and the Spaniards still held his country as firmly as ever. Nevertheless, those one hundred and sixty days which the Spanish king had given Morillo to reconquer South America had long since passed and he was still confined to the little northern rim of it—and having his hands full.

When Luís López Méndez, in London, received Bolívar's appeal for men, he set to work at once. In his years of agitating for the cause of South American independence he had won the financial support of many wealthy people and now he succeeded in borrowing a total of 200,000 pounds to equip an army. Nevertheless, what he had to offer volunteers for service with Bolívar was mostly promises. But his efforts began at an opportune moment. After Napoleon's final defeat at Waterloo, England and Ireland were teeming with discharged soldiers—venturesome young men who were trained for war and nothing else. In the great economic depression which gripped the nation following the long wars, these men found themselves in acute distress and with no hope of employment. Furthermore, Britain, freed from the necessity of maintaining an alliance with Spain, was willing to close her eyes to the open recruiting of men and the fitting-out of vessels to carry them to the American tropics.

The history of the foreign legionnaires in South America is a thrilling story in itself. In 1928 an exhaustive and authoritative book by Alfred Hasbrouck was published, covering it in all its colorful detail.

In London and later in Dublin, the appeals of Méndez for men to serve in Spanish America spread rapidly among the idle soldiers and they flocked to the recruiting offices in droves. So anxious were they that they signed up without any cash advance at all—on the strength, alone, of the promise of bonuses when they reached Venezuela. Nearly all of them joined from purely mercenary motives; but a few were moved by sincere convictions for the cause of human liberty. Daniel Florence O'Leary was of the great Irish patriot families Burk and O'Connell, Belford

Wilson was the son of Sir Robert Wilson, long a friend in England of South American independence and a constant correspondent with Bolívar, and Francis Burdette O'Connor was well known in Ireland as a patriot leader.

So anxious were the volunteers that, in the hands of some unscrupulous recruiting officers, the handing out of commissions became a racket. The men were actually forced to pay for their commissions. Instead of receiving an advance, in the nature of a guaranty, they handed out goodly sums of cash themselves; and the amounts asked rose daily until the recruiting officers were making a very nice thing of their little business.

Most prominent among those engaged in this profitable form of recruiting were John D'Evereaux, an Irishman who had become an American citizen, Colonel English, an Englishman, and Gregory MacGregor, the Scot who had been the hero of the retreat of Bolívar's men from Ocumare and of the battle of Juncal. MacGregor was married to Bolívar's own niece. He did very well in the selling of commissions in London and in addition he got a thousand pounds cash from Méndez which he appropriated to his own use. After his departure from Venezuela he had returned to England and raised men for several expeditions of his own. He had taken the fort at Fernandina on the coast of Florida, then made a raid on Puerto Bello, Panamá, and another on the coast of New Granada at Rio Hacha. In each instance he had remained only long enough to gather what loot he could find and then sailed away, leaving the Englishmen and their families to starve or be killed by the Spaniards. Hasbrouck relates that, of 344 officers, 1696 men, 99 women and 40 children who went out on his various expeditions, only three are known to have reached England again—and one of them was MacGregor himself. Later, after the success of the patriots in South America, he was involved in a fraudulent colonizing scheme in Paris and imprisoned in La Force. However, he was released eventually and returned to Venezuela in 1839 and demanded a pension. The government granted him the rank of major general on one-third retirement pay and an outright sum for services rendered. He lived in Caracas until he died in 1845, a respected and honored citizen.

In all, some seven or eight thousand men, largely commissioned or noncommissioned officers, were recruited and sent out for service with the patriots in Venezuela. They were mostly English and Irish and Scotch, but there were also some French and Italians; and there was a full battalion of Hanoverians, veterans of the German army.

The commanding officer of all the elements was Gustavus Hippisley, a half-pay lieutenant of British cavalry who was stepped up to the rank of colonel. The volunteers were organized into two main bodies—the British Legion, which sailed from England in December, 1817, in five ships, and the Irish Legion, which sailed in various detachments beginning in July, 1818. The names were largely irrelevant, for there were Englishmen and Irishmen in each.

The warehouses of British merchants were bulging at the time with war materials for which there was no sale whatever. The merchants were willing, therefore, to extend credit to López Méndez on the easiest of terms. They pressed upon the outfitters of the legionnaires the most expensive of their equipment. So the troops of the First and Second Venezuelan Hussars, the First and Second Venezuelan Lancers, the Grenadiers and Rifles found themselves decked out in uniforms that would have done credit to officers in the Royal Guards. They had both dress and service outfits and the service, in which they were to campaign in primeval tropic wilderness, was suitable for dress in any man's army. Everything was of the heaviest and finest material.

The First Hussars went in for green, scarlet and gold. They wore dark-green jackets with scarlet collars, lapels and cuffs, edged with gold lace, and gold epaulets and

gold-lace girdles. The dark-green trousers were piped with
gold and the sashes were scarlet silk, tied with an Aus-
trian knot. The officers had blue camlet cloaks lined with
red baize. The Second Hussars leaned toward light blue,
gold and scarlet. For full dress they had light-blue jackets
and pantaloons trimmed with scarlet and gold lace and
similar uniforms of gold, blue and scarlet for service. All
the other units were equally splendid in varying color
schemes. All wore Wellington boots and had forage caps
for service and tall plumed shakos for dress. They made
quite a stir about London, balls were given in their honor
and the papers were full of them. The Rifles had a fine
military band which played at all their gatherings.

The story of the journey to South America is mostly
one of disillusion and disaster. Many of the men, looking
forward to grants of land by way of reward when the conflict was over, took their families with them—so that the
hardships and suffering which befell them were shared by
gentle-born English women and children.

Scarcely had the first vessels left the coast of England
when a gale struck them and the *India* was sunk with all
hands. The other vessels, separated, found their way eventually to various West Indian islands.

Among the volunteers were many evil characters—adventurers and wasters who were seeking escape from debts
or worse. On the long sea voyage there was constant drinking, gambling and disorder. A man was killed in a duel,
there was open mutiny and Hippisley had to threaten the
men with hanging from the yardarm. Then, on the islands
where the various vessels landed—Haiti, St. Thomas,
Grenada, Trinidad—conditions were worse. Disillusion
awaited them there. The natives had far different stories
to tell of the land they were going to and of the character of the great hero they were to fight under than those
they had heard in London. Through the efforts of an
American press-agent employed by López Méndez—one
William Walton—all of England had been led to believe

that Venezuela was a tropical paradise, a land flowing with milk and honey; that the government was firmly established and well provided with funds and the Spaniards were practically annihilated; that Bolívar was the noblest character of the century. Now they heard that Bolívar was a tyrant who slaughtered women and children for sport, an ignorant savage who imposed his will upon a subjugated people; that Venezuela was a dark land of horrors, of naked Indians, pestilence and famine where there were no paths but the rivers, and those were choked with alligators and man-eating fish, and that the jungles were alive with centipedes, snakes, scorpions and jaguars. In some respects, as those few legionnaires and their women who eventually reached the country found out, the new picture of the land was hardly exaggerated.

The vessels spent long months in the islands. Funds had run low, provisions were exhausted and the captains waited for answers to their appeals to London for aid. The answers never came. The islands—small, isolated communities mostly—were ill prepared to harbor and feed the great numbers of strangers. Plagues broke out and scores died of typhus, dysentery, yellow fever, malaria and smallpox. In Grenada Hippisley was forced to quell a mutiny by training a brass cannon upon his men. In Haiti the artillery brigade disbanded, nearly all of the First Rifles deserted and the fine military band broke up and wandered away. Everywhere men deserted until all the brave battalions were reduced to mere skeletons. They sold their fine uniforms and equipment for what few dollars they could get and took passage in the first boat that would take them anywhere at all. Many of them wandered for years among the West Indies, penniless beggars. It is surprising indeed that any of them ever managed to make their way up the Orinoco to join the Venezuelan patriots. But some of them did, coming singly and in small groups, some of them with their wives and small children, making their way laboriously in flecheras against the current of that jungle stream.

Part of the Irish Legion arrived first in Margarita—a contingent numbering 1050 men. Arismendi, then in possession of the island, having few supplies and food stores for his own small force, was confounded at the number of strangers and refused to permit them to land. So the legionnaires had to force a landing on the soil they had come to deliver. They lay there for weeks, in agony for the want of food. Typhus broke out and 250 died in five weeks. Eventually Brión came with his fleet to bring them aid. Some of them went to New Granada with Montilla—who had got over his quarrel with Bolívar and returned from the United States—where they fought bravely and helped free the Magdalena from Spaniards. They did, however, cause a lot of trouble with mutiny and drunkenness, and they set fire to the town of Rio Hacha.

Another contingent, with some of the British Legion and Hanoverians, sailed for the mainland and were assigned to the command of Urdaneta. They, too, fought well and took the town of Barcelona; but there they broke into the stores, got raving drunk and sacked the town. They stayed fourteen days, brawling and fighting among themselves. Forty of them deserted to the Spaniards. Urdaneta succeeded in capturing five, three of whom he shot. Only the Hanoverians maintained their discipline. With killings, death from sickness and desertions, the original number of one thousand was reduced to 400, only 233 of whom were in condition to fight. Urdaneta asked to be relieved of the command. He said, "Six months with these men is worse than ten campaigns." Mariño was given the command and many of this body served bravely throughout the war.

While Bolívar was fighting the Spaniards around Calabozo, the first legionnaires began to drift into Angostura. They were sent up the river by the Council to join Páez at San Fernando. The llanero chief, finding them good horsemen, and immensely pleased with the gaudy uniforms they wore, took to them at once. He placed them on his staff and formed a guard of honor of those who still possessed the most finery. Fernando González says of Páez, "He was an innocent child, a primitive who looked on Bolívar as a god and at other times, when he was afar, as a devil. He was a child even unto his crimes, enamored of anything that shone." Anyway, the education of Páez began with the arrival of the British legionnaires. They taught him words in English and taught him to eat with a knife and fork.

Hippisley relates that the first meeting between Colonel English and Páez was after the battle of Ortiz. English had been sent out from headquarters at San Fernando and arrived just as the skirmish had been won. He found Páez lying under a tree in a stupor, frothing at the mouth. He gave him water from his canteen and brought him to. The llanero chief told him that he had killed thirty-nine Spaniards with his lance and was running through the fortieth when he had been overcome. He gave English the bloody lance as a memento.

Páez had a high old time with his new comrades between his skirmishes with the enemy. He was delighted with them and staged big rodeos at San Fernando and Achaguas, showing off his great skill at throwing the lance, lassoing steers and coleando bulls. He gave big feasts of the llanero kind, such as the one given that year on the day of San Juan. In the evening his men, full of "guarapo," a liquor made of cane-juice, went about the village playing guitars and demanding that everyone come out and dance. Those who refused were hauled out and rolled in the deep mud. The dancing went on all night to the music of guitars, native harps and marracas—the llanero dances, "La Maricola," "El Raspón," "La Zapa." The next day there was a feast, prepared over open fires, of beef, wild boar, venison, wild duck, fish, pheasant, native cheese and corn cakes. But such things were to be very rare in the life that was ahead for the strangers from London and Liverpool.

When Bolívar reached San Fernando, Páez was away in action against the Spaniards at San Carlos; but shortly, as the Liberator lay in his hammock in a delirium of fever, Páez returned to report that he had been forced to retire from San Carlos, then from Barinas and finally from Nutrias. Word came also that Zaraza had been defeated by Morales, who now occupied Calabozo. As soon as he was able, Bolívar set off down the river for Angostura.

The very day after he left, a group of the foreign officers, at the instigation of a Colonel Wilson, presented Páez with a written act, renouncing loyalty to Bolívar and declaring him to be the captain-general of the patriot army. So even the foreigners intrigued against the Liberator. Páez was flattered and at first inclined to listen; but his better judgment and the esteem in which he had come to hold his chief prevailed, and he reported the matter to him.

Chapter XVII

THE BOLÍVAR CONSTITUTION

✤

A COPY of the act which Wilson had written reached Bolívar in Angostura. The proof of the Englishman's guilt was conclusive. An order went to Páez for Wilson's arrest and he was sent down the river in chains. Bolívar had him confined in the prison at Guayana, but he contrived to escape and returned to England. It was proved later that he had been in the pay of the Spaniards, and was sent out with the legionnaires for the very purpose of causing dissension among the patriot leaders.

At the seat of government of the Third Republic there had now gathered many of the leading patriots who had served as civilian administrators in the past—among them Germán Roscio, Fernando Peñalver, Juan Martínez, Ramón Cádiz and Diego Urbaneja. Bolívar felt that it was necessary now, in view of the fact that President Monroe of the United States had recognized Venezuela as a belligerent and had sent out an agent to investigate conditions, to convoke a Congress. Therefore, he named those men to conduct an election. He formulated a plan by which the nation should be divided into six provinces —Margarita, Guayana, Caracas, Barcelona, Cumaná and Barinas—and each should elect five deputies. He ignored the fact that most of these localities were in the hands of the Spaniards. It was also provided that Mérida and Trujillo should elect deputies when they were able. Voting should be permitted all males over twenty-one if single, of any age if married, who owned land, had a profession, art or trade, or who enjoyed an annual income of 300 pesos or more. In his proclamation he said, "Elect to public office the most virtuous of your citizens and in the election forget if you can those who have liberated you."

Of the activities of Bolívar during this period Parra-Pérez says, "The labors of the Liberator were immense and covered all the branches of public administration. He was as many-sided as Proteus. Besides forming a government he was concerned with raising funds, reorganizing the army, commerce, taxation and emigration. No man in history has shown a greater energy and wiser intelligence or achieved greater results with such miserable tools. The country existed only through the will of the Liberator. He was not, like Washington and San Martín, merely the commander of a revolutionary army; he was the Father of the Revolution."

His principal worry was money—of which there was none at all. He garnered every bit of silver available, and, as Páez had done with the silver ornaments from the Spanish equipment he had taken, he melted it and stamped it out into smooth round pesos. These coins, known as "cut money," became almost the only currency in circulation.

He established a newspaper, *The Orinoco Post,* and published articles in it constantly.

The members of the foreign legions came drifting in with their families, all miserably in want, and he strove desperately to provide for them. Upon their demands for the payment of the bonuses promised, he had to resort to evasion and cajolery, trying to conceal from them the true state of the nation's finances. He invented an argument with which he answered all—that there had been a misunderstanding and that Méndez was to have paid them in London, that the matter would be taken up and the money paid when things were straightened out with Méndez. All were treated with uniform courtesy, consideration and good manners, and by superhuman efforts he managed to feed and shelter them. In fact, one of the legionnaires relates that there was plenty of food for all whenever the Liberator was present; but the moment he departed the food disappeared into thin air, and there commenced confusion and depredation by those whom he placed in trust.

Many of the new-comers refused to take the oath of allegiance when the bonus was not forthcoming; and with these Bolívar had to use his utmost tact and charm. Montilla, confronted with the same situation in another part of the country, ordered the men to be arrested and stripped of their uniforms—a policy which brought them to terms but scarcely won their sympathy for the cause. Bolívar, at one point, was on the verge of shipping the whole lot back to England.

However, there were many of the foreigners who won his immediate regard by their understanding attitude and spirit of co-operation. The hardships the legionnaires had endured in reaching their goal bespoke fortitude and had been a good weeding-out process—though there were still many unworthy ones among them. Bolívar, like Páez, formed a Guard of Honor and named several foreign officers to his personal staff. One of these was Colonel James Rooke, a huge, handsome, blue-eyed blond who had been a major in the British army and was the son of a general commanding a district of western England. He had brought his fascinating young bride with him from the island of St. Kitts and established her in a house amid the squalor and privations of Angostura. He was one of the first legionnaires to arrive and Bolívar came to love him as a son.

Strange and disheartening indeed were the conditions which the Europeans found in this remote corner of the New World. Had they first arrived at Caracas or one of the Andean cities, their impressions would have been vastly different. One of them—Dr. Robinson, an army surgeon—described his experiences. At Angostura he was assigned quarters in a great old Spanish house; but the

owner appeared in the middle of the night and put him
out. In the dark he entered an empty house adjoining,
hung his hammock from the ever-present hooks in the
wall and slept till morning. Then he discovered that the
hooks had been used for hanging Spaniards and the back
patio was heaped with their unburied remains.

He also described his first meeting with General Monagas and his army on the banks of the Orinoco. The soldiers, he said, ranged in age from eight to fifty and some
of them were completely naked, others wearing only a
short piece of cloth hanging front and back from the belly,
tied with a hair rope. The general, dark, wild-haired and
tattered, wore a blue jacket, a cap of jaguar skin, a white
vest and dirty white linen trousers. He had one fairly
whole shoe on a sockless foot and the other was a shape-
less flap tied to his ankle. But the legionnaires were to
find themselves as badly garbed, or worse, before very
long. Unused to the unsalted strips of dried beef called
"tasajo" which was their constant ration, they lacked the
knowledge to secure, as the natives did, such things as
wild honey, edible tubers and wild fruits. So, to get money
to buy them, they took to selling their fine garments piece
by piece. In a few short months, it was the native officers—
little fellows mostly—who were decked out in the Wellington boots and scarlet capes while the burly legionnaires
campaigned in alpargatas, jaguarskin caps and bare chests.
But even their size altered soon. They became, says Robinson, "shrunk and withered to mere walking skeletons . . .
struggling patiently with a combination of disappoint-
ment and disease . . . unparalleled in the history of the
world."

On one occasion, at a ball in Angostura, Colonel Rooke
appeared with his beautiful wife—and he wore no shirt
under his jacket. Bolívar, asking the reason, was told by
the grinning Rooke that his last shirt had been sold for
a nice fat wild duck. Bolívar called his servant and ordered him to get one of his own shirts for the colonel.

The servant, embarrassed, replied, "But, General, you yourself have only two shirts. Your other one is being washed."

Bolívar was excessively fond of such gatherings and he organized them on every occasion. At every village he called for the local musicians and gave dances that lasted till dawn. Even camping out in the bush, at times he danced by the fire on the bare earth with the women who always followed his troops. He loved to waltz and he would dance hours on end when he found a partner who pleased him. Dancing, he claimed, clarified his ideas, inspired and excited his imagination. He would leave the floor abruptly in the middle of a dance, dictate a letter to his secretary and return to dance some more. "There are those," he said, "who must be alone and away from all confusion in order to think and meditate. I can reflect and meditate in the midst of social gatherings, pleasures or the noise of battle. I am always alone in the midst of many people."

While the committee was engaged in arranging the election of members of Congress, he was busy laying his plans for the expedition into New Granada. He said nothing to anyone at all about it. To prepare the way he sent Santander into the bordering provinces of New Granada with a proclamation to the people in which he manufactured the deliberate lie that Morillo had been beaten, that 20,000 Spaniards had been killed and that Venezuela was now completely happy once more under a republican government and invited New Granada to send deputies to the Congress. Effect was what he wanted—and no one knew better than he how to achieve it, or had less regard for scruples in the process.

He made a rapid trip north to Maturín to inspect the army of Mariño and arrived to find that the patriot army in Cumaná had been completely destroyed by the enemy. He returned to Angostura, down-hearted for once. "Who would not lose hope and even his head," he said, "in the face of so many blunders. In addition to all the other evils that afflict us, we have to deal with incompetence, insubordination and presumption."

Almost immediately he set out again for Apure, mainly to assure himself of the continued loyalty of Páez. He met the llanero chief at San Fernando and read the law to him. He didn't spare words this time. He gave him to understand that he knew of his hesitation over the Wilson affair and that he would brook no such doings in the future. He would tolerate no pretension to authority that would tend to disrupt the solidarity of the Republic. He knew well how to maintain his power and dignity and he would not hesitate to act, no matter how valuable the guilty person might be. He said to him, grandiosely, "I am like the sun in the midst of all; my lieutenants have no other brilliance than that which reflects on them from me." This statement lends strength to the opinion of the Spanish writer Ciro Bayo, who said, "His career was a great vanity enlisted in the service of a noble cause."

But the illiterate Páez was impressed. He protested meekly his undying devotion to the person of the Liberator and declared his complete submission to his authority. Bolívar reviewed the llanero troops and made them a glowing speech in which he said, "The intrepid General Páez will lead you to victory and this genius of liberty will inscribe your names in the annals of glory! Llaneros, you are invincible!"

While he was in San Fernando, Colonel Hippisley, the commander of all the foreign legionnaires, arrived from Angostura. The meeting was unpropitious, for Bolívar was ill, and he had just received word of new patriot reverses on the llanos. Furthermore, Hippisley's men proceeded to get out of hand, raided the stores and got roaring drunk. Hippisley followed the Liberator about, pouring out his grievances—and he had a wonderful list of them. Bolívar had been hearing so much of the same sort of thing for so long that he was in no mood to hear more just then; and he carefully kept out of Hippisley's way. The next morning he set off down the river for Angostura.

The English colonel, finding him gone, immediately commandeered a flechera and went after him. There ensued a fine chase down the Orinoco that went on for days. Each evening as Bolívar's boat drew up to the bank to tie for the night, Hippisley approached and, observing all the formalities, ran up saluting flags and dispatched an orderly to request an interview with the commanding general. The answer was always the same—the general was indisposed. Hippisley, a determined Britisher, took to trying to approach him during the day. Speeding up his Indian paddlers, he would draw alongside the general's flechera, raise his signal flag—to which courtesy there was never any response—and call out a request for an audience. But the Liberator remained hidden away with one of his women within the cool shade of the thatched shelter on his narrow craft. So the chase continued all the way to Angostura.

There, of course, there was no getting away from the Englishman. Bolívar had to see him at last. He invited him to his quarters and sat beside him on the sofa, smiling and polite. Hippisley proceeded to pour out an amazing list of complaints. He, commander of the legionnaires, held only the rank of colonel, such as many another held under his command. Where were the two hundred dollars due him on reaching the country and where were the five hundred pounds which he had paid out for various necessities for his men? He wanted immediate payment in full. Bolívar could only evade and play for time. He couldn't reveal the fact that there never had been that much money in the national treasury. It had no effect whatever to point out to Hippisley that he had already been stepped up from half-pay lieutenant to full-pay colonel. The Englishman demanded the rank of brigadier general, no less. He claimed that that had been in his agreement with Méndez in London. Bolívar asked if he could produce a signature of Méndez's to that effect or an order from him for the sum demanded. Hippisley became very bitter and resorted to sarcasm; whereupon Bolívar politely terminated the interview. He offered his hand and Hippisley refused to take it.

For several weeks the Englishman bombarded the Liberator with letters; and he got a reply, finally, in which Bolívar said, "If you could present a single document in which you were offered the grade of brigadier you would have no more difficulty in obtaining it from me." Hippisley then demanded his passport and got it. In their final interview, Bolívar, with sly humor, offered to buy the Englishman's cocked hat and plumes. But there was no humor in Hippisley. He accepted eagerly and sold him his whole outfit for one hundred cut pesos; and the Liberator wore it about town with great aplomb and obvious delight.

When Hippisley returned to England, he brought legal action against Méndez and had him arrested; but he got nowhere and the Venezuelan agent was released at once. Then the Englishman sat down to write a scathing indictment of Bolívar and all his works—a book which was published in 1819 and has been used by all of the Liberator's detractors down through the years. It is a work of obvious pique and personal animosity.

Later, in 1825, Hippisley was involved in a fraudulent colonizing scheme—presumably the same one in which MacGregor was interested—and, like the Scotsman, he was arrested in Paris and imprisoned in La Force.

Bolívar traveled rapidly, always. The length of his daily marches was only governed by the strength and speed of his horse. Every one of the innumerable journeys of which we speak so glibly was in itself a test of physical endurance; and is so, even today—overland, of course, not by air. North Americans and Europeans now, more than a century later, making even one of those trips, will return home to write lurid accounts of "tropical exploration."

During that game of aquatic hide-and-seek down the Orinoco, the Liberator was not concerned only with his women and with dodging the pestiferous Hippisley; his mind was occupied with his plans for the Congress which was about to assemble and for the Constitution which he would propose to it.

With Francisco Zea as president, the Congress convened in Angostura on February 15, 1819. Only twenty-six deputies from the various provinces had arrived—and these, because of the Spanish occupation, were mostly representatives of the patriot military chiefs operating in those areas rather than civilians elected in the popular manner Bolívar had prescribed. But this was no time for rigid adherence to legality. In the morning of that day there was a great firing of cannon and the deputies took their places in the government palace. Present as observers were an Englishman named Hamilton and the agent whom Monroe had sent from the United States, a Mr. B. Irvine. Some historians identify this American as the famous author Washington Irving; but evidence seems to show that Irving was in England at the time, writing his *Sketch Book*.

The opening address and the Constitution which Bolívar delivered comprise the last of the three most important public documents of his career. They were translated into English and French and copies were sent to foreign governments. They are long enough to fill a book in themselves and there is no need here to consider them in detail.

He began by renouncing his civil power, now that a government was being established, and asked only that he be permitted to retain military authority. He reiterated his old declaration that "the first day of peace will be the last of my command." The dictatorship should not continue any longer "because nothing is so dangerous as permitting unlimited power to remain in the same citizen for a long period of time. The people become accustomed to obey him and he becomes accustomed to command them; from which are born usurpation and tyranny."

Then he reviewed, with considerable knowledge and clarity, the history of political trends throughout the world from the days of the Greeks and Romans. His style was grandiloquent as usual, but not overly so considering the times.

The bulk of his message was taken up with an explanation of the Constitution which he had prepared for their consideration. It was conceived, he said, according to the formula that "That system of government is the most perfect which produces the greatest measure of happiness, social security and political stability for its people."

That system, as he saw it for his people, could not partake of pure democracy nor federalism, for "We are not prepared for such blessings." "Our weak citizens," he said, "will have to strengthen their spirits greatly before they can take the salutary nourishment of liberty. Their limbs have been numbed by chains, their visions dimmed by the shadows of the dungeons. . . . Can they march with firm steps toward that temple [of liberty], sustaining its splendid rays, breathing without oppression its pure air?"

The North American Constitution, he declared, was ideal and excellent for the Yankees; but "It would be better for South America to adopt the Koran than the form of government of the United States, even though it be the best in the world." "It is a marvel to me," he said, "that it [the United States] has continued to exist and prosper, that it has not been overthrown at the first sign of danger. In spite of the fact that this people is a singular model of political virtue and moral enlightenment, that liberty has been its cradle, that it has been reared in and fed upon pure liberty, it is a marvel that a system so weak and complicated as the federal has been able to endure. . . . It has never even remotely entered my mind to consider a parallel between the positions and natures of two publics as distinct as the Anglo- and the Hispano-American."

The English system was much better suited to them; but it, too, failed to fit their conditions exactly, for there was no provision for the education of administrators. "Education forms a moral man," he said, "and to form a good legislator it is certainly necessary to educate him in a school of political morality, justice and law. . . . England, lacking such provision, is not entirely in conformity with the system I propose; but would not my system do much good in England? . . . Solon taught us how difficult it is to direct men by mere laws. . . . All the experience of history proves that men submit to the laws which capable legislators impose on them and then only so far as a strong magistrate applies them."

He declared strongly his opposition to a loose federal system and his belief in firm centralization. "Our slogan should be, Unity, Unity, Unity. The blood of our citizens is diverse; let us mix it to unite it. Our constitutions have had division of powers; let us concentrate them to unite them. . . ."

He recognized the inevitable evolution of a definite South American racial type and pled for acceptance of that fact in government; and in this he proved himself far more honest and daring than most Latin American commentators before his day—or since. He said:

We must face the fact that our race is not European or North American; it is rather a composite of Africa and America than an emanation of Europe, for Spain itself ceased to be European by its African [Moorish] blood, its institutions and character. It is impossible to determine exactly to what human family we do belong. The greater part of indigenous blood has been wiped out; the European has mixed with the American and African and this has mixed with the Indian and European. Even though all of us were born from the bosom of the same mother, our fathers, differing in origin and blood, are foreigners; and all differ visibly in coloring. This dissimilitude carries with it an obligation of tremendous proportion.

The Constitution which he submitted was a compilation, reduced to parliamentary form, of all those ideas he had expressed in his various manifestos in the past and which he had evolved from the theories inculcated in those early discussions with Miranda and from reading Montesquieu and Aristotle. It called for complete civil liberty and freedom of religion, and forbade slavery. It provided a general pardon for political offenses, applying to European Spaniards no matter what their actions had been, and regardless of rank or class. Suffrage was to be universal under certain qualifications. The government was to be divided into four branches: executive, legislative, judiciary and that fourth power which Bolívar dwelt upon so much, the censors—supervisory High Priests of government. The president was to be popularly elected for life, the senate was to be hereditary—elected for the first time by the Congress—and the lower house elective. The judiciary was to consist of a supreme court of five members named by Congress; and there were a multitude of laws for the different branches of government.

Bolívar concluded his address with the words, "Señores, begin your functions. I have concluded mine."

The English observer, Mr. Hamilton, was greatly impressed. He wrote, "General Bolívar gave so brilliant a proof of moderation and patriotism as is not found in the annals of any country."

The Congress set about its deliberation. The Republic of Colombia was solemnly declared re-established and Bolívar was elected president and commander-in-chief of the army—which offices he accepted, as usual, after a show of reluctance. Francisco Zea was elected vice-president. Bolívar selected a cabinet composed of three members and the Congress turned to the problem of the Constitution.

Bolívar harbored no illusion as to the legality of the Congress of Angostura, composed as it was of deputies

selected by God knows what haphazard methods and pre-
suming to represent communities which were under Spanish military governors; but he made the gesture anyway
and tried to give it the semblance of legality. The main
purpose, of course, was the effect upon foreign nations.
He wrote humorously to Fernando del Toro, who was in
Trinidad and who had been first considered for the presidency, "Something calling itself the government has
named you, or better stated, called upon you, to serve as
the executive power. Whether this be legal or not, I have
approved the action and I call you with even more insistence than the government."

The Congress was, on the whole, composed of a pretty
sorry lot of ruffians. They had never before heard such
noble words as poured from the mouth of the Liberator
and many wept, carried away by the sheer beauty of them.
They deliberated daily for several months over the question of a constitution. Barefooted and tattered, mounted
on mules and burros, they came to the assembly hall to
consider dutifully the affairs of state. When the Constitution was finally adopted, Bolívar was already far away
on a heroic project of which none of them, or anyone else,
knew anything.

When finally adopted, the Constitution made no provision for those pet projects that were so dear to Bolívar's
heart. The fourth branch of government—the educating
and inquisitory censors—was thrown out entirely. The hereditary senate was thrown out and also the life-term for
the president—who was to be elected for a term of four
years only. What remained, then, was a Constitution bearing a great resemblance to that of the United States—exactly what Bolívar had decried so vehemently. But the
federal system of the First Republic was not adopted and
the union of provinces was declared "one and indivisible"
—as was, in reality, the union of the United States, though
the fact was not established until later by the War between the States.

Chapter XVIII

"EVEN TO CAPE HORN"

✣

ONLY a few final preparations now, and he would be ready to set out upon that fantastic enterprise which had been simmering in his mind for so long.

Méndez had sent a shipment of 10,000 rifles and large quantities of munitions, and five armed war sloops had arrived from England to reinforce the squadron of Brión. Angostura, then, and the river would be well protected from enemy attack.

The attitude of foreign governments was beginning to favor the patriot cause; it was necessary to accomplish a spectacular maneuver quickly for effect. On March 28, 1818, Henry Clay had made an impassioned plea before the United States Congress for recognition of the South American states. The proposition was voted down, but considerable sympathy had been aroused; Clay was continuing his efforts and winning support.

Considerable numbers of the foreign legionnaires had arrived by this time—commissioned and noncommissioned officers mostly—and Bolívar had reorganized them, preserving somewhat their original units, though these consisted of little more than a cadre of officers for each. After the departure of Hippisley Colonel Rooke was placed at the head of the whole British Legion and of the First Rifles as his individual command. It was necessary to fill the ranks with native troops.

In the interior of Guayana, up the Caroní River, were those Indian missions which had been established by the Capuchín monks and which Piar had seized, needlessly slaughtering the Spanish priests in the process. There were nineteen missions in all, harboring some 7000 partially civilized Indians. Vast acres of rich land were under cultivation and there was food in abundance. Bolívar drew upon the missions to supply his men with corn, sugar, meat and casabe; and when he was confronted with the necessity of filling the ranks of the foreign battalions, he sent the officers to the missions to recruit men. There is no evidence that force or threats were used in this process. Presumably the Indians joined willingly, intrigued by the strange and colorful white men and delighted with the chance to see something of the outside world. At any rate the recruiting was successful and many of the foreign battalions, with their high-sounding names, came to number in their ranks hundreds of naked savages. Under the assiduous training of the foreign officers—Colonel Pigott and the Hanoverian Colonel Uslar in particular—the Indians attained a high state of discipline and proved themselves brave and efficient soldiers.

Shortly before his departure, Bolívar gave a huge ball in honor of the American agent, Irvine—whom he persisted in calling, incidentally, "the American Ambassador." At a long table a banquet was served to all the officers, civilian officials and their ladies. After toasts were drunk and while dessert was being served, the Liberator was called upon to speak. He was brilliantly dressed for the occasion in a uniform which had been sent him as a sample by a merchant in Trinidad. From his place at the head of the table he made a typically fiery and eloquent speech. Then, when he had brought his audience to a high pitch of excitement, he suddenly jumped upon the table and, oblivious of the wine bottles and flowers and crystal that crashed under his great boots, he strode the length of the board. "Thus," he cried, "as I cross this table from one end to the other, I shall march from the Atlantic to the Pacific, from Panamá to Cape Horn, until the last Spaniard is expelled!" Then, turning, he strode back. "And thus," he shouted, "I shall return, without having done harm to a single soul save those who oppose the completion of my sacred mission."

He wasn't drunk at all. He wasn't even carried away by enthusiasm. He acted coldly, with the studied calculation of the finished showman that he was. Whether or not the performance had the desired effect upon the staid Yankee, Irvine, is questionable. Bolívar had mastered the art of working upon the psychology of a more highly emotional people.

He was not a romanticist in the slightest degree. He was as coldly realistic always as anyone has ever been. He wore the mantle of romanticism deliberately for its appeal, knowing how well it fitted his personality and became his physical appearance. It was the costume of a superb dramatic actor, playing a heroic part in real life.

Only twelve days after the Congress had named him president, he started west with his army, leaving Zea, the vice-president, in charge of the government. No one knew where he was really going. No one suspected that his words at the banquet were spoken in dead earnest. He was careful not to enlighten them.

He left on February 27, 1819. There weren't enough boats available to transport his army and he took an overland route, paralleling the south shore of the Orinoco—a route of dense jungle and rugged hills and many streams, where there isn't a sign of a road or a trail even today. They crossed the Orinoco where it joins with the Arauca and turns abruptly south, building rafts for the men and equipment, swimming the pack-animals. They continued west and met Páez near Achaguas on March 16. In eighteen days they had marched 280 miles through country which could well be termed impassable.

While Bolívar was in Angostura, the Spanish forces had taken the offensive against Páez and had converged all their units from the llanos at headquarters in San Fer-

nando. There had been skirmishes almost daily and, while
the Spaniards had lost upwards of a thousand men, they
had driven Páez from his base in Achaguas. When Bolívar
arrived he decided to take the offensive at once. He attacked a Spanish force under Colonel Perera, dispersed
them after a sharp encounter and moved to a point on
the Arauca opposite Achaguas. Páez crossed the river with
only 150 picked horsemen, surprised the main army of
Morillo, dispersed it and captured all the artillery. The
llaneros lost but six men in the engagement, the Spaniards
500.

For several weeks Bolívar continued his offensive
against Morillo, hammering away at him with quick raids,
bewildering him with his rapid marches. Finally, as the
rainy season was upon them, Morillo withdrew far north
into the llanos to Calabozo and established winter quarters. (The rainy season is referred to in Venezuela as winter, although the weather is hotter, if anything.)

Santander, who had gone to New Granada with the
flagrant message Bolívar had addressed to the people there,
had raised an army and, with able tactics, cleared the
Spaniards from the eastern Andes slopes and the plains
of Casanare. Bolívar led his army from Achaguas and
met on the Arauca a messenger from Santander, who reported that the way was clear into New Granada, where
the people were eagerly awaiting liberation. On the night
of May 23, at Setenta—a little group of thatched houses
beside the river—Bolívar held a council of his officers. The
rains had begun and that was all he was waiting for.

They gathered in a mud hut by the light of a candle
stuck in the wall. There were no chairs. The officers
crowded together, squatting on the bare earth floor or on
the skulls of oxen. And there Bolívar revealed for the first
time his plan to continue westward across the plains, cross
the Andes and deliver the city of Bogotá. The route he
had chosen was the worst possible, over the mountains at
the highest point, where no one could possibly expect

him. The army of Morillo would remain inactive for several months at least, until the rains ceased and the rivers subsided. Páez would remain behind to cover the rear and engage Morillo, should he become suspicious, and to make feints in the direction of Cúcuta to draw the attention of the Spaniards there.

When Bolívar finished speaking there was a dead silence. The officers looked at each other as though to question if they really heard what they thought they had. For once Bolívar refrained from trying to persuade, to impose his will. He laid the plan before them and to their flow of questions he made frank and thoughtful answer. He had weighed every hazard carefully and he had full confidence that the project was feasible. The first officer to express agreement was Colonel Rooke, who blurted out, "Sire, I for one will follow you even to Cape Horn!" Finally they all agreed, some of them with trepidations. Bolívar swore them to secrecy. It wouldn't do for the men in the ranks to know, as yet. Then he dismissed them and flung himself into his hammock and swung rapidly, gazing at the flickering candle with his deep-set, burning eyes. The rain beat upon the thatched roof with a constant roar.

The next day at Mantecal, near by, he organized his forces in marching order, concentrated all the boats available and secured provisions and fresh horses. There were in all 1600 foot soldiers, 800 cavalry and several hundred women. The following day, May 26, they embarked on the canoes and rafts and headed upstream against the brown current in the teeming rain.

For eight days they poled and paddled their way up the ever-narrowing stream until it no longer carried them in the direction they sought. At Guasdualito they abandoned the Arauca and there the llanero officers, Iribarren and Rangel, fearful as always of mountains, deserted with their cavalry. Bolívar watched them go without a word of censure. He sent a message back to Zea, informing him for the first time of his intentions. Then he gave the order to continue the march.

The plains of Casanare lay ahead of them—endless, flooded, traversed by swollen streams with fringes of dense jungle on their banks. The rain beat down from a sky as dead gray as the herons that winged drearily across it and what once was land was now a boundless, leaden mirror, its surface broken by little islands of grass, shimmering like mirages. All life had fled from the land and the alligators had come out of the rivers to wallow in the slime.

The line of march stretched like a long thin serpent, dark and disjointed, writhing slowly forward. The men and women struggled through water to their waists, holding their muskets and their bundles aloft till their arms were aching with fatigue. The mud sucked at their feet with every step and they slipped and fell, face forward, to be jerked from the dark water by comrades. The herds of cattle stumbled along in stupid complacence and pack-mules foundered, sometimes to drown before their burdens could be removed. At night the men and animals crowded on the grassy tufts that rose above the flood. There was no dry wood to build fires. The tortas of casabe and corn had melted in the constant wet and the only food was beef, eaten raw, stripped from the warm and bloody carcasses of steers. There was no sun to dry it and the rain washed the salty sweat from under the mule-packs.

Day after day the column wallowed forward in the silence of exhaustion. The clothing rotted on their bodies, the shoes fell away from their feet. Sores opened on their bare limbs and leeches hung in clusters like brown grapes. Their flesh was torn from their bones by the vicious caribe fish that swarmed in the water.

The rivers were the worst. There a path had to be cut through the tangled bush, and at the banks crude rafts were made from logs and cowhides. The mules were all unpacked, the equipment was lashed to the rafts and

poled across. Then the cattle and pack-animals were
herded and driven into the stream, many of them to be
carried away in the swift current. Finally the troops and
women crowded onto the frail craft and were ferried
across. A full day was spent at the rivers; and there were
many of them.

The patriots plodded on doggedly, none of them, save
a few officers, knowing where they were going or for what
purpose. They followed Bolívar trustingly, mute as the
cattle they drove. He was everywhere among them, labor-
ing with the fallen animals, helping with the sick and
faltering. "Only a little farther now," he told them constantly. "Only a few more leagues. The worst is over."
But the worst, he well knew, was to come.

Of them all, only Rooke kept up his spirits. The big
Englishman was irrepressible. Everything was wonderful.
The country was wonderful, the climate was wonderful.
There was no burning sun to plague them, the rain was
wonderful and cool. He was pleased with everything and
everybody, particularly himself. He had only a pair of
tattered pants to clothe his big white body and his hair
hung in long wet curls and he laughed from his shaggy,
reddish beard. He worked like one possessed, hauling logs
for the rafts, dragging the unwilling animals into the
streams. His voice, shouting commands to the men,
boomed over the silent wastes.

They were three weeks crossing the plains of Casanare.
Slowly, out of the west, the Andes rose like gray specters.
On the fourteenth of June the column arrived at a little
cluster of huts called Tame, at the first slopes; and there
part of the army of Santander awaited them. The naked,
exhausted men from the plains and the lowland Indians
looked upward in astonishment at the towering peaks.
They had never before seen anything rise so far above
the horizon. Many of them had never even heard of the
Andes.

Bolívar stayed at Tame for three days, resting his men

and organizing his army. Santander, already ahead in the mountains with the main of his army, would advance as the vanguard. He had two battalions of infantry and a squadron of cavalry, numbering 1200 in all. With his own 2000, Bolívar's army now totaled 3200 men. Bolívar was thirty-six years old. His chief of staff, Soublette, was twenty-nine, Santander was twenty-eight, the commander of the rear guard, Anzoátegui, was thirty. They were all able, experienced officers and all thoroughly loyal—even Santander, at this time. Rooke was in command of the British Legion, composed of several hundred English and Irish, and the bulk, Indians; and Colonel Daniel O'Leary, the Irishman who was to remain with the Liberator until his death, was an aide to General Anzoátegui.

The troops suspected now, of course, that they were going into the mountains. Bolívar quieted them with the assurance that they were going in only a little way.

For the first few days the ascent was gradual; but slowly the trail grew steeper, the crags closed in and the ground grew rocky. One by one the unshod horses from the plains went lame or flagged from the unaccustomed effort of climbing—and the llaneros scrambled along on their spindly legs, bewildered, as men who had been maimed.

A force of 300 Spanish troops was strongly placed among the crags at the pass of Paya, at the foot of the abrupt rise of the mountains. Santander's advance guard stormed the pass in an adroit and daring action and destroyed the enemy force. When Bolívar reached Paya, five days after leaving Tame, all his horses were gone. Only a small herd of cattle and some of his mules remained. The cavalry of Santander, mountain men, had mounts which were accustomed to the terrain.

From Paya Bolívar chose an abandoned and difficult trail in order to keep the enemy in ignorance of his whereabouts; and from that point began an ascent which has probably never been equaled in military history. Bolívar had crossed the Andes before with the army of New Granada. But his men then were those strong young patriots from the Andean country, fired with the zeal of holy crusaders. Now he had men and women from the lowlands, exhausted by six hundred miles of march from Angostura, burned out with malaria, starved, almost naked. He could only urge them on with that constant phrase, "Only a little farther now. We're almost there."

The rock faces rose almost perpendicular. The army scrambled up them, clinging, their hands and bare feet bleeding. Mountain torrents fell from the ledges and the cold mists rose, wrapping the struggling column in clammy folds. The ravines fell away into dark voids and the men and animals that slid into them sent back no sound when they crashed far below. Crossing them, they had to make bridges of plaited vines and weave slings for the cattle and mules. Gradually, as they rose, the vegetation thinned out and the air grew chill, moaning among the crags. Most of them had never felt cold before; and now it struck them like a new pain, and they were naked in it. In the brief moments of noon, when the thin shafts of sunlight darted into the dark chasms, they flung themselves on the rocks full-length, to absorb it into their numbed bodies. The air grew thin, their hearts raced and a strange lethargy spread into their limbs. The constant voice of the Liberator and the arms of their comrades urged them on. Higher and higher they climbed, day after day, and soon all vegetation had vanished and there was no wood for fires at night. The winds grew colder and stronger and the men and women huddled together to warm each other with their bodies. In that bleak region there was only one lone plant, the fraylajón, rising gauntly among the rocks, waving ghostly arms in the moonlight. Rooke plucked its yellow blossoms and declared they were the most beautiful flowers he had ever seen.

They climbed for six days. Black squalls moved among the ravines, cutting them with hail, numbing them with sleet, blinding them with snow. Hundreds lay down to freeze, more hundreds to yield in peace to the "soroche." When at last they came out onto the bleak Páramo de Pisba, all the mules and cattle were gone. Among the British legionnaires alone, fifty men had succumbed to the mountain sickness. The army had climbed thirteen thousand feet.

The night spent on the páramo was the worst of all. Icy winds screamed about the huddled people, biting into their frozen bones. The stars seemed strangely bright and infinitely remote and the moonlight spread, as O'Leary described it, with a "metallic luster."

Many died that night of cold, starvation and soroche. Among them was a woman and her whole family of children who had come with the army for protection on their journey home. Another woman bore a child that night, too, and the next day she marched with the army, carrying it in her arms.

At last the worst was over. A few days of easy descent and the army straggled into the high, green valley of Sogamoso, bright with sun and painted with flowers.

Bolívar had crossed the Andes. Thirty-two hundred men had begun the ascent on the other side and twelve hundred scarecrows wandered into the village of Socha.

The villagers stared at the apparitions that appeared among them suddenly as though from out of the ground; and when they were told it was the army of liberators, they crossed themselves and hurried to heap them with all the food they could gather from their rich valley.

Colonel Rooke had been left behind to bring up the ammunition, the abandoned equipment and the stragglers who still survived. He showed up in Socha a few days after the vanguard and hurried to Bolívar's headquarters, where the staff officers were seated at lunch. Beaming as usual, he had nothing but good word to bring; everything was lovely, the survivors were all in, in fine shape. Anzoátegui, always a gloomy man, carefully read his writ-

ten report. He broke into Rooke's exuberant flow to remark drily that he noticed Rooke had lost a fourth of the
men and officers of his command. Rooke gulped a mouth-
ful of the food that had been given him and answered
airily, "That's nothing at all, General. They were the most
worthless of the lot. I'm glad to be rid of them."

Bolívar learned in Socha that the Spanish General
Barreira was concentrating some 3000 troops between him
and his objective, Bogotá. His own men were in a frightful condition and there wasn't a single horse, not even
one for himself. He sent out Colonel Lara to recruit
among the surrounding country and bring in what mounts
and food supplies he could. Within a few days Lara returned, bringing 800 men and over a thousand horses
from neighboring villages.

Bolívar took three days only to rest his troops and to
remount his cavalry—July 7 to July 10, 1819. He had
marched 750 miles from Angostura, fought several battles
and crossed the Andes in four months' time, accomplishing one of the greatest military feats of history; and after
three days he marched again and engaged an army of
Spanish veterans who had fought under Wellington.

Chapter XIX

BOYACÁ–NEW GRANADA
LIBERATED

✤

BARREIRO knew now that Bolívar was there. He determined to take the offensive at once and strike quickly. From his headquarters at Tunja, on the main road to Bogotá, he sent out two columns to scout the Sogamoso Valley. On the same day Bolívar, knowing his only chance lay in assuming the offensive himself, marched out from Socha; and his advance cavalry attacked and destroyed the enemy squadron of 300 men. This was Bolívar's first action after crossing the Andes and the victory, insignificant though it was, put new life into his army of scarecrows.

The following day Barreira came up with his main force and crossed the Rio Gameza. Bolívar, effecting a union with Anzoátegui and Santander, made a rapid march of fifteen kilometers in the early morning and arrived at the Gameza so suddenly that Barreira recrossed the river and took a strong position on a hill opposite. Bolívar sent four battalions to attack at once, among them the Rifles of Colonel Rooke. This was the first time Bolívar had seen the foreign legionnaires in action; and their behavior delighted him. The battalions stormed the hill, took it and drove the Spaniards to a new position. There Bolívar attacked them with his advance and center in successive charges for eight solid hours, but he couldn't budge them. He withdrew to the village of Tasco where he concentrated his forces, joining with the rear guard under Soublette.

For a week the two armies jockeyed for position in the valley and among the rugged hills, each striving to hold the offensive. Bolívar made several feints to draw Barreira out into battle; there were skirmishes daily by the flanks; but the Spaniards, though numbering 3000 to the patriots' 2600, failed to respond. Bolívar had to act fast before reinforcements should arrive from Bogotá. He made a quick march against the enemy's right flank, turned it and opened the pass of Tunja.

On the morning of July 25 the patriot army marched south on the main road. Barreira, perceiving Bolívar's intention, made a rapid oblique movement and intercepted the patriot route at a narrow pass where the road crossed the Sogamoso—a place called Paso La Balsa. He placed his army among the rocky heights, covering the road. Bolívar, coming up, scouted the position and placed his forces as best he could, fronting the enemy. He was in bad terrain, his right in a great swamp called Pantano de Vagas, his left at the foot of the heights occupied by the enemy. He ordered Santander to occupy a rocky knoll fronting them.

Barreira, seeing Santander's movement, attacked at once and drove the patriots back, inflicting heavy loss. Bolívar ordered counter-attacks by the British Legion in the center and by Carvajal by the swamp on the right flank. The English, Scots and Irish charged the hill in rigid formation in the face of heavy fire from the crags above. O'Leary fell wounded, then Rooke. Mackintosh took command, rallied the faltering troops and led two charges with bayonets that carried the heights.

Meanwhile, fresh Spanish troops arrived and attacked Soublette's rear guard on the road. Barreira threw a vigorous counter-attack against the British Legion and Bolívar was completely encircled. He had one cavalry squadron in reserve under Colonel Rondón—llaneros, happy once more with horses under them. Bolívar turned to Rondón and said, "Colonel, save your country." Ron-

dón shouted an order to his men, spurred his horse and
charged directly into the Spanish cavalry holding the narrow pass. The Spaniards yielded. Bolívar threw in his infantry, cleared the defile and struck the enemy's rear by
both flanks. The Spaniards, routed, withdrew in confusion. Night had fallen with the suddenness of the tropics
and a thunderstorm broke that hurled torrents of rain
into the pass and lighted, in blinding flashes, the mangled
bodies of men and the stark, silent crags. It was the storm
and the night that saved the Spanish army from total
destruction. Bolívar was unable to follow up in the darkness and Barreira retired safely to Paipa. The patriot
losses had been heavy but the enemy's had been greater
still.

In the official report of the Spanish commander on the
action at Pantano de Vargas there is this comment: "The
destruction of the rebel army seemed inevitable and
should have been so complete that not a single one should
have escaped death. Desperation inspired in them resolution without parallel. Their infantry and cavalry, surging from those chasms in which they were trapped, hurled
themselves against the heights with fury. Our infantry,
which became confused by their excessive ardor and the
difficulty of the terrain, could not resist their force."

That night the patriots camped there in the pouring
rain. Colonel Rooke lay in a crude shelter of cowhides
and the patriot officers stood over him in silence. The
yellow light of a lantern flickered on the deep-lined and
harried face of Bolívar. Doctor Foley bent over, busy
with his instruments, and Rooke grinned up at him from
a drawn face, pale with the loss of blood. Foley worked
quickly, talking pleasantly in his Irish voice. The eyes of
the watchers followed the movements of the surgeon's
hands with morbid fascination and then at last they
turned away. Foley straightened up.

"There we are, my lad," he said. "All done."

"Well, let me see it then," Rooke said.

"See what?"

"The arm, man. Give it to me."

He reached out with his hand, grasped the great, mangled, severed arm and held it aloft. He examined it critically, grinning.

"Isn't it a beauty, doctor?" he said. "A perfect arm if ever I saw one. Look at the strength of it, will you? Did you ever see a more beautiful arm?"

"It isn't bad," Foley said. "Not bad at all; but I've cut off better ones."

"You lie in your teeth. You never saw a better arm."

He waved it weakly in the air and cried in a feeble voice, "Viva la patria!"

"What patria? You've fought for England and Ireland and you've got the blood of each."

Rooke was silent for a moment and his hand fell and released its grasp on the thing it held. He spoke gently and all the mockery was gone from his voice.

"I mean the land I'm dying for," he said.

The next day Rooke was still alive; and while he lived they carried him with them. But a few nights later Bolívar sat down to write a letter to the young woman who waited for her husband in Angostura; and later, when he had accomplished the liberation of New Granada, he said, "To Rooke I owe all my good fortune in New Granada, and Venezuela is indebted to him for the preservation of its president and will hereafter have to attribute her liberty mainly to him."

Bolívar's army was sadly depleted once more; but he was faced with the necessity of keeping the offensive and trying to win a decisive victory over Barreira before Sámano, the Spanish viceroy in Bogotá, should arrive with reinforcements. He returned to Bonza and made desperate efforts to fill up his ranks. He decreed martial law in the province and ordered all able-bodied men to

present themselves for fifteen days' service, bringing their
horses with them.

Meanwhile, Barreira waited at Paipa, also refilling his
ranks from the surrounding country. The amazing thing
of this whole action in New Granada was the hesitancy
and indecision of the veteran Spanish general before the
scarecrow patriot army. The skillful maneuvers of Bolívar
and the rapidity with which he executed them seem to
have bewildered Barreira completely.

Bolívar spent only five days recruiting and training his
new troops—farmers and cattlemen who knew nothing
whatever of warfare.

The battle of Boyacá, as Bolívar's first great decisive
victory, reveals the Liberator at his best as a military
leader, demonstrating the rare talents which were always
most acute in him in the face of great odds.

He didn't make a single mistake. Perceiving at once
every intention of the enemy, he anticipated their action,
trapped them into errors of judgment and took quick
advantage of them; at the same time he observed strictly
the primary principles of military tactics—concentration,
offensive action and security. In addition, he employed
ruse and the unconventional tactics of guerilla warfare,
with never a violation of the principle of safety that so
often accompanies them. He knew this country well from
his campaign of the Magdalena in 1812; and he had that
mental trait so necessary to a commander of troops—the
ability to absorb topographic details at a glance and retain
them.

On August 4 the armies faced each other, jockeying like
wrestlers, their outposts in plain view. Bolívar made three
separate moves, trying to draw Barreira out; but the
Spaniard refused to budge. As dusk fell the patriot army
abandoned its position and crossed the Sogamoso, apparently to occupy Paipa. But an hour after dark Bolívar
countermarched rapidly, recrossed the river, circumvented
the Spaniards by a back trail and came out on the road to

Bogotá behind them. His army marched all night and surprised the small garrison at Tunja at daybreak, capturing 600 muskets and large quantities of munitions and food. It was a masterly maneuver, putting the enemy behind on the road to the capital and cutting them off from their base.

Barreira, learning of the patriot movement, attempted to employ a similar maneuver himself. He marched south by a back road, skirted the village of Tunja and advanced with the intention of blocking the road to Bogotá where a narrow bridge crossed the Rio Boyacá sixteen kilometers to the south. These two roads, the main one occupied by Bolívar and the side road to the west followed by the Spaniards, converged slowly and joined at the foot of a hill a short distance north of the bridge.

Bolívar's scouts watched the enemy movements constantly and he himself went out, climbed the rough slopes separating the two roads and observed the marching formation. Seeing at once Barreira's intention, he gave the order to march at the double in close order, Santander with the advance, Anzoátegui with the rear. Barreira failed for his part to scout this movement—a fatal error. Furthermore, his column was strung out, the advance well ahead of the main, the artillery well behind. Then, to cap his string of errors, he called for a rest at midday within a short distance of his objective, the bridge. His advance had already reached the junction of the roads and he, with the main, was half a mile behind. And there they rested—with that space between them and the enemy advancing rapidly on an almost parallel road only a few hundred yards to the east.

The Spanish advance, composed of a squadron of dragoons and two battalions of that famous corps called Numancia—which Bolívar had met in battle before in Venezuela—were resting under the trees on a small knoll beside a farmhouse. Santander's advance squadron was almost upon them on the road below before it was discov-

ered. The second battalion of Numancia opened fire and
the dragoons hurried to remount. The patriot squadron
fell back at once, pursued by the Numancia battalion.
Santander came up quickly, concentrated the whole advance and ordered a counter charge. Meanwhile, the main
column, with the British Legion at the head, followed in
close support. Under the attack of Santander the Spaniards
abandoned the knoll and the dragoons hurried south to
hold the pass at the bridge. Santander deployed his advance guard in a wide front and began a circling movement that sent the Numancia battalions after the dragoons. This action was possible, of course, only because
of that space between the enemy columns, permitting the
patriot main to protect the advance guard's rear.

The Rio Boyacá, flowing east to west, was ordinarily no
more than a brook; but now it was swollen to a brown
torrent by the rains. The banks were thick with tangled
brush, the bridge at the pass was narrow and the hills rose
steeply on all sides. All the surrounding country was
broken with low, rocky ridges, thickets of stunted trees,
and shallow, steep-sided ravines where small streams
flowed. The Spanish advance guard crossed the bridge
and occupied the heights along the south bank. Santander
deployed his battalions on the opposite shore and attacked
vigorously across the bridge with one charge after another.

Meanwhile, Bolívar formed his main columns in company fronts and advanced west in open order across the
rough land and the small creek that separated him from
Barreira. The enemy forces were thus stretched for half a
mile, facing each other, the Spaniards along the west road.
The British Legion, in the van and in contact with Santander's troops at the river, began a flank movement across
the road, turning the enemy battalions and driving a
wedge which ruined all hope for the Spanish main force
to establish contact with their advance guard. At the
same time the patriot rear, under Colonel Rondón, also

began a flanking cavalry movement that turned the Spanish rear—thus forming a crescent that gradually approached a circle, driving the Spaniards toward its center. Barreira, in face of Anzoátegui's vigorous frontal attack, fell back from the road and placed his artillery on a ridge within that ever-diminishing circle.

Thus there were two battles raging simultaneously, a quarter of a mile apart. It was all over in two hours. Santander, at the bridge, fought his way across at last and drove the Spanish advance from the heights. Anzoátegui, with a bayonet charge, forced the Spanish center and silenced the artillery; and all the while the British Legion to the south and Rondón's squadron to the north continued doggedly, finally closing their circle on the banks of a creek to the Spanish rear. Then Bolívar threw in his reserves at the center—a battalion of lancers and two battalions of the new recruits from the neighboring provinces. Barreira was done. He threw down his sword and surrendered to a private in the First Rifles, Rooke's old battalion. None of the force in that circle got away. Only 50 men escaped in all—these the few that fled south from the heights along the river. They kept going all the way to Bogotá; and their story of the battle so frightened Sámano, the viceroy, that he fled the city in haste, leaving behind him half a million pesos of royal funds.

Bolívar had won a glorious and decisive victory. Sixteen hundred men and thirty-nine officers surrendered with all their munitions; and his losses had only been thirteen killed and fifty-three wounded.

Among the Spanish prisoners Bolívar found one whom he was delighted to see. It was Colonel Francisco Vinoni, his old subordinate in the Aragua Militia, the man who had betrayed the patriot cause and aided the uprising of Spanish prisoners at Puerto Cabello seven years before. Bolívar took sweet revenge and hanged Vinoni at once.

The battle of Boyacá was fought on the seventh of August, 1819. Bolívar set out with three squadrons of cavalry on the hundred-mile journey to Bogotá, leaving the rest of his army to bring in the prisoners. Three days later he entered the capital of New Granada.

The reception accorded him in the old city of Santa Fé was of the same nature and equal enthusiasm as the one he had received when he had delivered Caracas, but perhaps slightly less garish; for Bogotá was a city of older culture and more discriminating taste. Besides, the people had less time to prepare. Nevertheless, there was much of the same sort of thing. His way was strewn with flowers; the people jammed the narrow streets, crying his name in a delirium of joy; an old woman fell to her knees, clung to his leg and called him a "holy vision." A bevy of girls attended him once more. This time there was no chariot; but they did press on his brow a wreath of gilded laurel. He removed it promptly, declaring that it fitted better those who deserved it more, Santander and Anzoátegui. In his triumphal march to the palace, the scarecrow remnants of the British Legion followed behind, grinning as señoritas rushed out to kiss them. Not one man of them had either shoes or stockings and the officers had only alpargatas.

At the steps of the palace the leading citizens waited to greet him. He remembered them all, called them by name and inquired for all of those he had known five years before who weren't there. Most of them had been put to death by the Spaniards. His manner was easy, unassuming and gracious, his questions rapid, clear and penetrating. An eyewitness recorded the scene and said that all were impressed by the energy and grace of his movements, the fine modeling of his head and the extraordinary brilliance and expression of his dark eyes. He hadn't stopped to get dressed up; this time he wore an old black dress coat and white trousers, worn cavalry boots and a cap of rawhide. He had come, he declared, to repay the debt which Venezuela owed to New Granada.

Chapter XX

THE COLOMBIAN UNION

✣

THE critics of Bolívar who charge him with an inordi-
nate appetite for popular acclaim and with the loss
of time indulging it, need only to examine the records of
his activities to be refuted. Three days after he entered
Bogotá he sent off to Zea, in Angostura, a complete report
of all his movements since leaving Venezuela—a voluminous composition which would be a good three days' task
for anyone.

He ordered Soublette and Anzoátegui to continue the
persecution of the few Spanish forces remaining in New
Granada—which they did so successfully that in a few
weeks' time the whole viceroyalty was cleared, except for
a strip along the north coast. But the patriot cause suffered
a great loss when the loyal and brilliant Anzoátegui died
in Pamplona from sickness contracted in crossing the
Andes. Meanwhile Bolívar had proposed an exchange of
prisoners to Sámano, offering him the valiant and—rare
among the Spaniards—honorable Barreira. Sámano didn't
even answer. He descended the Magdalena and sailed for
Spain.

The liberation of New Granada was a tremendous
boost for the patriot cause. This land had not suffered the
fearful depredations of the Spaniards, as had Venezuela;
and, although the most illustrious citizens had been executed, the country was overflowing with food and rich
in man power. Bolívar found himself for the first time
with an abundance of materials of war at his command.

He took steps immediately to make it available for use in the field.

He organized a provisional government, naming Santander acting president—officially, Vice-President of the republic. A popular assembly had proclaimed Bolívar president and commander-in-chief of the army, and had solemnly conferred upon him the title of Liberator of New Granada. He make a quick inspection tour into the various provinces—a journey which became a triumphal procession with arches of flowers and crowds of cheering people awaiting him at every village.

On his return to the capital he received bad news from Venezuela. Hardly had he left Angostura before the old dissensions began. It was Arismendi, in Margarita, and Mariño this time. Refusing to recognize the authority of Urdaneta, who had been keeping the Spaniards busy in the east, they had declared against the government of Angostura. Urdaneta arrested Arismendi, took him to the capital on the Orinoco and put him in prison. But the intrigue went on. Bolívar was accused before the Congress of desertion in having gone into New Granada without permission. The friends of Arismendi worked assiduously toward the overthrow of Zea, and they were so successful that Arismendi was released and went directly from his cell to the presidential palace to assume the office of head of the government. Mariño was named commander of the army—and this capricious young man had done absolutely nothing of value to the patriot cause since his liberation of the east seven years before. When Bolívar learned these things he decided to leave immediately for Angostura. The sweetness of his triumphs turned to gall almost before he could savor it.

In turning over the government to Santander before he left, he charged him particularly with humane treatment of the many Spanish prisoners and respect for the property rights of civilian royalists. He had decreed the end of "War to the Death," and he meant it. Santander made a proclamation to the people declaring his intention to carry out the wishes of the Liberator faithfully. The statement ended with the words, "Granadans! Remember always that your regeneration in 1819 was the work of the immortal Bolívar!"

The Liberator left Bogotá late in September, only a month after he had arrived there from the victory of Boyacá. Scarcely had he gone when Santander ordered the execution of Barreira and thirty-seven other prisoners. The Spaniards were dragged from the prison and shot in the plaza. When Bolívar learned of it he sent a scathing rebuke to Santander. The Vice-President attempted to justify himself on the plea that he had acted in the face of public demand. The Spanish commander, Calzada, who had fled with the garrison from Bogotá, had marched south into Quito, murdering and committing typical Spanish atrocities in every village in his path; and the people of the capital clamored for vengeance. Further, Santander claimed, there had been evidence of plotting among the prisoners to create favor in the people for the royalist cause. In the interest of preserving solidarity, Bolívar pretended to accept the explanation.

Santander was a brilliant, well-educated man, a jurist by profession. An extremely able organizer and administrator, his talents were mainly political. Bolívar recognized this and placed him in the positions where such talents were needed. It is an interesting insight into the perception of the Liberator, his knowledge of psychology and his versatility of expression, to compare the letters he wrote to Santander with those he wrote to Páez. They are completely different in style and tone. To Santander he wrote with precise phraseology and logic, using somewhat technical terms, and always with a certain reserve and dignity. To Páez he wrote in simple words, almost in the vernacular of the llanos, and his letters abound in undisguised flattery. Even in his reprimands there is a tone of gentleness and affection such as one would use in correcting a misguided child.

Santander, though he had apparently forgotten his clash with Bolívar at their first meeting and now labored assiduously at his side and under his orders, was fundamentally in disagreement with him. He was still, as he had always been, strictly a regionalist, opposed to the union with Venezuela, opposed to Bolívar's policy of strong centralization of government, and a firm advocate of federalism. He was to render Bolívar invaluable aid in achieving still greater glory—and he was to cause, at last, his downfall.

Back once more along that arduous trail to Angostura . . . but this time he traveled almost alone and followed the main routes. He went incredibly fast, changing mounts at every village, riding from daybreak till long after dark. Down the swift rivers he traveled in the lightest dugouts, paddled by the strongest Indians. At Barinas he met Páez, embraced him, told his story of triumph and spent the night with him, discussing plans for future action.

Descending the Orinoco one day, Bolívar sighted another flechera coming up the river, flying a pennant with the device of a patriot general.

"Who is this coming upstream?" Bolívar asked.

"General Sucre, sire," a man answered.

"Sucre? There is no such general. Signal him to put to shore."

The two flecheras came together on the bank and a young officer presented himself to the Liberator. He was about twenty-five, handsome, not unlike Bolívar himself in countenance; but his features were less mobile, lacking in the easy humor that was always just under the surface in the Liberator's face.

He introduced himself to Bolívar and gave him an account of his career. He had been born in Cumaná and studied engineering in Caracas. When the war broke out he was only seventeen, but he joined the patriot forces

under Mariño and fought during the liberation of the
east. After the downfall of the Second Republic he fled
to Trinidad; and he returned to fight under Mariño as a
staff officer when Bolívar arrived with his expedition from
Haiti. When Mariño formed his government at Cariaco in
opposition to the Liberator, he had refused to be a part
of it and went south to Guayana to join the patriots there.
During Bolívar's absence in New Granada he had been
active in holding the east against Morillo and Morales;
and Zea, as acting president, had commissioned him brigadier general. "But I would never think, sire," he said,
"of retaining my rank without your approval."

Bolívar studied the young man carefully and was pleased
with him. He smiled and said that he was sure the president of the republic had acted wisely. He expressed the
hope that they should be friends, embraced the young
general and bade him good-by.

As the two flecheras drew apart on the wide river,
Bolívar pondered the impression Sucre had made upon
him. He remembered that he had heard very favorable
reports of him in the past. He didn't know then that before long Sucre was to become his "right arm" and his
most loyal friend—"the son which Providence has sent me
as a recompense for leaving me childless." He didn't know
then who it was he had met for the first time. Antonio
José Sucre. The white knight, the undefiled. The only
figure perhaps in all the history of South America against
whom no one has ever risen to charge self-interest, ambition or incompetency. He remains through the centuries—
blameless, heroic, the symbol of abnegation.

Bolívar arrived in Angostura so suddenly that Arismendi was taken completely by surprise. The Liberator
presented himself affably, pretending that he had no suspicion that anything was amiss. The clouds of dissension
disappeared at once before his warm glow. His mere presence was enough. Arismendi tendered his resignation and
entertained the Liberator at a great ball to which five

hundred people were invited. Mariño came forward, too, and offered his congratulations, and even Montilla apologized for his behavior in the past.

Things were in pretty good shape in Angostura; Arismendi, for all his disloyalty, had governed ably, and he had retained the cabinet which Bolívar had appointed. The Liberator reinstated Urdaneta and Bermúdez in their commands and, as a reward to Montilla for his contrition, sent him to New Granada to lay siege to the city of Cartagena, now held by the Spaniards. He sent Zea to London to work for recognition of the republic.

There it was again—that need for a firm hand. Zea was an able man but he was weak. Arismendi was an able man and he was strong. The people, in that fatal hunger for strength to rely upon, had demanded Arismendi in the absence of Bolívar. It was the people, in spontaneous action, who had overthrown Zea and released Arismendi from prison. And before the superior hombría of the Liberator the confidence of the people shifted and settled upon him once more. Bolívar used that weakness for his purposes; but inwardly he deplored it.

Within a few days after his arrival he assembled the Congress and procured the adoption of the Fundamental Law of Colombia, creating a single republic comprising the old captain-generalcy of Venezuela and the viceroyalties of New Granada and of Quito. The inclusion of the latter was a bit premature in view of the fact that Quito was entirely in the hands of the Spaniards—but Bolívar was already forming plans for its liberation. And to him the conception of an idea was exactly the same as an accomplished fact.

The first Congress of Colombia was to meet in May of the coming year at Rosário de Cúcuta on the border of the two countries. Bolívar was elected President of the Republic of Colombia, Santander Vice-President—acting President in New Granada. Bolívar sent the proposition off to Santander, who, though it was against his political doctrines, labored for it and secured its ratification by New Granada.

Bolívar set out for Bogotá once more on December 24, 1819, only twelve days after he had arrived in Angostura. Back again, that long journey. Just one of them would provide a modern man with something to talk about all his life. Bolívar made three of them in less than a year. This time he went rather slowly, in a roundabout course, visiting all the provinces along the way, drumming up favor for his new union, conferring with the military commanders.

In the capital of New Granada he was welcomed with wilder acclaim even than he had been after Boyacá. Everywhere his plan for the Republic of Colombia was hailed with enthusiasm. Even Santander proclaimed, ". . . Your Excellency has freed it [the republic] from tyrants, has defended it, preserved it, reunited it and will also present it free, independent and established to the eyes of the universe. Colombia is the daughter of the immortal Bolívar!" Strange words these, in view of the fact that Santander was himself calling Bolívar a tyrant a few years later; but he was always a smooth politician and he saw then that the Colombian idea had caught on overwhelmingly with the people.

Even the Franciscan monks of Bogotá hailed Bolívar. They sent him an invitation to some function or other which was addressed thus: "To the Supreme, the Incomparable Hero, the Terror of Iberia and the Glory of his country; to the Peerless Warrior, the Scourge of Tyrants, the Protector of Mankind; to the Genius of Independence, serene in adversity, modest in triumph, the Ever-Great Simón Bolívar, Liberator, President and General of the Army of the Republic of Colombia." There was nothing said of the fact that five years before, when Bolívar had appeared before the city to subdue the insurrection against the government of Tunja, the archbishop had excommunicated him. On this occasion he didn't accept the invitation in spite of the attractive salutation.

During the following months of summer Bolívar was active throughout the whole of New Granada, making innumerable journeys into the mountains, down the Magdalena, south along the Cordillera toward Quito. He organized armies everywhere and directed their movements. Montilla had arrived on the coast and was opening his campaign with Cartagena as the objective, and Valdez was sent south to open the way into Quito for the next great project the Liberator was dreaming of. Bolívar was in constant communication with all these forces and with all his officers in Venezuela as well—Páez, Briceño Méndez, Soublette, Urdaneta, Bermúdez, Sucre, Arismendi, Monagas, Zaraza. In addition, he wrote personal letters to the families of all those who had died in battle under his command, and he obtained pensions for them from the Congress. Many of them he aided from his private funds—when he had any. He seldom had a cent. As soon as his salary was paid he gave it away. He had to borrow from his aides when he needed a few pesos. His back salary for the year 1819—25,000 pesos as commander of the army and 50,000 as president of the republic—was due him, and he wrote to Congress asking that it be distributed among the families of the soldiers who were in need. Fernando González said that, throughout his whole life of action, glory, companionship of men and favors of women, he was always "the lonely soul, without funds, without lover, without family."

Morillo, the Spanish general in Venezuela, that veteran field marshal of Wellington's army who had been sent out by the King of Spain to subdue all of South America in a hundred and sixty days, wrote to Fernando VII: "Nothing can compare with the untiring activity of that leader. His fearlessness and his talents entitle him to his place at the head of the revolution and of the war; but he possesses as well, from his noble Spanish strain and his education, also Spanish, qualities of elegance and generosity which elevate him far above all who surround him. He is the revolution." Morillo was speaking of the man who, as a youth, had impudently lifted the cap from the head of that same king at a game of lances.

Morillo also wrote, urgently calling for reinforcements. "Bolívar," he wrote, "is an indomitable soul whom a single victory of the smallest nature is enough to make master of 500 leagues of territory."

Fernando heeded the words and made plans for another expedition—a big one this time, composed of 24,000 men, ships, artillery and munitions in tremendous quantity. But the expedition never sailed. The ruthlessness of the Inquisition which Fernando had re-established had caused widespread discontent in Spain; a certain sympathy for the colonies had grown among the Spanish people. On the first day of 1820, when the expedition was about to sail, a revolution, headed by Rafael Riego, broke out in Cádiz. By March, Fernando had to compromise with the revolution and agree to re-establish the liberal constitution which the Regency had granted in 1812. Since the constitution was to apply to the colonies, Fernando felt that the warring ones would be willing to talk peace. Accordingly he issued orders to his generals throughout the colonies to negotiate an armistice with the rebels for the purpose of urging the acceptance of the constitution and a return to the Spanish fold.

General Morillo received the order with considerable disgust; but there was no way out. The royal command was explicit and he had to obey. Reluctantly he sent out commissioners to Bolívar, to the Congress at Angostura and to various provincial commanders.

Chapter XXI

CARABOBO—VENEZUELA
LIBERATED

✤

W HEN Bolívar was approaching Cúcuta after a journey to the coast for a conference with Montilla,
General Sucre rode out to meet him.

One of his officers asked, "Who is this bad horseman
coming?"

"That," Bolívar said, "is one of the best officers in the
army. He has the professional knowledge of Soublette, the
kindly character of Briceño, the talent of Santander and
the activity of Salóm. For some reason I didn't know of
nor suspect his aptitudes before. I intend to bring them
into the light; for some day he is going to rival me."

The communication which Bolívar received from the
Spanish general was addressed to "His Excellency, the
President of the Republic"—quite a difference of attitude
in those who had refused to address him at all only a
short time before, and who had persisted in regarding
him as an insignificant leader of bandits. But Bolívar
wasn't impressed. To the proposition that Colombia submit to the domination of Spain he replied heatedly that
the idea was the height of folly. The moment was most
inopportune for the Spanish proposal; Bolívar was riding
high on the wave of success. He had succeeded at last in
winning the people of all classes to his cause. The mestizos, pardos, blacks and Indians, weary at last of the
atrocities of the Spaniards and won by the noble words
and brilliant victories of Bolívar, were now completely

united in sentiment throughout the two countries. Nevertheless, the idea of an armistice appealed to the Liberator and he agreed to negotiate for its realization. Any temporary cessation of hostilities could only be an advantage to him. It would give him a chance to rest his troops, train the new recruits who were pouring in, concentrate his resources and establish his armies in positions which would be favorable to his new project when hostilities should be resumed. Besides, he was anxious for an agreement which would humanize the war on both sides, bring an end to atrocities, permit the exchange of prisoners and establish the war in general on a more formal basis.

The negotiations for the armistice went on through emissaries for several months, during which Bolívar made all haste to strengthen his positions. Morillo, with his army, established headquarters at the village of Carache near the New Granadan border and Bolívar occupied Trujillo, a short distance away. To a Spanish officer who came to lunch with him and who suggested that Morillo thought he should withdraw from the province, Bolívar answered, "Tell your chief that he will retire to Cádiz before I to Cúcuta." He appointed Sucre, Briceño Méndez and Colonel Pérez as his agents to draw up the terms of the armistice. On November 25, 1820, at the city of Trujillo, the same spot where Bolívar had decreed the "War to the Death" seven years before, an agreement was reached and the articles signed. In diplomacy, Morillo was no match for Bolívar. The terms of the armistice were advantageous to the patriots in every way, though the facts were ably disguised. All hostilities were to cease for a period of six months and could be resumed by either side only upon a notice to be given forty days in advance.

Morillo had long since conceived a high regard for Bolívar as a man. Perhaps out of curiosity and certainly from a sense of chivalry, he now proposed that they meet in person at the village of Santa Ana between the two positions. Bolívar accepted warmly.

The Liberator planned his behavior at this meeting carefully, regarding it purely as a show, as one of those performances he excelled in. It would increase his own prestige at home and abroad and let the world know that Colombia was now treated by Spain as one nation to another. He was serenely confident of his intellectual superiority over Morillo and of his ability to dominate him by the force of his personality, his hombría.

On the morning of the day agreed upon, Daniel O'Leary was sent to Morillo as Bolívar's representative. He found the field marshal of Spain, veteran general of the Napoleonic Wars, Count of Cartagena and Marqués of La Puerta, in full regimentals, his breast gleaming with all his orders, and surrounded by his staff officers and a regiment of hussars in dress. "How many will accompany General Bolívar?" Morillo asked. "Only ten or twelve officers of his staff, Your Excellency," O'Leary answered. Morillo exclaimed, "Por Dios! My erstwhile enemy has outdone me in gallantry." He dismissed the hussars and ordered the march toward Santa Ana.

As the two groups of horsemen approached each other, the Spanish general turned to O'Leary and asked, "Which one is General Bolívar?"

The Irishman pointed out the Liberator and Morillo exclaimed, "Is it possible? The little man on the mule, in the blue coat and forage cap?"

Bolívar had once been impressed by the simplicity of Napoleon amid the magnificence of his officers.

The two commanders dismounted and embraced. Then they entered a small house, dined and spent the rest of the day within. When they came out they rolled, together, a large boulder to the spot where they had met and marked it with their swords.

Morillo wrote of that meeting:

. . . I spent one of the happiest days of my life in the company of Bolívar. . . . No one could imagine the interest

that interview held nor the cordiality and love which reigned
between us. All of us committed absurdities of happiness. It
seemed like a dream, reunited there as Spaniards, brothers
and friends. Bolívar was carried away with delight and we
embraced a million times. We determined to erect a monument as an eternal memorial to the beginning of our reconciliation on the spot where we had first embraced.

But Bolívar kept his wits about him during that feast
of love. He used every opportunity to impress Morillo
with his capabilities, the righteousness of the cause he
championed, the strength of the patriot forces, the abundance of their resources and the impossible task confront-
ing Spain in making war against a united people in such
an immense and primitive country. He succeeded so
well in his purpose that almost immediately after the
meeting, Morillo resigned and returned to Spain. La
Torre, the general whom Piar had defeated at San Félix
to open the Orinoco, and who had evacuated Angostura,
was given his command.

Bolívar looked upon the meeting only as a great political victory. "It discouraged Morillo and caused him to
leave the country, to be replaced by La Torre—an officer
less active, less capable, less a soldier. . . . I was convinced I could dominate Morillo in a personal encounter."
Of the armistice he said, "It was an excuse for time to
regulate the war and was adopted exactly as I had written
it. It was a sane, humane and politic treaty which put an
end to that horrible butchery of slaying the conquered,
of giving no quarter to prisoners of war—Spanish barbar-
ism that the patriots were forced to adopt themselves in
reprisal, that had pushed back civilization, made the soil
of Colombia an abode of cannibals and soaked it with
innocent blood until all humanity shuddered. It was an
advantage to us, fatal to the Spaniards. Their forces could
only diminish, mine augment and organize."

The movement of troops had been limited by the terms

of the armistice to certain localities; but Bolívar had arranged these provisions so astutely that all during its duration he was busy shifting his men into the best strategical positions. He called upon Montilla, on the coast, to send 2000 troops up to the Venezuelan border, "rapidly, rapidly, rapidly." La Torre, on the other hand, lay inactive.

The armistice didn't run its full course. In the city of Maracaibo, of all places—that old royalist hotbed and thorn in the side of the patriots from the time of the First Republic—a rebellion occurred in favor of the patriot cause. Bolívar probably anticipated it, for Urdaneta was right on hand with troops to march into the city at once. La Torre declared the action a breach of terms and Bolívar promptly gave the forty days' notice. On April 28, 1821, the war was on again. The Liberator issued an order for the execution of any patriot soldier who killed a prisoner or committed any other atrocity.

Bolívar was all prepared. He had planned to drive the Spaniards from Venezuela before he went south into Quito. He marched rapidly from the frontier toward Caracas; Páez came out of Achaguas with his llaneros and the British Legion; Urdaneta hurried east from Maracaibo, occupied Coro and turned south; Mariño, Cedeño and Zaraza came out of the east. All of them had skirmishes with small enemy forces along their way, but they defeated them and advanced rapidly. In less than a month they concentrated south of Valencia, the gateway to the capital. Sucre had been put in command of the forces remaining behind in New Granada. Meanwhile, Bermúdez had been ordered to march from Barcelona in the east along the coast and strike at Caracas from the rear. He moved so quickly that he occupied the very outskirts of the city and took a position within sight of the central plaza. There he kept up a continuous action that distracted a large part of the Spanish force from Bolívar's movements to the south.

La Torre remained supinely at Carabobo while Bolívar

concentrated within a few miles of him. Almost the whole Spanish army in Venezuela was confined to a small area between the patriots and the capital. On June 23 the Liberator reviewed an army of 6500 men—infantry, cavalry and artillery—the largest he had ever commanded as a unit. Facing him was the Spanish army of 5000; for the first time in his career as a warrior he outnumbered the enemy.

As Boyacá was the decisive victory which drove the Spaniards from New Granada (now Colombia) for all time, so Carabobo was for Venezuela. Bolívar had won an earlier battle in the same place in the campaign of 1814.

The savannah of Carabobo is a broken plain in the shape of a tilted saucer, covered with sparse grass and clumps of low bush. Around it rise rugged hills, cut by small streams with tangled vegetation in the deep defiles. Through its center from southwest to northeast ran the road to Valencia, the second city of Venezuela; La Torre's army occupied the center of the plain along the road. Between him and the patriot army stood the broken ridges along the south rim.

Early in the morning of June 24 Bolívar arrived at that south rim. There he detached three battalions of infantry and two squadrons of cavalry to hold the main road while he advanced with the rest of his army along a side trail to the left, in the direction of the north end of the savannah. Why La Torre remained upon the plain with his main army, instead of placing it among the defiles, is incomprehensible. He stayed where he was while Bolívar occupied the hills and won the opportunity of selecting the place of battle. The movement of the patriots circumvented the enemy artillery, which was placed on a knoll above the main road where it came out of the hills into the savannah.

Bolívar climbed to the thatched roof of a small house. The morning was dazzling bright, the foliage sparkling and the mountain air crisp and clear from the rain that had fallen during the night. Through his glass he could see the army of Spain spread out on the rolling savannah. The battalions of infantry moved slowly into their positions, solid masses of brilliant color—green, yellow, scarlet—and the squadrons of cavalry maneuvered rapidly, their pennants fluttering. The bugle notes rang faint and clear.

The whole patriot army was charged with eagerness and a sort of nervous gaiety, sensing that the final issue of the long struggle faced them at last. The llaneros of Páez, fresh and confident after the whole year of idleness in Achaguas while Bolívar was fighting in New Granada, were spoiling for battle. Their sleek horses pawed the earth and raised their heads to sniff the tingling air.

El Negro Primero, the giant black who followed Páez like a dog, sleeping at his feet and keeping his saber polished like a curved slice of mirror, harangued the troops in grotesque imitation of the grandiose phrases of the Liberator. "Nothing," he shouted, "shall be in front of me today but the neck of my little horse!" The llaneros guffawed and the negro's speech trailed off in confusion when he saw Bolívar listening to him, smiling.

Only the British Huntsmen—a battalion composed entirely of Britishers—remained unperturbed, showing no sign of emotion.

Bolívar issued his orders to the officers and the march was resumed. The army continued in the same direction, keeping to the protection of the narrow ravines, wading in the shallow streams. It was not a flanking movement Bolívar had conceived but a maneuver of the main of the army to place the battle at the north end of the savannah. As they neared the edge of the hills, La Torre saw the intention and sent two battalions north across the plain to intercept it—an error, for he should have sent his main force. Bolívar, with a battalion of infantry as guard, occupied a knoll from which he could observe the whole battle. The army, with the cavalry of Páez at the head and the British battalion immediately behind, continued the march. The route became so narrow and tangled that it had to be cleared with machetes and the troops could only pass in file—a fact which put them at a great disadvantage, preventing the formation of an attack in mass, giving the Spaniards time to reach their position.

The battle began at eleven o'clock. Páez, from the bottom of a narrow ravine, found himself confronted by the two Spanish battalions massed on a hill above. He ordered up the British infantry in support. They advanced in perfect formation, drums beating, colors flying. Then he ordered a cavalry charge which met a withering fire from 1400 muskets and was halted in its tracks. A second charge failed as well; and on the third, the llanero ranks broke entirely and the horsemen went scrambling out of the valley in all directions. From the hilltop, the Spanish infantry charged down the slope after them. At the bottom waited the British battalion—alone, unsupported—to take the shock.

Colonel Farrier formed his line, standing and kneeling in perfect ranks. "They became no longer a body of human beings; they took roots in the earth and became a mass of granite." Farrier called the orders. "Aim!" "Fire!" The muskets blazed in one voice. "Load!" "Aim!" "Fire!" The rifles came up, the ramrods went home, the hammers clicked, the barrels reached out and spat flame—all together, in cold precision. Farrier fell dead, breathing the words, "Stand firm!" Major Davy took his place and the orders went on—"Load!" "Aim!" "Fire!" Gaps opened in the front ranks and men stepped up from the rear to fill them. The Spaniards came on in waves that melted before the line of flame but more waves rolled down the hill after them. Davy fell dead and Lieutenant Scott replaced him. The orders went on. Scott fell and Lieutenant Minchin stepped up. Here and there a rifle remained silent. The

ammunition was running low. The men fired their ramrods in place of a ball for the last shot.

Bolívar, from his high post, had observed the predica-
ment of the British battalion and ordered the infantry
which was guarding him to advance at the double in support. The terrain, broken and swept now by enemy fire,
delayed their movement. They arrived behind the Britishers when the ammunition had all but given out. Cases
were torn open and rifles loaded quickly.

Meanwhile, Páez had reorganized his scattered cavalry.
The "Bravos de Apure"—the battalion that had van-
quished La Torre at Queseras del Medio—came charging
in, striking the Spaniards on the hill from the north.
Lieutenant Brandt, then commanding the Britishers, ordered a charge from the ravine. The rigid ranks, gaping
with holes now, changed shape, fixed bayonets and went
up the hill. The Spaniards fell away before them. In less
than a half hour the British had lost seventeen officers and
a hundred and nineteen men—half their force.

La Torre at last sent his squadrons of cavalry up from
the road in the middle of the savannah to support the infantry. It was much too late. Páez charged south to meet
them, dispatching two squadrons against the Spanish infantry from the rear as they gave way before the Britishers. Surrounded, the two enemy battalions threw down
their arms.

Páez, a general now, watched the combat between the
llaneros and the Spanish cavalry from the rear. A horseman detached himself from the patriot squadrons and
dashed toward him. Páez rode to meet him, a reprimand
ready at his lips. The lone horseman was El Negro Primero. He reined up beside his commander and saluted
with his lance. "I came to say good-by, my general," he
said. "I am dead." He opened his shirt to expose his gaping wound and fell from his horse.

Meanwhile, at the edge of the south ridge on the main
road, the patriot infantry and cavalry advanced against the

Spanish artillery which was supported by the famous infantry battalion, "Valencey." La Torre, faced by disaster on the plain behind them, ordered these units to fall back to his aid. They withdrew slowly, abandoning their cannon, and the patriots stalked them step by step. Once clear of the hills, Rondón's cavalry came from behind the infantry and struck "Valencey" by the right flank. Cedeño's cavalry and infantry came down from the north and attacked the left flank. "Valencey" formed a hollow square and, fighting from all sides, slowly fell back in perfect order. Cedeño fell dead but his battalion kept on, dogging the Spaniards. "Valencey," keeping its formation, joined with La Torre and his staff and carried them along in safety. Of the whole Spanish army, only this battalion and the general staff escaped. The cavalry of Morales, which hadn't arrived in time for action at all, fled into the llanos.

The victory was complete. Forty per cent of the Spanish army was killed, wounded or taken prisoner. Bolívar ordered Páez to pursue La Torre, and the Spanish general was driven all the way to Puerto Cabello on the coast. The way was cleared into Caracas.

Because of the conditions of the battle, Carabobo was mainly the work of Páez. Bolívar planned the maneuvers but upon Páez fell nearly all the action. The Liberator gave him full credit, praised him in extravagant terms and made him commander-in-chief of the armies of Venezuela. The battle marks the height of the llanero chief's accomplishments. He was never to fight in a major battle again—and, on the strength of the fame he won there, he rose to the presidency of Venezuela and became an honored figure in foreign lands. He was never again to occupy the place in the hearts of his countrymen which he held then.

At the approach of Bolívar, the Spaniards of the garrison in Caracas fled to La Guaira. Once more he entered the city of his birth and the capital of his country in triumph. Once more the people poured into the streets to cover him with flowers, kiss his hands and tear pieces from his garments. He visited his hacienda at San Mateo, the beloved retreat of his youth and of his brief married life. Of the 1200 slaves who had once lived there, he found only three dwelling among the tumbled, battle-torn walls and weed-choked gardens. He gave the three their freedom.

Bolívar immediately set about raising funds to feed and clothe his troops. He levied upon the merchants of Caracas and La Guaira for the sum of 25,000 pesos and contributed from his own properties, which now came back into his hands. The war had indeed taken on a new character, for La Torre, in Puerto Cabello, agreed to the exchange of prisoners, addressing Bolívar in the most gracious terms, and Bolívar granted passports to the Spanish troops who had fled to La Guaira. He found time, also, to remember Don Francisco Iturbe, the Spaniard who had given his guaranty for Bolívar and secured a passport from Monteverde, and who was now destitute in Curaçao. He asked the Congress to restore Iturbe's properties, which had been confiscated.

The Congress of Colombia had been in session in Rosário de Cúcuta since May 6, considering a constitution; and there was a growing ill-feeling over the fact that the President wasn't on hand. Bolívar was anxious to go back before Congress should adjourn.

Soublette, who was now Vice-President of Venezuela, came up from Angostura and established the government in its proper capital city. With him, too, came all those wanderers, those fine ladies who had fled the capital before the wrath of Boves years before, who had survived that fearful trek to Barcelona, wandered among strange islands of the West Indies and returned with their warrior husbands and lovers to live in a primitive outpost far down on the Orinoco. Among them were Juana, Bolívar's sister, and her grown daughter; and there were Señorita Pepa and Isabel Soublette. But the Liberator apparently had lost all interest in both of them. It had been a long time since he had left them in Angostura to begin his famous march into New Granada. Isabel was consoled, perhaps, by the fact that her brother was now Acting President of Venezuela.

Bolívar, fearing still the opposing ambitions of his generals, placed them strategically about the country. Mariño was made commander of the west—far removed from the seat of his greatest influence, his native Cumaná; Páez, chief of all the armies, was made commander of the center; and Bermúdez of the east. He wrote to Pedro Gual, in connection with this arrangement:

You can have no idea of the spirit which animates our military officers. They are no longer the men you knew. They are men who have fought for years and believe themselves superior; and yet they are humiliated and impoverished, with no hope of enjoying the fruits of the work of their lances. They are often resolute llaneros, ignorant men who think themselves superior to those of greater accomplishments. Even I, who have always been at their head, cannot say of what they might be capable. I treat them with the greatest consideration, but it doesn't seem to inspire them with the spirit which ought to exist among comrades and fellow-citizens. Believe me, Gual, we are over a volcano about to erupt. I fear peace even more than I fear war.

Chapter XXII

THE PATH LEADS SOUTHWARD

✤

IN this pessimistic spirit, in spite of his great victories and the knowledge that the final liberation of his country was at last accomplished, Bolívar set out for Cúcuta to face the Congress and to begin his heroic project in the south.

He had hoped to secure the adoption by the Colombian Congress of that idealistic and perhaps too complicated Constitution of his which the Congress of Angostura had turned down. But here again he was disappointed. The code which the Congress finally adopted was even more inclined to federalism than that of Venezuela. All Bolívar's pet ideas—censors, hereditary senate and president for life—were thrown out and the senate, president and representatives were to be removed, by half their numbers, every four years, thus staggering the renewals among the legislators.

Bolívar was elected Constitutional President. Once more he demurred, sought to resign his dictatorial powers, was overridden by the acclaiming Congress, and yielded. He said to them, "History will say, 'Bolívar took command in order to liberate his countrymen and, when they were free, he left them to govern themselves by their own laws and not by his will.' " But apparently by liberation of his countrymen he meant liberation of all of northern South America—for he accepted the dictatorship for the duration of the project he had conceived for liberating the southern colonies. The Congress also voted him the authority to organize governments for any territories he might emancipate.

Bolívar took the oath of office, swearing to uphold a constitution which he disliked intensely—and proved himself thereby a true liberal, to the confounding of those who claim otherwise. He made a sincere and moving address to the Congress expressing his attitude; and Parra-Pérez says of it, "No assembly since the days when Athens heard the glorious voice of Pericles has listened to nobler or more lofty ideas from the mouth of a soldier or statesman."

In all Bolívar's dictatorial and usually illegal governing, his words and his writings prove that he never believed for a moment that he was usurping the rights of the people. He believed sincerely that, by some sort of mystic ordination, he was the embodiment of the people, their voice, their instrument of action. Studying his words, one becomes conscious of his deep conviction that he alone knew what was best for them, he alone stood between them and the evil interests which sought to oppress them—an attitude not greatly unlike that by which most dictators have deluded themselves before and since. An aristocrat, he identified himself always with the common people and, in the very execution of autocratic powers, considered himself a Voltairian. He frequently spoke of himself as such. He sought to govern arbitrarily and at the same time legally, in conformity with the codes which he was forever advocating—an obviously impossible task which even he couldn't accomplish. The result was a soul-shattering struggle within himself. He knew well the difficulty of making his people and the world understand. Ravaged by his consuming thirst for abstract and enduring glory, he was pathetically fearful that his paternalism would be mistaken for ambition. He strove desperately to clarify his attitude to his people and to the outside world—an effort which glutted his proclamations with contradictions and drove him to puerile gestures of abnegation and insincere posturing. It wrung from him such hypocritical statements as:

A man like me is a dangerous citizen in a popular government. He is an immediate threat to the national sovereignty. I want to be a citizen in order to secure my own freedom and the freedom of everyone else. I prefer the title of citizen to that of Liberator, because the former comes from war and the latter comes from the law. Change, I implore you, all my titles for that of good citizen.

Believing sincerely in freedom of speech and of the press, he always granted them to the fullest extent, even against the urgings of his supporters; yet he suffered intensely when the press attacked him.

The continuous psychological struggle within himself made of him a fundamentally unhappy man. It showed more and more in his countenance—which became, with the years, a mask of tragedy. But through it all he never wavered an inch from the supreme conviction that he was right.

There was so much to be done, so many letters smothering him, pouring in daily in a constant deluge. Pacing the floor with rapid strides, his index finger tapping his long upper lip, the words rolled out and the three secretaries strove to keep up with them. Their quills raced over the long sheets of paper—but they were never fast enough. O'Leary was his chief aide now. "Get me faster penmen, O'Leary, faster ones!" he charged him. "These fellows can't keep up with my thoughts."

Appeals poured in on him, appeals that he had no resources to meet. The unworthy ones he answered brusquely, sometimes with a cold humor. To a priest who had ardently supported the royalist cause and now begged a favor he replied, "I suggest that you ask the King." To a New Granadan general who had taken no part in the war and who now appealed for back pay he wrote, "There are no funds to buy the necessities for those who have liberated your country, much less for the salaries of those who left her in slavery." A young English officer had married a Venezuelan woman, much older, rich and avaricious. The officer died of fever. While he was alive the woman had collected his salary regularly and after his death she annoyed Bolívar with demands for its continuance. He wrote to her, "Refused. The infant, to whom we were godparents, is now dead."

To others he wrote with kindliness and sympathy and he strained his own resources to the utmost to help them. The widow of Camilo Torres, who had been executed by the Spaniards, and who had been president of the old Congress of Tunja and the champion and ardent admirer of Bolívar, was found to be living in direst poverty. Bolívar wrote an order that 10,000 pesos of his own salary of 30,000 should be paid to her yearly.

María Antonia had returned to Caracas from her exile in the West Indies and Bolívar wrote to her constantly— long, affectionate letters, inquiring after each of her children individually and suggesting plans for the education and welfare of the orphaned children of Juan Vicente, whom he had adopted. He assigned to her the management of his mineral property in the valley of Aroa—the only productive property remaining to him—and instructed her about the use of its income. She was hard put in that task, for the numerous orders he sent her to pay out sums to old friends and former slaves who were in want far exceeded the property's yield.

He wrote to Juana also, but less frequently and with less intimacy. He had never been so close to her as he had been to María Antonia, even though the lovely Benigna, her daughter, was his favorite niece.

Things were shaping up nicely for the project of liberating Quito and Perú. Bermúdez had succeeded in driving the last Spanish force in eastern Venezuela from Cumaná;

and Montilla, after a siege of fourteen months, had taken that walled city of Cartagena. La Torre had fled to Cuba. Morales, in Puerto Cabello, commanded the only Spanish force remaining on Colombian soil. Again, siege of that port was impossible because of the lack of naval facilities for closing its access to the sea. But Morales was confined to operations in the immediate vicinity by the constant action of the patriot forces of Páez.

After Cartagena was taken, Bolívar ordered Montilla to sail for Panamá to attack the Spaniards there; but the expedition proved unnecessary. The Panamanians broke out in revolt themselves, won their independence and applied for admission to the Republic of Colombia. So Bolívar acquired for his nation a large province, the only one he didn't have to fight for in person.

He ordered Montilla to send 2000 troops up the Magdalena to aid him in the project he was preparing for.

His efforts had now liberated Venezuela—a country as big as France and Germany combined—and a part of New Granada of equal size. Quito, now the Republic of Ecuador but then a part of the old viceroyalty of New Granada, remained in the hands of the Spaniards. It is a territory as large as Italy. But the plans he was now forming didn't stop there. They included as well the liberation of the viceroyalty of Perú—a country which included then the present Republic of Bolivia and covered an area twice as big as France, Germany and the British Isles, six times as big as Spain. His idea was not to include the latter country in the Colombian Republic but to form it into independent nations, bound to Colombia by treaties of mutual friendship, commercial co-operation and military defense—the South American Union of his earliest dreams.

He had long since prepared the ground. While he was engaged in the campaign in Venezuela which ended with the battle of Carabobo, he had assigned to Sucre and Valdez the task of carrying the struggle against the Spaniards south into Quito. These two, aided nobly by the

British battalion, "Albion," had fought desperately in that awful terrain among the peaks of the main Andean range and succeeded in clearing the way as far south as the city of Popayán. Then Bolívar ordered Sucre to proceed south by sea with 1000 troops to occupy Guayaquil, the port of Quito, the capital city of the province of the same name. Sucre sailed from the Pacific port of Buenaventura and occupied Guayaquil without resistance. Thus, between Popoyán on the north and Guayaquil on the south, there was a large stretch of the province still in the hands of the Spaniards. In it lay the rugged mountain valley of Pasto, a hotbed, since the beginning of the wars, of ardent royalist sympathy. It was the well-nigh impregnable home of fierce mountaineers, fighting men who were fanatical in their opposition to the cause of independence. This, then, would be Bolívar's first objective in his drive southward.

Since 1812 another great Liberator had been waging constant warfare against Spain in the cause of independence. He was José San Martín. He occupies a position of fame in South American history rivaling that of Bolívar— though Bolívar's field was wider and his achievements accomplished in the face of far greater difficulties. But in some ways San Martín, in character, was the nobler of the two. Austere, completely devoid of self-interest or any desire for fame, he lacked the charm of Bolívar, the ability to win and hold the affection of troops, to inspire them to superhuman deeds. He could never have succeeded under the conditions which had faced Bolívar constantly during his ten long years of war—not for lack of military ability or determination but simply because he could never have survived the psychological struggles which were so large a part of those conditions.

Like Bolívar he was an aristocrat and like him was educated in Spain. There the similarity ends. Five years older than Bolívar, he was thirty-four when he took up arms

against Spain and he had had twenty years of service in
the Spanish army on the Peninsula. His native land was
Buenos Aires, the name given then to the whole viceroyalty which is now the Republic of Argentina. He
played an active part in the war which won independence
for that country, and rose to be commander-in-chief of
the army. Assigned to an inactive post far in the west at
the foot of the Andes near the border of Chile, for several
years he planned and prepared for a drive across the
mountains to liberate that neighboring country. He felt,
as Bolívar did, that the independence of any nation was
in danger so long as Spain held colonies adjacent, and that
liberation, therefore, was a continental project, reaching
beyond provincial borders. In January, 1817, he marched
his army across the Andes—an amazing feat which rivaled
that of Bolívar, though the elevation of the passes was not
so great and his army was magnificently equipped, fully
uniformed and rationed, accompanied by sleds and thousands of mules and cattle. Further, the march had begun
from the army base at the foot of the eastern slope and
the troops had had no long, debilitating journey through
steaming and flooded jungle as a prelude.

Within four weeks after he had left his base in Buenos
Aires, he met the flower of the Spanish army on Chilean
soil at Chacabuco and defeated it decisively. A year later
he won another great victory at Maipú, to complete the
liberation of the Chilean nation. These two victories were
as brilliant, as masterly in execution, as any Bolívar had
achieved.

Offered the dictatorship of the new nation, San Martín
refused. The man selected to head the government was
Bernardo O'Higgins, the son of an Irishman who had
risen to become viceroy of Chile under the Spaniards. The
younger O'Higgins had revolted against the government
his father had served and devoted his life to the patriot
cause.

Now San Martín began to look northward toward Perú

as Bolívar was beginning to look southward toward it. He raised funds in Buenos Aires, purchased warships in the United States and built up a navy under the command of the Englishman, Admiral Lord Alexander Cochrane. Cochrane attacked the fortress of Valdivia from the sea and forced its surrender, thereby driving the last Spaniards from Chilean soil.

San Martín and Cochrane were ready, then, to sail north against Perú. They landed at Pisco in the southern part of the country. San Martín sent a land force north which marched seven hundred miles through the Spanish lines and laid siege to Lima, the capital city, while Cochrane appeared with his fleet off Callao, the port of Lima. After ten months of siege the city was starved out and San Martín marched in, amid a tremendous ovation, to declare the Independence of Perú on July 28, 1821. San Martín had no taste for such festivities and he hid out from as much of it as he could. There was still a large force of Spaniards under General Canterac in Peruvian territory; but San Martín, instead of acting against them as Cochrane urged, spent several months in Lima organizing a government. Canterac seized the opportunity to strengthen his position close to Callao. Cochrane, angry with San Martín, deserted him and sailed back to Chile with the fleet. There he resigned and went to Brazil, where he took command of the fleet of that country. Meanwhile, Buenos Aires withdrew its support from the long-absent commander-in-chief, Chile clamored for the return of her troops, and the pleasure-loving people of Lima began to resent the dour demeanor and stringent measures of her Protector.

That was the situation when Bolívar was preparing for his expedition to the far south.

He had long been in communication with O'Higgins, Cochrane and San Martín, and knew perfectly the conditions that existed. He was facing a campaign into territory which extended 1500 miles along that great chain of breath-taking, marching peaks—a route that is well-nigh impassable today. He pored over the few crude maps then existing and fixed every detail in his mind. He spent only several weeks planning for a military expedition over an extent of territory on which today a modern expedition, organizing for mere exploratory purposes, equipped with every modern facility and comparatively accurate maps, would spend months of study.

From every source available, he studied the personalities and talents of all the Spanish officials, civil and military, with whom he might have to deal. That was a custom, characteristic of him, which he always adhered to. In all his campaigns he sought to know his opponent thoroughly, to judge his capabilities and to ferret out his weaknesses. He sought, as he expressed it, to learn "Upon which foot he limped."

He sent off envoys by sea to Mexico, Perú, Chile and Buenos Aires to foster the idea of a Hispano-American Union, and to the United States and other foreign governments for the purpose of securing recognition of the Republic of Colombia; and then he was ready. The troops had come up from Cartagena under General Salóm, his chief of staff, and he had organized battalions of Venezuelan troops and troops of New Granada. His final act was a proclamation to the people of Colombia, urging them to support Santander in his absence. "Colombians!" the decree said in part: "The law designates the Vice-President as the chief of state while I remain a soldier. He will be a just, beneficent, diligent and altogether worthy leader of Colombia."

On December 13, 1821, he marched out of Bogotá for the south with 3000 soldiers. Five years were to pass before he returned.

Chapter XXIII

PICHINCHA—QUITO LIBERATED

✤

HIS original plan was to take his army by sea to join Sucre in Guayaquil; but the arrival of a Spanish fleet on the Pacific coast made that impossible. There was nothing for it but a march southward overland.

The first phase, as far as Popoyán, was relatively easy—down the valley of the Cauca, cleared beforehand of the enemy, between the mighty ranges of the Andes. There he rested his army and there, too, he won a bloodless victory—not an important one at all, but interesting as an example of the tremendous power of his personality. Upon Bolívar's approach to the outposts near the city, Colonel José Obando, the commander of the small Spanish garrison, came out under a flag of truce and asked for an interview. The request granted, the two officers met in conference. Obando succumbed completely to the Liberator's charm, hombría and persuasion. He ended up, not only by surrendering, but by offering his services and the services of his officers and troops to the patriot cause. He fought under Bolívar loyally and valiantly for the rest of the war.

Southward, those mountains went mad. Their ordered ranges snarled themselves into a mighty jumble of shining glacial peaks that pierced the clouds and reared beyond them into thin blue space; of dark, bottomless gorges and raging streams and thunderous cataracts that clothed the narrow passes in cold mists. It was a country where some giant, creating gods had run amok. In the very heart of it, on a high plateau, was the town of Pasto.

Bolívar marched his army into it. Once more the frightful nightmare of those other Andean crossings. Once more the appalling ascents, the lacerated feet and hands, the bitter cold, the starvation, the pounding hearts. The route was marked again with corpses of men and beasts. They slipped from the ledges, collapsed from exhaustion, turned to ice in their sleep, yielded blissfully to the soroche. The hempen bridges they strung across the chasms swayed and broke with the burden of them.

Of the 3000 troops who had marched out of Popoyán, only 2000 reached the gorge of the Guaítara below the town of Pasto.

Bolívar had hoped to avoid the town entirely, to pass it by a side trail without the knowledge of the Spanish army that occupied it. But his hopes were in vain. The enemy had scouted his movements and took a position blocking his path.

Bolívar didn't know then that, at that very time, the government of the United States was about to recognize the Republic of Colombia, the nation he had created. For five years Henry Clay had labored constantly in the interest of the struggling colonies of South America and on March 28, 1822, his efforts brought about that formal act of recognition.

There was no retreat back along that awesome route. Bolívar had to fight. The Spanish commander, Colonel García, with 2000 troops, artillery and hundreds of native sharpshooters of Pasto, confronted him near a place called Bomboná. Bolívar scouted the position himself. The enemy occupied the heights above the gorge in which the patriot army found itself. The left was upon the rocky slopes of the volcano of Pasto, the center in a dense forest that was matted with breastworks of felled trees, the right upon the foaming Guaítara—a stream that was impossible to ford and crossed by a single bridge exposed to fire from two angles. There the enemy waited in supreme confidence—and with every reason in the world.

Desperate as it seemed, there was no course open but a direct frontal attack. Bolívar instructed his officers. Glancing upward at those awesome heights, he said calmly, "The task seems impossible; but we must conquer and we will." Always, in his marches, in his political activities and his preparations for battle he was restless, impatient and garrulous. In the midst of military action he at once became serene and completely self-contained. His manner became pleasant, almost light-hearted, but oddly reserved. His speech shed its usual intimate tone and came slowly, in formal phrases.

The battle began at three in the afternoon. Bolívar ordered a full advance against the enemy, holding in reserve one battalion of infantry and two squadrons of cavalry. All afternoon the patriot forces charged against the rocky heights in the face of terrific fire from the woods, the stone parapets and from the artillery on the volcano. They fell in bloody heaps and their comrades came on behind. In an hour of battle all the field officers were down. A battalion sought to turn the enemy flank by the stone bridge and every man who tried to cross was killed.

Bolívar, with his reserve force and his staff, watched the battle from below. The task was hopeless. His whole army would be annihilated, flinging itself against those ragged slopes. Then, suddenly, as the sun dropped below the peaks in the west and shadows filled the gorge, Bolívar saw an amazing thing. Valdez, on the right flank, was leading his men up the face of a sheer cliff. They clung, suspended like flies, between earth and sky. Making a ladder of their bayonets stuck into crevices in the rock, they were mounting slowly and surely, protected from enemy fire by the cliff itself. Bolívar called off the attacks on the center and held his forces on the north side of the ravine, to prevent, by constant fire, the sending of reinforcements to the enemy flank above the climbing men. Standing there, the whole staff strained their eyes, fascinated, watching the thin column mount higher and higher.

Then, with the chill of approaching darkness, a mist rose
from the gorge and hid the climbers from sight. There
was an hour of anxious waiting. Suddenly a last ray of
sunlight broke through, the mist lifted and, far above,
the Spaniards were breaking from their defenses before
the patriot bayonets. The battalion of Valdez had
mounted to a crest above the enemy flank, descended a
thousand feet, fixed bayonets and charged without firing
a shot. The Spaniards, out of ammunition, broke and fled.
Quickly then Bolívar threw in his reserves and ordered
an attack on the center. Darkness fell suddenly. The flash
of muskets winked, the rock faces shuttled the roaring
echoes back and forth. The Spaniards fell back slowly,
the patriots advanced up to the breastworks on the crest.
As they emerged on the heights, the full moon opened
from a cloud and spread a ghostly light over the volcano.
For another hour the patriots pursued the retreating Spaniards, searching them out among the boulder shadows.
But the ground grew rougher, the advance more difficult.
The Spaniards escaped into the darkness and Bolívar
called off his men. They fell in their tracks, exhausted, to
sleep in the full moonlight.

The Battle of Bomboná was fought on April 7, 1822.
It was not decisive, for García got away to re-form at
Pasto. But Bolívar won a better position and the royalist
confidence was broken. Also, García was prevented from
sending aid south to General Aymerich, the Spanish captain-general of Quito, who was opposed by Sucre in brilliant and energetic action. Bolívar had sent O'Leary to
General Sucre with instructions for carrying a campaign
northward against Quito.

The Liberator, ill with fever, established headquarters
near Pasto to await the arrival of reinforcements from
Bogotá to fill up his ranks—gravely depleted from the
losses at Bomboná—and to keep García occupied while
Sucre drove north. . . .

In Guayaquil, Sucre had faced difficulties that would have taxed the abilities of the Liberator himself. Entering a strange city with nearly a thousand foreign troops, he was without funds to pay his men or rations to feed them. Besides, the government of Guayaquil, though it had declared against the Spanish domination, was wavering between the proposition of joining with the Republic of Colombia, under Bolívar, or with Perú, under San Martín. Sucre was forced into the diplomatic mission of persuading them into the Colombian fold and winning the co-operation of their troops with his army. In the latter object, at least, he met with success, employing such tact as would be worthy of Bolívar. But there were other troubles as well. There was a revolt among the patriot ranks; a large contingent of soldiers boarded six armed vessels in the harbor of Guayaquil, proclaimed the King of Spain their sovereign and sailed away. Sucre commandeered two ships, embarked with the British troops of the Albion Battalion, pursued the deserters and captured them.

Immediately he had to open operations against the Spanish army under Aymerich, which was threatening Guayaquil. From August until November of 1821 he was in constant action in the environs of Guayaquil, fighting against great odds in difficult terrain. He won several splendid victories and suffered as many defeats; and his efforts resulted in an impasse. He wrote to Bolívar at that time, saying, "How vain is hope and how fickle is victory!" In November he signed an armistice with Aymerich which was to last for ninety days. He took the opportunity afforded by the cessation of warfare to reorganize his army and to appeal to San Martín for Peruvian troops to aid him. San Martín complied; and when the Spaniards broke the armistice, Sucre was joined by General Santa Cruz with a sizable force of Peruvians. With these, the remnants of his Colombian army and the invaluable Albion Battalion of Britishers, he was ready to march north in compliance with the orders he had received from Bolívar.

His first action was at Riobamba, where he defeated a
detachment of Aymerich's army and caused the Spanish
captain-general to retreat north toward Quito. On May
23, while Bolívar was keeping García occupied around
Pasto, Sucre confronted Aymerich at Pichincha, twelve
miles from Quito.

The next day a decisive battle was waged among the
forests and crags on the slopes of a volcano. Largely
through the brilliant action of the Albion Battalion, a
wedge was driven into Aymerich's army, three Spanish
companies were destroyed and the rest broke and fled into
the city. O'Leary went in under a flag of truce and demanded capitulation. Aymerich complied, surrendering
all his officers and men—nearly 2000—fourteen pieces of
artillery, 1700 muskets and all his ammunition and stores.

Pichincha was a brilliant victory for Sucre. García,
learning of it in Pasto, surrendered to Bolívar; and the
province of Quito was liberated. Aymerich, as viceroy of
the King, ceded the territory and shortly afterward he and
García departed for Spain.

So Bolívar and Sucre, working in perfect co-operation
from north and south, had added another vast province
to the Republic of Colombia. The decisive battle, Pichincha, was the work of Sucre; but Bolívar had prevented
the union of García and Aymerich and had conceived the
plan of advancing against Pasto and Quito from two quarters. Hasbrouck says, "The plans for the campaign of the
south, conceived by the genius of Bolívar, had worked
out to perfection."

The Liberator came down from Pasto and joined Sucre
in Quito amid a tremendous public ovation. He hadn't
seen the young Venezuelan for nearly two years. He embraced him, heaped him with extravagant praise, called
him his "right hand." Together they organized a provisional government and instituted the Fundamental Law
of Colombia.

In this campaign and in all the campaigning which was

to come still farther south, the efficient support of Santander, in Bogotá, should not be overlooked. Holding in
abeyance, for the time, his political nonconformity and
his personal ambitions, he lent his extraordinary admin-
istrative talents loyally to the support of Bolívar's campaign. He labored magnificently, raising funds, organizing a service of supplies, equipping and sending out fresh
troops as they were needed. Without his efforts the liberation of Quito, and later of Perú, would never have been
accomplished.

Bolívar had received from San Martín, his rival liberator who was holding on so precariously in Perú, an invitation to meet and confer in Guayaquil. It was more than
an invitation, it was an appeal. "Protect," San Martín
wrote, "this unhappy nation! You alone, Bolívar, are
capable of delivering it from its madness. God himself
would be powerless but I know you and have confidence
in you." Bolívar hastened to accept. Turning his back on
the great festivities in his honor that were in full swing,
he hurried south toward Guayaquil. There were certain
things about the political ideas of this man San Martín
which he didn't like, and he knew the advantage that
would fall to him by arriving at the meeting-place first.
  With all speed, changing horses at every opportunity,
he rode down along that chain of breathless, shining,
snow-capped peaks. Chimborazo rose 21,000 feet, showing
its gleaming cone detached, far above the high-riding
clouds. Bolívar gazed on that mighty peak with emotion;
but just then he was hurrying, urged on by the ever-
beckoning chimera of glory.
  He reached Guayaquil on the Pacific coast fourteen
days before his rival from Perú; and he used that time
to good advantage. The people, who had long been wavering between allegiance to Perú and to Colombia, and even
considering complete independence of both, received him
with the usual ovation—the arches of flowers, the thunder-

ing cannon, the military bands and the mad throngs. One arch bore the words, "To Simón Bolívar—The Lightning of War, The Rainbow of Peace. From the people of Guayaquil." Hastening to direct the enthusiastic admiration for his person to political channels, he exerted to the utmost his charm and eloquence to win support for union with Colombia, and won it to the extent of being officially accepted as the Protector of Guayaquil.

He was ready to meet San Martín.

The liberator of Argentina and Chile was indeed in a precarious position in Perú. He was unpopular with the people there; the Spaniards still held large sections of the country; and in addition, the Marqués de Torre Tagle, a converted royalist who had raised the whole northern province of Trujillo for the patriot cause and who had been made President of Perú, was making secret overtures to the Spanish general. The people were clamoring for the annexation of Guayaquil. Without any resources at all save those which the Peruvians yielded him grudgingly, San Martín faced the necessity of seeking them elsewhere and accomplishing something that would bolster his declining prestige. His attention settled upon the annexation of Guayaquil as an answer to his problems. He sent envoys there for that purpose—but their efforts were largely nullified by the activities of Sucre, who was occupying the city at that time. When Sucre actually proposed union with Colombia to the government of Guayaquil, San Martín was so desperate that he even considered a declaration of war; but his better judgment prevailed against so calamitous a step; and besides, news came of the Colombian victories at Bomboná and Pichincha. Joaquín Mosquera, Bolívar's commissioner to San Martín, arrived with a treaty between Perú and Colombia for a perpetual alliance in the interests of mutual protection; and in it Guayaquil was tacitly regarded as part of Colombia. A long series of discussions, reaching rather violent pitch, ensued between the emissaries of the two republics over the problem of Guayaquil. It was out of this turmoil that San Martín determined upon a personal conference with Bolívar; and the winning of Guayaquil for Perú was one of the principal objects he hoped to achieve by it. He didn't know, yet, the kind of man with whom he was dealing.

He sailed from Callao on the armed vessel *Macedonia*.

The meeting between the two most famous men in all South American history is important because of its political consequences; and it holds considerable human interest as well, for it represents a psychological conflict between two great personalities.

San Martín, always completely devoid of any self-seeking, approached the meeting innocently, without guile, without any other purpose than the hope of working out the political happiness of the South American nations. His plan to secure the incorporation of Guayaquil into the Republic of Perú was born of a sincere and disinterested conviction that it was necessary to appease the Peruvians and to win them away from their drift toward reconciliation with Spain. He admired Bolívar unreservedly and looked forward to the meeting with honest pleasure—with no feeling of rivalry whatever. He wrote to him, "We shall meet and I predict that America will never forget the day on which we embrace." His best-known biographer, Mitre, says, "The Liberator of the north, possessor of his territory, which he trod with firmness, had on his side the sun and the wind. He of the south presented himself in a false position, without a fixed plan, without solid base for his own power and, upon touching the soil of Guayaquil, to use his own expression, was defeated out of hand in the questions with which he had proposed to treat as one equal to another."

Bolívar, on the contrary, approached the meeting with careful plans and after deliberate preparations to enhance his position. He regarded it definitely as a conflict with a political rival. He had very clear objectives—principally the incorporation of the Peruvian army with the Colombian under his own command. And in justice to him, it must be said that he had good grounds for suspicion as to the political leanings of San Martín, for there was considerable evidence that the liberator of the south favored the establishment of monarchies for the liberated nations. Bolívar, much as he opposed pure democracy, opposed monarchy more.

Already Mexico had made a deal with Spain and established a monarchy with Iturbide sitting upon the throne— thereby fulfilling the prophecy Bolívar had made in his Jamaica Letter years before. San Martín had signed an armistice with the Peruvian viceroy, La Serna, and had conferred with him at great length in secret meetings at which, rumor had it, a similar plan had been evolved for Perú and Buenos Aires. There was evidence, too, that after the conferences, in December, 1821, San Martín had sent a delegation to Europe for the purpose of finding a prince among the royal families to sit on the throne of Perú. Long before the meeting with San Martín was proposed, Bolívar knew of these things. In fact, amazing as it seems in view of the slow means of communication of the day, he was always well informed of events throughout the whole world.

As early as September, 1821, while Bolívar was still in Bogotá, he had written to Colonel Ibarra,[1] his envoy to Perú, "Learn the truth of these notices, with all details, antecedents, present status and probable results, so we can form a just opinion. If the notices are true, endeavor to penetrate and sound out the spirit of General San Martín and try even to persuade him to relinquish the project of erecting a throne in Perú, which would be scandalous."

[1] A direct descendant of this Ibarra, who enjoyed and merited Bolívar's friendship, is the distinguished American journalist and author, T. R. Ybarra. Interesting observations upon the spirit in which the Liberator was served by his loyal adherents may be found in Ybarra's colorful book, *Bolívar, the Passionate Warrior.*

It must be stated here that the monarchial ideas of San
Martín, the result of sincere convictions that such governments were necessary to the consolidation and happiness
of the nations, bore no trace of self-interest whatever.
There has never been the slightest suggestion that he himself desired a throne. On the contrary, he had always exercised civil powers with great distaste, hated pomp of any
sort and desired above everything a quiet private life
under a firmly established government.

Since the time of the First Republic, Bolívar had
fought, and was to have to fight again, the ideas of pure
democracy and federalism; and now he was confronted
with a struggle against the idea of monarchy. He stood,
armed with his hereditary senate, strong union and life-
term presidency, between the two extremes. It was a political war, much more bitter, nerve-racking and distasteful to him than military warfare ever was. Nevertheless, he had excellent talents for it.

When the *Macedonia* anchored in the harbor of Guayaquil on July 25, 1822, a delegation from Bolívar went
aboard to welcome the Protector of Perú to "Colombian
soil." San Martín, surprised and thoroughly taken aback,
decided to remain aboard his vessel overnight, in spite of
the fact that a reception had been planned in his honor.
The following morning Bolívar himself came aboard, embraced San Martín and welcomed him with his usual gracious charm. Together they went ashore, where the city
was adorned with flowers and a multitude of people
waited to greet them. Side by side they rode through the
cheering throngs—San Martín, tall, grave and silent, obviously ill at ease; Bolívar, slight, active, smiling, talka-
tive, thoroughly in command of the situation and at home
in such surroundings. A group of girls placed a gilded
wreath on San Martín's head and he, blushing, struck it
off rudely; but he recovered his wits in time to remark
that he'd keep it for a souvenir. A "sumptuous house"

had been prepared for the liberator of Chile and the Protector of Perú. There a banquet was served and San Martín writhed under the barrage of glowing words that were poured upon him. Seated at Bolívar's side, he whispered to him, inquiring if he didn't find such acclaim suffocating. The dinner over, the two men retired to a small room and were left alone.

During that day and the following one there were three conferences between the two liberators. One of them was merely a formal visit to present various staff officers but the other two lasted several hours.

For more than a century what was spoken in those meetings remained a matter for conjecture; but recently several documents have come to light which enable us to reconstruct the discussions with reasonable accuracy.

There were three main points to be considered by the two leaders: the status of Guayaquil; the best way to finish the war in Perú against the Spaniards; and finally, the form of government which should be established in the new states.

On the first point, with which Bolívar opened the conversation, San Martín had nothing to say. He had already been defeated there and he knew it. Bolívar stated that he was willing to leave the matter entirely to a popular vote by the people of Guayaquil—an election which had already been arranged for. San Martín agreed, knowing well that Bolívar's influence had already won the people and assured the outcome of that vote.

On the second point, San Martín discussed at length the military situation in Perú and suggested a plan for a campaign utilizing the troops of Colombia. He thought naïvely that Bolívar would turn his command over to him in its entirety. Upon Bolívar's flat refusal, he flushed with dismay. He had attributed to the Liberator of the north the same generous, impersonal patriotism which animated himself. Bolívar, to appease him, offered three battalions, some 1800 men, to operate independently under the command of General Castillo. But even that offer was only a gesture which he had no intention of fulfilling, for he knew of San Martín's weakness in Perú. Then San Martín, feeling that his leadership was the cause of Bolívar's hesitation, made the supremely generous offer to place himself and his army under Bolívar's command. It was Bolívar's turn to be taken aback. Undone in the face of this unexpected and convincing gesture of abnegation, he could only hedge, murmuring that he would have to get permission from the Congress of Colombia before he could pass the limits of the state into Perú—an argument which held a degree of truth.

San Martín was totally incapable of fathoming this wary and complicated man. Embarrassed, he dropped the subject of armies and brought up the question of governments. He admitted frankly that he believed monarchies were necessary, that he had planned with La Serna to obtain independence for Perú under a constitutional monarchy and had sent a delegation to Europe to find a prince. Bolívar listened to this, pretending surprise. "Consider," San Martín said, in effect, "the uncivilized state of the Spanish colonies, the heterogeneity of races, the unbalanced division of property, the unity between the aristocracy and the Church, the ignorance of the priests in general, the military spirit of the masses as a consequence of the prolonged civil wars. All this presages anarchy when we conclude the war of independence, and we will be forced to repent having founded democratic republics in these countries. . . . When I left Spain for La Plata I expected to find the people of the whole hemisphere disposed to establish republics and, with the highest patriotism, came to work for that end; but I confess to you now that I haven't the least hope of seeing a republic realized in these countries. And I confess also that if you refuse to aid the plan I propose, I shall not stand in your way. I shall turn over to you the direction of the war in Perú."

Bolívar launched at once into an oration on the glories

of democracy; and San Martín listened, fascinated—not convinced but unable to reply to such a flow of eloquence. Bolívar denied that there was no real sentiment for democracy in the New World, declared that the people of Colombia had ordained him to work for its ends and that he would be unworthy of the trust they had placed in him if he failed to do so—unworthy of the title of their Liberator.

"Democracy," he said, "which has flourished even in the polluted soil of Europe, would certainly thrive in the virgin soil of America. Here there is no real element of aristocracy, nothing but a sorry caricature. There are not then, my dear general, elements of monarchy in this land of God. Let a republic be formed here and dignity will grow in men, the necessity and habit for work for social benefits will be created and these will produce territorial wealth and commercial industry which will attract immigration from Europe where the proletariat lack lands and can find them here. It is impossible to hold back the progress of the human race. A monarchy established here would be of short duration, for an idea, once implanted in the people, is impossible to extinguish; and the idea of democracy has been firmly rooted here during twelve years of glorious struggle, full of examples of abnegation and patriotism."

Then, with San Martín confused and inarticulate before his barrage of words, he suddenly played his trump card. He reached into his coat and handed San Martín a letter which he had just received from Colonel Juan María Gómez, his agent in Lima, Perú. It contained the notice, he said, that a revolution was being planned against San Martín in Lima by officers of the Peruvian army who were opposed to his political principles—proof of the things he had just stated. San Martín read the letter in silence. He handed it back to Bolívar and walked the floor for a long time, his head sunk on his breast. Then he said slowly:

"If this is true, I have finished my public life. I shall go to Europe and live in retirement. I hope, before I close my eyes, I shall celebrate the triumph of the republican principles which you defend. Time and events will say which of us has seen the future with more clarity."

Bolívar sought to console him with a few parting words. "Neither our generation nor the generation to follow ours will see the brilliance of what we have founded. I see America in chrysalis. There will be a metamorphosis in the existence of its inhabitants, and at last a cast of all the races will produce a homogeneous people. We cannot stay the march of human progress with outmoded constitutions which are foreign to the virgin soil of America."

That was the last conference, on the afternoon of the second day.

That night there was a great ball in honor of San Martín. He attended, but the strain of hiding his bitterness became more than he could bear as the evening progressed. When the festivities were at their height, when the music was playing and the lovely ladies were dancing with the brilliant officers, he left quietly and walked into the darkness toward the harbor. Bolívar followed him and met him at the dock. A few words of farewell, a last embrace, and San Martín stepped into a longboat and was rowed away.

When he reached Lima, San Martín learned that the notice Bolívar had received was true. The revolution had occurred and the minister he had left in charge had been deposed. He wrote Bolívar a letter full of bitterness, suggesting that he wasn't convinced the arguments the Liberator had given for refusing his offer to co-operate in the liberation of Perú were sincere; that he didn't find them plausible. He sent with the letter a gift of a fowling piece, a pair of pistols and a horse. "Accept," he wrote, "this gift from the first of your admirers." He lived up to his promise to leave South America forever, and sailed to France where he died twenty-seven years later. After thirty years, his body was brought back to Buenos Aires and buried in the cathedral with full honors.

Before he died, after time had eased his bitterness, he wrote of Bolívar, "It may be said that his military achievements have, with reason, entitled him to be considered the most extraordinary man that South America has produced."

Chapter XXIV

THE LAND OF THE INCAS

✤

BOLÍVAR was ready to begin the task of liberation in Perú, the project which had so long filled his dreams; but circumstances held him in the province of Quito for more than a year. Envoys came up from the government of Lima with urgent appeals couched in the most grandiose and flattering terms, and Bolívar sent them back with the assurance that he would come to their aid with his conquering army as soon as conditions allowed and when permission arrived from the Colombian Congress. Four such delegations arrived in Guayaquil during that year. But the permission was slow in coming and the Liberator, as always, had a thousand other things that demanded his attention.

Word came from Venezuela that the Congress there was playing with the idea of renouncing the Colombian Constitution in favor of the old, federalistic code of the First Republic—the code to which Bolívar had always attributed the republic's downfall. The Colombian Constitution had been specifically adopted for a period of ten years. Seeing the hand of Santander in this intrigue, Bolívar wrote him a stern letter in which he said, "The Constitution of Colombia is sacred for ten years. It will not be violated with impunity while blood flows in my veins and the army of Liberators is under my orders." The letter had the desired effect, for the time being at least.

In his campaign in the province of Quito, he had defeated the Spanish armies and driven them from the land; but he had not quenched the fanatical spirit of the native royalists in Pasto. Word came to him that an uprising there had routed the garrison he had left under the command of Colonel Obando. He ordered Sucre to march north from Guayaquil to quell the revolution. At first, even the brilliant Sucre was repelled by the obstinate resistance of the Pastusos; but a second battle, in which the royalists fought every inch of the way back into the center of the town itself, brought the rebellion to an end. Bolívar made a rapid journey to Pasto, established a strong military government and returned with Sucre to Guayaquil.

Then more disturbing news arrived from Venezuela. Morales, long pent up in Puerto Cabello, had succeeded in getting away by sea and had landed at Goajira, defeated a republican force and marched into the state of Zulia. At this time the government of Perú was clamoring more loudly than ever for aid and Bolívar determined to send Sucre to Callao while he sailed for Venezuela to combat Morales. Sucre, with a large contingent of the Colombian army, embarked from Guayaquil as the Liberator's Minister Plenipotentiary to Lima.

As Bolívar himself was about to depart, more news came from Venezuela—good news this time. Páez had succeeded in driving Morales into Maracaibo, shutting up the Spanish fleet inside the lake, and besieging the city. Before this he had assembled a fleet of twenty-two small vessels under the command of Captain José Padilla. The 1300 sailors who manned the fleet were largely North American volunteers, Yankee seamen from New England, and the second in command was Captain Walter Chitty, an Englishman. During the night of July 24, 1823, Chitty with a few boats had drifted with the tide across the bar at the entrance of the lake, under the guns of the fort at San Carlos, and appeared in the midst of the Spanish fleet. In a sharp action, ten Spanish ships had been boarded, one sunk and all the officers and men taken prisoner. Morales had surrendered the city shortly after and was permitted to sail

away to Cuba. The last Spanish force was driven from
Venezuela. It is interesting to note that the only important naval action of all the wars of northern South America was a victory largely by North American sailors and
an English captain.

Bolívar received the news with great relief; he could go
to Perú now, as soon as permission arrived from Bogotá.
But, as usual, his satisfaction was of short duration. The
Pastusos broke out in rebellion once more; and this time
they succeeded in capturing the city of Quito.

Most of the army had been sent to Callao with Sucre.
Bolívar hurriedly raised what troops he could in Guayaquil, levying upon the people for supplies and conscript-
ing old men and boys, and marched north. After a hard-
fought campaign in that awesome mountain country, he
finally defeated the Pastusos. He was determined to put
an end to the business this time. He exiled the priests—
ringleaders in the agitation against the cause of liberty—
by the score and imprisoned the rebellious people by the
hundreds. On the long march back to Guayaquil the
fanatical Pastuso prisoners refused food and many of them
died of starvation by the roadside. Others flung themselves
into the mountain streams to drown rather than submit
to the enemies of the Spanish king. Bolívar's action
brought the Pastusos into final subjection; but he never
succeeded in breaking their royalist spirit. In that remote
mountain province, even after half a century of life under
the rule of the Colombian Republic, toasts were drunk
to "our sovereign, the King of Spain."

Meanwhile the government of Riva-Agüero in Perú
had been overthrown and the Marqués de Torre Tagle
was once more made President. Torre Tagle added his
voice to the clamor for the Liberator's presence in Perú
and when his envoy arrived—the fourth that had come to
Guayaquil—Bolívar decided to wait no longer. He wrote
Santander a letter to that effect, and was in the act of
sealing it when he received a communication from Bogotá,

giving him the permission he had been waiting for so long.

Within an hour he was aboard a vessel and sailing down the estuary, bound for new and greater glories.

Perú, the fabulous land of the Incas, was a strange and bewildering world to the men of Colombia, hardened and brutalized by twelve years of desperate warfare. The richest land in America, it had been largely untouched by the ravages of prolonged struggle such as had impoverished their own countries. Here the division of wealth was more unequal than anything they had known—the rich were infinitely richer and the poor infinitely poorer. All the conditions created by the extremes of class inequality—the great gulf which had existed between the aristocracy and the peasants in the northern colonies before the revolution, in their way of life and social privileges, and which had been wiped out by the scythe of war so long ago now that few even remembered it—were presented here in exaggerated form. In that legendary land of gold and precious gems the wealth was concentrated in the hands of the aristocrats, the noble descendants of the Conquistadores.

In the tropic hothouse atmosphere of Lima there existed a worldly and brilliant society that was unequaled anywhere in America. It was steeped in the ideas and traditions of the courts of the viceroys, dominated by great lords who were jealous of their hereditary privileges and bloated by the sense of their importance. In its heavy, perfumed air there lurked a faint odor of decay, of indolence and moral corruption. The men, even to the army officers, lolled upon the silken divans in their luxurious chambers, discussing in soft and lazy voices the political or military problems that confronted them. Their eyes were dilated from the effects of chewing the leaves of the coca plant—a habit to which all, lord and peon alike, were addicted.

It was a land of women—beautiful, worldly, seductive.
In contrast to the traditional restrictions placed upon the
highborn women of Spain—probably a relic of the Moor-
ish invasion—here they enjoyed amazing freedom and fantastic privileges. They gambled to excess, drank, smoked
and made love openly. They walked the streets alone by
day or night, dressed in rich gowns that showed their
soft, perfumed bosoms and clung to their curved thighs as
they moved with voluptuous and studied grace. In the
parade of fashion in the late afternoons, they rode astride
prancing palfreys that jingled their silver ornaments. They
wore sheer, ruffled white trousers under white gowns, and
small stiff hats like men's. Their tiny feet, with satin shoes
and light silver spurs, were tucked into little silver stir-
rups.

On the bleak mountainsides the naked and dull-eyed
Indians scraped away at the stony earth, producing gold
and crops for their masters.

The tendency to monarchy was strong among the ruling
class. As in Venezuela, there had been great dissatisfaction
with Spanish rule because of economic abuses and commercial restrictions. The colony had, true enough, declared for independence and established a government;
but here, even more than it was in the northern colonies
in the beginning, the struggle was between the creole aristocracy and Spanish overlords. The peons looked on with
indifference. There had been numerous backslidings, dissensions and intrigues with the Spanish commanders, and
almost nothing had been done to drive the large Spanish
army from the country. For over three years the capital
city had been periodically invaded and sacked by the Spaniards, its treasures seized, the gold and silver and jewels
stripped from its many churches. As a result of this, the
aristocratic rebels were fast being shorn of their wealth;
and it was because of that fact, mainly, that they had
turned in desperation to Bolívar, begging his help. . . .

When Bolívar landed in Callao on September 1, 1823, a reception awaited him that outshone anything he had ever seen before. The road from the port to the capital city was lined for its whole length with cheering multitudes. Gorgeously attired officers dashed about holding the people back, cannon thundered, drums rolled, hundreds of beautiful, dark-eyed horsewomen rode ahead to strew his way with flowers. He was given a luxurious villa called Magdalena on the Pacific a few miles from the city, where the dinner service was of gold. The festivities lasted without pause for a solid week. There were fireworks at night, brilliant balls and performances at the opera house. His name was on every lip. The climax was a government-sponsored bullfight for which the best matador of Perú was brought from a distant city and for which the people stormed the gates during the whole night before.

Sucre had been acting as commander-in-chief of the Colombian and Peruvian armies; but when Bolívar arrived the post was given to him, with wide civil authority as well.

The splendor of his reception did not blind his all-seeing eyes to the truly deplorable state of the Peruvian independent government. A magnificently equipped and trained Spanish army of 18,000 men occupied almost the whole country and had its headquarters in the ancient city of Cuzco. The patriots held only a narrow strip along the Pacific coast, Callao, Lima and Trujillo. And in Trujillo the deposed Riva-Agüero had set up a rival government and had been declared a traitor by the Lima government of Torre Tagle. Then, too, in spite of the opulent existence of the patriot upper classes, the treasury was empty and the troops were in dire want. Bolívar sent communications to his agents in Chile and in England, begging them to arrange loans if possible. Previously he had asked for troops from Chile and for troops and supplies from Santander in Bogotá. The latter were forthcoming as rapidly as the able Santander could send them;

but the Chilean troops, arriving on the Peruvian coast just as word came of a Spanish victory, lost heart and sailed back home.

That victory had been an eye-opener to Bolívar, showing him just how much he could expect from the undisciplined, lazy and ill-led Peruvian troops. The Peruvian General Santa Cruz had declined to co-operate fully with Sucre. With 5000 troops he had set off, over the violent objections of Sucre, on an ill-conceived expedition into difficult country. The Spanish army had blocked his action and, without even coming into battle, forced him into a retreat over country so frightful that only 600 men out of his whole army survived.

The outlook for the Peruvian patriots was dark indeed. They turned to Bolívar as their savior, their only hope.

In his efforts to build up his army and to arouse the Peruvians to united action and enthusiasm for the cause, Bolívar outdid himself. He rose to new heights of eloquence in his speeches, his proclamations rang with new nobility of expression and with sentiments of exalted patriotism. Larrazábal said of him, ". . . His speech broke forth like a meteor, splendid with images, irresistibly moving. . . . It was in Perú that the imagination of Bolívar shone most and where his discourses were truly inspiring." Bernardo O'Higgins, the Irish patriot President of Chile who had worked side by side with San Martín and who was in Lima during this time, was moved to exclaim, "Bolívar is the greatest man in South America."

But it was a heart-breaking task. "The country receives us with enthusiasm but gives us nothing," he wrote to Santander. "We have need of much tact and great moderation to prevent this nation from becoming entirely reactionary. Money is needed but we ought not and cannot demand it of these unfortunate people, for here the era of home government has been one of crime and pillage. The inhabitants are sound but they are disinclined to

military service and it is difficult to organize an army. The
natives are what they were at the beginning of the world.
. . . The country is patriotic but unadapted to military
service; it is good, but apathetic. There are provisions and
transportation but no will to furnish them. . . . The difficulties are immense, there reigns a disorder that appalls
the most determined. The theater of war is equatorial
America; our enemies are everywhere, our soldiers are
men of all parties and all countries, of different dialects,
color, laws and interests. Only Providence can bring order
out of this chaos." No wonder San Martín had cried to
him, "Come and deliver this nation from its madness!"

As soon as he had organized a semblance of an army
he marched northward toward Trujillo to put down the
rebellious faction of Riva-Agüero—a distasteful task from
which Sucre asked to be excused, but which was imperative, for the dissenting patriots were making overtures to
the Spaniards. Happily, Bolívar was able to accomplish it
without bloodshed. He sent a staff officer ahead to treat
with the Peruvian troops who were loyal to Riva-Agüero
and he himself had an interview with Colonel Gutiérrez,
commander of the rebellious leader's army. He won
Gutiérrez completely and got his word to deliver Riva-
Agüero as a prisoner. Torre Tagle's government condemned the former President to death but he got away—
some say with Bolívar's aid—and sailed for Europe. Bolívar established army headquarters in Trujillo and sailed
south to Lima.

Suddenly stricken with a violent illness, he retired to
the seacoast town of Pativilca, ninety miles north of Lima.
Mosquera, his envoy to Buenos Aires, went to visit him
there and found him a small bundle of skin and bones.
His cheeks were sunken so that the outlines of his teeth
showed through, and his knees protruded from his trousers like points. But his eyes burned still. "What do you
intend to do now, Excellency?" Mosquera asked him.

Bolívar looked up in surprise. "Why," he replied, "conquer, of course."

As he lay there in the warm sunshine, with damp cloths
laid across his eyes to cool the fever, his mind was visualizing that vast landscape of all his past actions, reviewing
the conditions that existed in all the liberated provinces
and planning what still remained to be done. He pictured mentally a relief map of the whole land of Perú,
spotted upon it the disposition of the Spanish forces and
conceived to the last detail the actions he would use
against them. But his pondering was disrupted by bad
news from Lima, very bad news. On February 4, 1824, the
troops of Buenos Aires which had come with San Martín
and had held the garrison in Callao rose in revolt, freed
the Spaniards from the prison, raised the flag of Spain and
threatened Lima. In the face of this the Congress made
Bolívar Supreme Civil and Military Chief with dictatorial
powers over the President. Scarcely had this been done
when Torre Tagle reverted to his old royalist sentiments,
went over to the Spaniards with over three hundred of
the officials of his government and surrendered the capital. So Bolívar, ninety miles away, was, with his officers
and army, the sole defender of independence in that foreign land.

Under such circumstances the Liberator showed once
again his unconquerable spirit. Rising on his tottering
legs, he drove his sick body and fever-ridden mind into
frantic action. To his brave and beloved Sucre he wrote,
". . . I must decide with you here on various plans which
are necessary for you to know of in order to advise me and
to learn the part in their execution which you will play.
I have a great scheme which should finish this war." Later
he wrote, "We must, dear general, be deaf to the clamor
of the whole world because war thrives on despotism and
is not made from love of God. Stop at nothing, show yourself to be a terrible, inexorable character." Still later he
wrote to General Heres, his chief of staff, "This half

month must be spent in preparation, that of May in marching, June in fighting." Then, again to Sucre, "I am ready for anything. I am possessed of the very demon of war and am in the mood for putting an end to this struggle. . . . The enemy will come with 8000 and we shall go to the battlefield with as many. Victory must be ours." This from a man who could scarcely walk.

Word of dissatisfaction over his long absence reached him from Colombia and he wrote to Santander, resigning his presidency—a position which he had never exercised anyway. Then he rode two hundred miles up the coast to Trujillo, where his army was encamped.

The preparations required five months—five months of activity more amazing even than any that Bolívar had displayed before. Out of nothing he equipped an army of 9000 men. He conscripted horses and men, seized all available food supplies, raised money by force, took the gold and silver from the churches. He built foundries for repairing and manufacturing small ordnance, forges for pounding out lances and sabers and making horseshoes, towers for making shot. He directed in person the organizing and training of troops, inspected equipment and managed everything to the last detail. He made long journeys into remote corners of the Andes, penetrating to spots where white men had never been before, garnering men, food, horses, llamas and anything of metal he could lay his hands on. He wrote to Salóm, in Guayaquil, "We must liberate these people in spite of themselves, in order to end this war and return to our homes; otherwise we shall be campaigning till the end of the world." To Sucre, "I am resolved to spare no pains whatever and will compromise my soul to save this land."

By the end of May he was ready to march. He had 5000 Colombian troops and 4000 Peruvians, established at different points in northern Perú. Sucre commanded the Colombians and General La Mar the army of Perú. The efficient and meticulous Daniel O'Leary was Bolívar's chief aide; there were several hundred British officers scattered among the different battalions and General William Miller, an English adventurer, was in command of the Peruvian cavalry. Bolívar sent messengers to the various divisions with orders to march south and concentrate near Pasco.

Those marches of the patriot armies are epics in themselves. Moving southward in parallel valleys between the Andean ranges, they encountered all extremes of weather and topographical condition. To reach the designated spot, some of the divisions had to cross the mountains at their worst places by passes which are among the highest in the world.

Sucre's march lay along three hundred miles of blinding desert; and though his army marched at night to avoid the heat, three hundred of his men died of exhaustion—one for every mile.

The division which General Miller accompanied had the worst task—a march of six hundred miles down the Cordillera. Miller recorded the events of that march and expressed the opinion that it was the most difficult ever made by an army—but he hadn't been with Bolívar on his other Andean crossings, which were worse. The whole army, including the officers, marched on foot, leading the horses to save them. Six thousand head of cattle were herded along to provide food. The temperature, during the whole march, seldom rose above zero and nearly every man suffered from snow-blindness. They fell by the wayside, blood gushing from their nostrils, and slipped into the dizzy chasms. It was such a march as had become almost routine to the Liberator.

On August 2 all the divisions had joined on the great plain between Cerro de Pasco and Rancas, twelve thousand feet above the sea. Bolívar reviewed the troops and addressed them: "Soldiers! You are about to complete the greatest work which Heaven can confide to man—that of saving an entire world from slavery!" The men broke out into wild cheering. Four days later, through a gap in the mountains, they saw the magnificent army of Spain marching in a valley below.

Canterac had marched toward Pasco from his headquarters at Jauja when he learned of Bolívar's movement; but he was too late to prevent the concentration of the patriot divisions.

Scouting the advance of the enemy, Bolívar sent his cavalry ahead to intercept them and followed with his infantry at the double. The Spanish cavalry, among the finest that Europe could produce, also moved in advance of their infantry. The two mounted divisions met on the wide plain of Junín, under the escarpments of the Andes, beside the Lake of Reyes. Drawn up in line of battle, facing each other, the commands were given to each almost to the second, the lances dropped, the horses leaped forward. The dust rose and the two columns came together with an earth-shuddering shock. The Battle of Junín lasted one hour. Not a shot was fired. It was charge and countercharge over the high Andean plain, Venezuelan llanero with long hair and jaguar cap, pigtailed and helmeted Spanish dragoon and grenadier, Peruvian montonero with poncho of llama wool, lances and sabers ringing, flashing in the bright sun, dripping crimson. Slowly the patriot cavalry gained ground, slowly the Spaniards gave way, falling back into the confused columns of their infantry. Bolívar was coming up fast with his foot soldiers. In the face of his advance, the whole Spanish army retreated, leaving on the field 1000 men, 700 muskets, ammunition, horses and cattle. They kept going for four hundred and fifty miles back among the mountains. Canterac himself couldn't explain the defeat. He wrote, "My army being superior in numbers and its officers valiant without exception, it was natural to expect a victory and I had counted upon it. . . ."

The battle was indecisive, for Canterac got away; but it worked wonders for the patriot morale and broke the confidence of the Spaniards. They began to feel that this man Bolívar was indeed, as he claimed, invincible, possessed of the demon of war.

Junín, too, marked the turn of luck in favor of the Liberator. Word came that Lima had gone patriot once more, that a loan of three million pesos was on its way from England, that three thousand fresh troops were due to arrive from Colombia. Leaving Sucre in command, with detailed instructions for pressing the campaign against the Spaniards, Bolívar hurried to Lima. Already his mind was soaring far beyond the problems of Perú, which, characteristically, he now regarded as solved. Inspired by the doctrine of all America for Americans only, which President Monroe of the United States had declared less than a year before, he was beginning to ponder upon that congress of South American nations in Panamá which he had conceived in his Jamaica Letter.

He rode into the city at night and almost escaped the crowds who had been waiting for him all day. They mobbed him, lifted him from his horse and carried him through the streets on their shoulders.

Chapter XXV

AYACUCHO—PERÚ LIBERATED

✤

THE end came even more quickly than Bolívar, with all his confidence, had hoped. The Battle of Ayacucho was fought only a month after he arrived in Lima. It was one of the decisive battles of the world.

The Colombian government, under the spur of Santander, had declared that, in accepting the dictatorship of Perú, Bolívar had automatically sacrificed his official position in Colombia and his authority over Colombian troops. Therefore, Sucre was named commander-in-chief of the army in Perú, superseding him. The Liberator took the announcement from Bogotá very hard; but he swallowed his resentment, wrote a polite letter of compliance to Santander and informed Sucre of his elevation. Sucre, always loyal to Bolívar, protested. He signed, with all his staff officers, a declaration of refusal to accept the mandate of the Colombian government; but Bolívar dissuaded them, expressing his complete confidence in Sucre and assuring them that he derived as much pleasure from Sucre's achievements as though they were his own.

So, though the troop movements and the tactics which determined the site of the action were his own, the actual execution of the battle that climaxed the Liberator's career fell to his beloved Sucre. Sucre took over the command with detailed instructions from Bolívar and with orders to avoid combat until reinforcements should reach him. Then, in Lima, Bolívar organized the fresh troops and supplies that arrived from Colombia and dispatched them to the field as rapidly as possible.

287

After the defeat of Canterac at Junín, La Serna, the viceroy, marched from Cuzco to join him in the valley of the Apurimac. Sucre attempted to prevent the union but was defeated in several minor skirmishes and found himself obliged to confront the combined Spanish forces. He did, however, succeed in maneuvering the enemy into the position which Bolívar had designated as the place of battle. On December 8, 1824, the two armies confronted each other near the plain of Ayacucho, 11,600 feet above sea level. That evening the opposing generals scouted each other's movements and drew up their lines. They spent the night quietly within sight of each other's campfires. Breakfast was eaten on the morning of the ninth, and then the officers of both armies visited each other, embraced and fraternized in all friendliness. At eleven o'clock the Spaniards went back to their lines and La Serna sent Sucre a formal announcement that he was ready to begin battle. All, patriots and Spaniards alike, knew that the fate of South America was to be decided. Far different, this, from the savage and ruthless warfare that had raged between the patriots and the armies of Morales and Boves in the northern countries.

The bugles sounded almost simultaneously in the opposing ranks. Sucre commanded in all 5780 men, with but one piece of artillery. The Spaniards numbered 9310 and had eleven cannon. Addressing his troops, Sucre said, "Upon your efforts today depends the fate of South America. This shall be a day of glory that will crown your long struggles. Soldiers! Long live the Liberator! Long live Bolívar, the Savior of Perú!" With these cries on their lips, the men went into action. Under the gleaming heights of Condoranqui, the battle lasted only one hour.

It was a battle of generals, of formal tactics, of maneuvering of infantry, cavalry and artillery. The outcome was decided sheerly upon the merits of the contending officers; Sucre and the other patriot leaders proved themselves the masters by far. Silva, La Mar, Lara, Miller and

Córdova executed their movements with precision, led their troops with inspiring valor. Silva, severely wounded, stuck to his saddle and charged at the head of the Colombian cavalry. To Córdova belongs renown for the most spectacular individual action of the day. He was only twenty-four, the youngest general in the Colombian army. At first the tide of battle favored the Spaniards and Sucre ordered Córdova to charge with his reserve force. Córdova, at the head of his infantry, dismounted and killed his horse with his sword. "I want no means of escape," he said. He gave his subordinate officers their instructions. "The orders are," he said, "advance, arms at will." "What step, General?" he was asked. "Step? The step of conquerors," he answered.

With that order ringing in their ears, the patriot column advanced. The Spanish center gave way before them, retreated to the heights at the edge of the plain. Up the slopes the patriot infantry charged, Córdova at their head. Sucre, seeing the wavering of the Spanish line, threw in his whole army. Córdova gained the heights, planted his flag and accepted the surrender of La Serna himself and thirteen of his generals. Canterac, seeing the capture of the viceroy, withdrew from the field. The battle was won.

That night, in a small hut, Miller, the Englishman, served tea to the Spanish generals while the terms were discussed. The royalists had lost 2100 men killed or wounded and all their guns; the patriots 979. Canterac, under orders of La Serna, also surrendered his entire command—16 colonels, 68 lieutenant-colonels, 484 minor officers and 3200 men. There were more Spanish prisoners than there were patriot troops to guard them.

As the battle had been vastly different from the early battles of the revolution, so the terms which Sucre dictated were different. All the Spanish officers were to retain their uniforms and swords. Every Spanish soldier was to be returned to Spain at the cost of the Republic and was to draw half-pay until he reached his homeland. In return, La Serna agreed to surrender all the Spanish forces remaining in other parts of Perú.

Sucre wrote to Bolívar at once:

The entire royal army, all the provinces which it occupies in this Republic, all its parks, storehouses, and generals, are offered to your Excellency by the United Army as a testimonial to the illustrious Savior of Perú who, since Junín, has pointed out the plains of Ayacucho as the place upon which to complete the glory of the liberating arms. . . . The campaign of Perú is ended. Its independence and the peace of America have been signed upon this battlefield. The United Army hopes that its victory of Ayacucho is a worthy offering to the Liberator of Colombia. . . . The only reward I ask for myself is that you continue to be my friend.

Bolívar received the report in the salon of his house in Lima. He read it quickly and then jumped to his feet, waving the letter, crying, "Victory!" He danced about the room, singing and shouting with joy. He snatched his sword from its scabbard, tore off his uniform jacket, threw them to the floor and cried that he would never use them again.

His reply to Sucre was grandiose but full of sincere praise. It gave full credit for the victory to the young officer whose talents he had brought into the light. Conferring on him the title Grand Marshal and Liberator of Perú, he wrote:

The Battle of Ayacucho is the climax of American glory and the work of General Sucre. His dispositions for it were perfect and their executions flawless. Quick and skillful movements destroyed in an hour the victors of fourteen years—an enemy perfectly organized and expertly commanded. . . . General Sucre is the father of Ayacucho; he is the redeemer of the Children of the Sun [the Incas]; he has broken the chains with which Pizarro bound the empire of the Incas;

Posterity will picture him with one foot on Pichincha and the other on Potosí, bearing in his arms the cradle of Manco Capac and contemplating the chains broken by his sword.

From nothing the patriots had accomplished everything. Holding only one small town on the Pacific coast, they had, in less than a year, organized and equipped an army of 9000, killed, wounded or captured more than 18,000 Spanish troops and liberated an immensely wealthy land, twice as large as France, Germany and the British Isles.

There was still a little mopping up to be done. In Alto Perú, now Bolivia, the Spanish commander Olañeta refused to recognize the surrender of La Serna and held on to the country in the name of the King. Bolívar sent instructions for Sucre to open a campaign against him. Within a few months, Olañeta was killed in Potosí and his army surrendered.

In the port city of Callao the Spanish commander Rodil also refused to acknowledge La Serna's surrender. Shut up with his troops within the city, there was nothing he could do, but he held out for over a year in brave but foolhardy defiance. General Salóm threw a tight siege about Callao and the terrible suffering that had marked the siege of Cartagena years before was repeated—but it was the royalists who suffered this time. Finally, on January 23, 1826, when the last crawling thing had been eaten, Rodil surrendered to Salóm and the last Spanish flag in South America was lowered.

Salóm, asking Bolívar what punishment he should impose upon Rodil, received this answer, "Heroism never calls for punishment and generosity becomes the conqueror. I know you have a thousand just causes for fury against Rodil; but consider what pride we would take in him were he a patriot." No punishments were inflicted and the Spanish troops were permitted to embark for Spain. . . .

Bolívar was at the very height of his glory. His long war with Spain was over at last. He had fought for fifteen years, directed nearly 500 battles over 3,000,000 square miles of territory; and he had accomplished everything, in the way of liberating at least, that he had ever dreamed of. He had made good all the mad boasts of those dark days on the Orinoco, when, hiding in the bushes from the Spaniards, his orderly had thought he had lost his mind.

He had broken the power of Spain for all time in Venezuela, New Granada, Quito and Perú—territories that comprise today Venezuela, Colombia, Ecuador, Bolivia and Perú. And Panamá had come under his protection of her own will. In all, it was a land more than ten times the size of Spain. He had indeed "struck with his sword the fairest jewel from the crown of Fernando VII." He had fulfilled the vow he had taken in Rome twenty years before.

But unfortunately for him, perhaps, his dreams went beyond mere liberation. They included as well the establishment of permanent governments under constitutions based upon the principles which he had conceived and which he was convinced were the only ones suited to the lands he had liberated. And his nature was such that he could never rest so long as one of his dreams remained unfulfilled.

The physical war was over. The bitter, soul-shattering, political and psychological warfare went on, more violently than ever. He was forty-two years old.

Lima went utterly mad with joy. Church bells clamored for days, throngs paraded the streets and every appearance of the Liberator was the signal for new demonstrations. He no sooner rode out on his horse than he was lifted from it and carried on the people's shoulders and the horse was led behind, garlanded with flowers. Te Deums were sung in the churches, the priests offered prayers of thanks to God for sending them Bolívar and called down blessings upon him. The Villa Magdalena where he lived was converted into a palace of splendor by the adoring women. Its spacious salons were heaped with fresh flowers daily and it was tended by lovely señoritas as though it were a holy temple.

In the midst of all this, Bolívar was busy with his schemes. The time had come now, he felt, to take a definite step toward the formation of that international Congress of Panamá he had long dreamed of. Accordingly he sent communications to all the Latin American countries and to the United States and England as well, inviting them to send representatives to meet in Panamá the following year, in June of 1826. He said afterwards that he had no real hope of success for that first Congress, that the time wasn't ripe for it; but he initiated it for its effect abroad—to show the world the liberal and advanced philosophies which animated him, and in the hope that some day it might bear fruit. Among the duties of the Congress which he planned were the interpretation of treaties between nations, the settlement of all differences by peaceful means and the reviewing of questions of international law. What he proposed was, in effect, an international court of arbitration. The Congress of Panamá actually met on schedule; but few of the delegates of the nations he invited ever arrived and nothing was accomplished. The Congress eventually ended in failure; but so has every such effort down to the present day. Bolívar was initiating, over a hundred years ago, something for which the world is still not ready. Even the Pan American Union existing today, fine and successful as it is, is largely cultural in function and has no such judicial powers as Bolívar conceived for his Congress; nor, in fact, does it dare to touch upon the subjects which were to be the chief concern of his assembly.

One of his first acts after Ayacucho was to announce that the circumstances which had necessitated his exercise of dictatorial powers existed no longer, and that the

Peruvian Congress should convene as soon as possible to name a president. On February 10, 1825, he opened the session in Lima and addressed the delegates. "It was praiseworthy," he said, "for the Congress, in order to pass through the abyss and weather the terrific storms, to substitute the bayonets of the liberating army for its laws; but now that the country has secured domestic peace and political freedom, it should permit no rule but the rule of law."

The Congress, however, thought otherwise and devoted itself mainly to heaping more honors upon him. It voted for an equestrian statue to be erected in the main plaza, for an engraving of him to be placed in every provincial capital and for a gold medal to be struck, bearing his likeness and the words, "To its Liberator, Simón Bolívar—Perú, Restored, Ayacucho, 1824." It also voted for a sum of 1,000,000 pesos to be distributed among his soldiers and an equal sum to be awarded him as a gift. Bolívar refused to accept the latter and then the Congress proposed that it be paid in his name to Venezuela for educational and charitable purposes—which he agreed to.

On the question of the dictatorship the representatives insisted unanimously that conditions still necessitated his unhampered authority, that dangers still threatened the nation and only he could avert them. They voted the suspension of the Constitution and placed all law in his hands. Bolívar was sincerely reluctant this time, for word of fresh trouble in New Granada and Venezuela had reached him and he was anxious to return to those countries. But he was anxious, also, to establish a permanent government in Perú and secure the adoption of his constitution. So he agreed to continue as Supreme Chief and to remain for a year, until the next session of Congress, when the question of a constitution would come up.

With all his old energy, he plunged at once into the political, commercial and social problems of the nation. He appointed twelve jurists to draw up civil and criminal codes. He established normal schools throughout the provinces, undertook the construction of roads and irrigation projects, established civil courts and local governments and a bureau to study and promote modern methods of mining and developing the mineral resources of the country. He organized public charities and passed laws to aid agriculture and commerce and to distribute lands to the Indians. He removed all tariff from mining and farming implements. In the midst of it all he kept up his voluminous correspondence with individuals and governments throughout the world.

Interlude

AN AMAZON AND JEWELED
WREATHS

✤

IN recording the stream of events in the Liberator's
career during the southern campaigns it has been
necessary, in order to preserve continuity, to neglect his
private life. Not that there ever was much of it. It consisted almost entirely of the five or six hours a night when
he slept, sometimes in a hammock under a thatched roof,
sometimes on the ground on a square of rawhide, rolled
in his cloak, sometimes—but very rarely—on the silken
bed of a Spanish governor's palace in a strange city.

In 1822 he met a woman who became more important
to him than any since Fanny Villars and who came as
near to winning the complete surrender of his heart as
any mortal woman could. She never wholly succeeded in
that but she made a valiant effort; and her failure was due
only to the fact that Bolívar's psychological make-up rendered such a thing impossible.

He saw her first in Quito after the Battle of Pichincha,
when he rode into the city in triumph. She smiled at him
from a balcony and tossed him a flower. That night he met
her at a ball and found her the best dancing partner he
had ever had. Hard and sinewy as himself, she was soft
where a woman should be soft and her movements were
light and graceful as a dove on the wing. He danced with
her till dawn, forgetting everyone else, including the
lady's husband.

Bolívar was thirty-nine then. In spite of the worries that
had plagued him for so long and the spells of sickness that

were coming upon him with more and more frequency, the youthful spring was still in his step, the fine-drawn muscles still played like rippling cords. His face still lighted with eagerness and his figure retained its slender grace.

Manuela Sáenz was twenty-two. She was married to a staid English physician, Dr. Thorne, who adored her and looked upon her wayward behavior with gentle dismay. She had lived her girlhood in Lima, breathed its air of happy freedom, absorbed the unconventional customs of its women; and she added a few that were entirely her own. Beautiful, vivacious, daring, utterly charming, in remote Quito, in the Englishman's ordered household, she was stifled.

The Liberator had known many courageous women before, women who had forsaken lives of luxury and faced the hardships of the jungle and the savagery of Spanish soldiers without qualm; but none of them compared with Manuela. She had a fine figure that was entirely feminine, yet she had an amazing strength and was a true Amazon within her gentle-appearing body. A superb horsewoman, she could fence and use firearms with the best of men.

The wooing between two such people was naturally a very brief affair. Bolívar, anxious to hasten to Guayaquil for his meeting with San Martín, left Quito within a few days; but those few days were enough. Manuela followed him, accompanied by her personal slave, a big laughing negress.

During the year in Guayaquil and the province of Quito, Manuela was with Bolívar wherever he went. Dressed in the uniform of a dragoon, lance in hand, she followed him in his campaigns against the Pastusos. Mounted on a white stallion, she charged into battle with the Colombian troops. The men made her presents of the beautiful mustaches they cut from the fallen Spaniards and she collected them, stitching them on a silk scarf. "La

Libertadora," the patriot men and officers called her; and Bolívar called her "amable loca," the "lovable fool."

Thorne wrote her constantly, sending her money and begging her to return to him. She refused, none too gently, and returned the money. She was too much woman for poor Thorne, far too much.

After nearly a year of her company, Bolívar began to feel the tightening of the strings around his heart, and his pride, his sense of hombría and instinct for complete self-dominance, revolted. With other women, a single cold glance from his hawklike eyes, his rigid, unyielding manner, were enough to keep them at a distance; but not Manuela. She wanted him completely; and her determination was almost as great as his own. When he sailed from Guayaquil for Lima, he deliberately left her, to escape what he feared she would do to him. He calmed her storm of protest by the promise that he would send for her.

During that first year in Perú, in the hectic struggle against the political and economic chaos that reigned there and in the campaigns against the Spaniards, Bolívar got along quite well without his lovable fool. But after peace came with the Battle of Ayacucho and he relaxed somewhat in the idyllic surroundings at Villa Magdalena, the old spell began to work in spite of himself and in spite of the abundance of other women only too anxious to please. Thorne had gratefully taken Manuela back, and Bolívar wrote her a pious and noble letter of renunciation:

My beautiful and good Manuela, each moment I am thinking of you and the fate which touched you. I see that nothing can unite us under the auspices of innocence and honor. I see well and deplore the horrible situation for you. You must be reconciled with one you do not love and I must be separated from one I adore. Yes, I adore you today more than ever before. Tearing myself from your love and your possession has multiplied in me all the sentiments which bound me to your soul and heart, that heart without equal. When you were mine I loved you more for your enchanting nature than for your delicious attractions. Now it seems to me that an eternity separates us. . . . My own determination has put me to torment. . . . In the future you will be alone, even at the side of your husband; I will be alone in the midst of the world. Only the glory of having conquered ourselves will be our consolation. . . .

But scarcely had he written it than he repented and followed it with a letter begging her to come to him. That wasn't necessary, however. Manuela had already taken things into her own hands and was on the way to Lima.

The worldly and pleasure-loving capital of Perú was a perfect background for the mistress of the Liberator. She was received everywhere with the courtesy and honors she would have merited as his wife, and her colorful antics were regarded with amused approval. By day she rode about the city dressed in a uniform of her own design—tight red trousers, dragoon boots, a black velvet cape and plumed hat—and attended by two lancers. She created a furor wherever she appeared, joking with the common people in the markets, playing tricks on the palace sentinels. At the Villa Magdalena she spent whole days riding, fencing and shooting with the officers. She was extremely fond of animals and filled the house with them. Her special pet was a bear cub which she kept near her always.

In the evenings, at the fashionable affairs that were given nightly at the villa, she appeared completely transformed. All feminine then, beautifully gowned and coifed, she sat at the end of the long table, opposite the Liberator. He, splendid in his blue and gold uniform, smiled quietly at her across the myriads of candles. Intelligent, sharp-witted, she dominated the gatherings and kept the guests amused with her caustic and humorous comments upon the personal peculiarities and doings of people in

high places in the country. Her negro maid had a fine
gift for mimicry. It was one of Manuela's delights to dress
her up and have her perform in ribald and hilarious
burlesque of prominent citizens. Bolívar's British aides,
the methodical O'Leary, the dour and loyal Ferguson, and
his physicians, Doctors Moore and Foley, became Manuela's devoted slaves.

The strong monarchial sentiment which had always
flourished in Perú, that land of concentrated wealth and
ignorant masses, was still very much alive. Now that independence was won, there was born in the minds of the
ruling classes an idea for an "Empire of the Andes," with
Bolívar occupying the throne—an empire quite different
from that "Empire of the Incas" which Miranda had
dreamed of. The aristocrats were convinced that a monarchy was necessary and they couldn't believe that Bolívar
was really opposed to it. They felt approvingly that in
spite of his declarations to the contrary, the motive behind all his political moves was the establishment of a
monarchy. The belief was disseminated far and wide and
reached to other countries. As a result of Bolívar's victories in Perú, the Congress in Bogotá once more restored
him to the presidency. Only a few days after Ayacucho
he wrote to Santander, resigning the office for the sixth
time. He begged Santander to induce the senate to accept
his resignation. The insinuations and the casual acceptance of the belief that he had monarchial ambitions were
creating in him a sort of frantic dismay—aggravated perhaps by the fact that the idea really tempted him. He
wrote:

Por Dios, my dear general! Interest yourself in this business
as if it were your own. All the world knows that Colombia
has no need of me now. No harm will be done by my leaving
and it is better that I go with permission than without it.
The whole world is torturing me with the belief that I am

ambitious, that I wish to crown myself. The French are saying it, they say it in Chile, in Buenos Aires, they say it here.
. . . By resigning I will answer them all. I do not want more
glory or power or fortune; but I do want much, very much,
my peace of mind. I cannot accuse myself of selfishness in this,
for I have served during the whole revolution. A third of my
life remains to me and I wish to live it. . . . I want nothing
for myself—nothing, absolutely nothing. You, who know me,
and the others who ought to know me, will do me this justice.

The idea of a crown for the Liberator was spreading
in Venezuela as well; and María Antonia wrote him, even
before the victories in Perú:

Divine Providence, which has always protected and watched
over you, has made you superior to everything; and men will
see that, having won so many great triumphs with your sword,
you will retire to your home and be only a good citizen, mock-
ing those who foster ambitions, scepters and crowns. This I
believe and hope of your great soul; for not only North
America has produced great men like Washington.

During this period in Lima, while he was so busy with
all his projects for bringing order out of chaos, he was in
constant correspondence with the sister in Caracas who
held him in such high regard. He gave advice for the
education of all the children and was particularly interested in young Fernando, his dead brother's son, whom
he had adopted and sent to the University of Virginia.
He had great hopes for Fernando and inquired about the
conditions he found at the school, the curriculum, the
abilities of the professors, the grades the boy was making
and if the money he sent was sufficient. He was anxious
to dispose of his last remaining property, the mines of
Aroa, in order to provide funds for all the people he was
supporting; María Antonia was charged with the task.
A lawsuit arose in the courts of Caracas over the title
and his sister wrote him the details at great length. One of

his letters dealing with the matter said in part, "I will not write to any judge in regard to this suit, as you suggest. I do not wish to exceed the limits of my rights. . . . Fate has placed me at the pinnacle of power but I want no other rights than those of the most humble citizen. . . . I hope that justice will be done and that I will be given what is mine. If not, I will accept without protest the decision of the tribunals." In this attitude, Bolívar showed himself far superior to others in authority, who almost without exception placed their kinsmen in high government positions and availed themselves of every personal advantage their powers allowed.

He was greatly interested, too, in the marriages of his nieces. His old and loyal friend Briceño Méndez, who had been in love with the beautiful Benigna ever since the days of Angostura, apparently hadn't got on well with his suit. Bolívar came to his rescue, urging María Antonia to use her influence with the girl's mother. "Tell Juana," he wrote, "that Benigna should marry Briceño, who is going there for that purpose. He is the best man in the world and I shall love him above all my nephews." His efforts bore fruit quickly. Within a few months he had word of the impending marriage. He wrote to Briceño, expressing his great delight and deploring the fact that he couldn't send them any money. "I haven't a peso," he wrote. "Will you believe me, I gave away 20,000 pesos this year? In this same post I am sending 10,000 pesos to two persons who are in want and to whom I owe debts of gratitude."

About this time, too, he had news of another old friend —Simón Rodríguez, the eccentric tutor of his youth, the apostle of Thomas Paine and Rousseau, who had wandered through Europe with him and who had inspired his famous oath on a Roman hill. Rodríguez had appeared in Bogotá out of nowhere, after all these years. Bolívar at once wrote him a letter of impetuous warmth. "You shaped my heart," he said, "for liberty, for justice, for everything that is great and beautiful. I have followed

the path you showed me. . . . I long to know what plans
you have for everything. . . . Since I cannot come to
you, you must come to me. You will lose nothing by it."
Rodríguez came to Lima, as tattered as ever and even
more eccentric.

By the middle of April, 1825, things were pretty well
organized in Lima, and Bolívar was anxious to join Sucre
in Alto Perú and establish a government there. He left
on the fourteenth, taking Manuela, O'Leary, Rodríguez
and a large staff with him.

He had experienced the acclaim of grateful people
many times before, but nothing to compare in lavishness
and enthusiasm with the homage that met him in his last
journey through the land of the Incas. At every village
the poor Indians and the wealthy lords came out for miles
to ride in with him and strew his path with flowers. There
has never been another such march in the history of
America. At Arequipa he was given a horse whose trappings were decorated with solid gold. At Cuzco a thousand
ladies gave him a gold wreath set with pearls and diamonds. There he received word that the assembly of Alto
Perú, which had met at Chuquisaca at his orders under
the authority of Sucre, had, on August 6, 1825, declared
the province an independent nation and adopted the
name, República Bolívar. Bolívar was decreed the Father
of the Republic and the Supreme Chief of State. He sent
a messenger to convey his gratitude and his refusal to
accept the executive office, naming Sucre in his place.
Thus what is now the Republic of Bolivia was created and
Sucre was its first president. The name of its capital city
later was changed from Chuquisaca to Sucre.

Continuing his journey he entered La Paz and was
given another jeweled wreath. This one he sent to Sucre,
saying, "He is the conqueror of Ayacucho and the true
Liberator of Perú."

At every town he studied local problems, conferred with

merchants, farmers and miners, discussed plans for improving conditions and established schools.

The city of Potosí had spent six weeks in preparing his reception. General Miller, whom Bolívar had appointed as governor of the province, had employed two hundred Indians to build arches and plant trees along the road. As the Liberator approached over the barren plain, twelve thousand feet above sea level, painted and feathered Indians danced beside him and the city officials, dressed in robes of office and carrying gilded staffs, met him with the keys to the city. As he entered the plaza bombs burst and the flags of all the liberated nations were unfurled to the breeze. At the great arch before the government palace, two children, dressed as angels, were lowered and showered him with flowers. Six women bore a laurel wreath that was placed on his head. General Miller, writing of the occasion, says in his memoirs:

In extemporaneous speech Bolívar had no equal. In a single day I heard him reply to seventeen successive harangues, with the most marvelous propriety and with a coloring of which I can give not the slightest idea. What liveliness of imagination, poetic imagery, grace, ease, and surprising turns! In proposing a toast, in returning thanks or in speaking on any subject, Bolívar is unsurpassed.

On December 9, the first anniversary of the Battle of Ayacucho, he was with Sucre in Chuquisaca. There both he and Sucre were presented with silver caskets containing swords, scabbards and uniforms. The uniforms were encrusted with jewels, heavily embroidered with pure gold thread, and all the buttons were of solid gold, beautifully chased with laurel designs and initials. The hats were draped with gold lace and had cockades of white plumes. The swords and scabbards, hand-wrought in the most elaborate and expert workmanship of the Incas, were jeweled and the hilts were of solid gold. They were set with 1433 diamonds, large and small, weighing 73 carats in all. All the honors that were heaped on them in that far Andean city were on an equal scale of lavishness.

The next day Bolívar received a letter from Páez, bringing disturbing news from Venezuela. Conditions were very bad there. Páez, in a disguised but perfectly obvious way, suggested that the only solution was for Bolívar to crown himself king. "The situation," Páez said in the letter, "in this country is very similar to that of France when Napoleon was away in Egypt and was recalled by the leaders of revolution who were convinced that a government which had fallen into the hands of the rabble would not survive; and you are in a position to say what that great man said then, 'The conspirators endanger the existence of the nation; let us save it.' "

The Liberator knew then that he must hurry back to the northern countries or everything he had accomplished would be destroyed. He left the capital of Bolivia on January 6, 1826, arrived at Tacna on the coast four days later, sailed for Lima and arrived there on February 10. He was anxious to provide these southern nations with a constitution before leaving them.

He had left Rodríguez in Bolivia as head of the school system. The old scholar failed miserably in his task. With the years his eccentricities had grown and his mind had weakened. He horrified the people by appearing before his classes stark naked, trying to impress upon the children the glories of an existence in complete harmony with nature. In no time at all he dissipated all the funds allowed him in fantastic experiments and innovations, and soon left, to wander the face of the earth once more.

V: LAURELS, NOT A CROWN

Chapter XXVI

THE PINNACLE

✤

H E had achieved now, surely, all the glory that any man could want; but still he was dissatisfied. This glory he enjoyed now, the acclaim that fell upon him with it, he regarded merely as a transitory thing, the result of his feats of arms alone and not of the noble purposes behind them which he was unable to make the people see. His great hunger was for a glory that would last through the centuries after he was dead, that would reach to the far corners of the earth; and the things that were happening now in the nations he had created gravely threatened the fulfillment of that dream.

In answer to the letter of Páez, he wrote a stern reply. "Colombia is not France," he said, "nor I, Napoleon. . . . The title of Liberator is superior to every other that human pride has conceived; it is unthinkable that I should degrade it."

From other sources, too, he learned of the chaotic conditions that existed in Venezuela. The old forces were at work, the jealousies among the officers, the clamoring of the people for a strong hand to guide them. Páez was strong but not strong enough. He thought only of his little "patrecita," his llano homeland. As President of the nation, treating with foreign diplomats, the old vaquero succumbed to the influences of "culture," became avaricious and grew rich from his misuse of public funds. From Soublette came word that conditions alarmed him, that Páez and Mariño were committing abominations. Under their rule, he said, nothing moved smoothly in accordance with the law. There were no taxes organized, "nothing to give strength to our forces. . . . They know that you are in Perú and are wasting no time."

María Antonia wrote him a loving but disturbing letter:

I shall rejoice on the day that you come here with troops. . . . This land has grave need for your presence. There are a thousand abuses and political factions; but the moment you arrive all will disappear. Now they are sending a commission to you to propose a crown. Receive it as the infamous proposition deserves; and try, without resorting to the methods of Europe, to bring an end to this miserable existence at the hands of factions. Say always, as you said in Cumaná in 1814, that you "will be Liberator or dead." That is your true title, the one which has elevated you above other great men and which will preserve for you the glories you have attained at the cost of so many sacrifices. Detest all who propose a crown to you, for that will procure your ruin. Remember Bonaparte and Iturbide and the many others you are not ignorant of. I am well satisfied with your mode of thought and I believe you incapable of such things; but I can do no less than declare to you the sentiments of my heart out of the interest I have in your happiness. . . . Will you come quickly? How shall I prepare for you and for the troops you will bring? Here there is nothing, nothing. . . . Shall I prepare a house, and which shall it be—mine, yours or another?

She signed the letter, "Yours, who loves you and desires your happiness." A postscript reveals her nature still more. "Send a passport for that old man, Juan Esteban Echezuras, who is eighty and ill. Don't forget. Also, send me a picture of yourself, for I have none."

New Granada, too, was in a frightful state. Only the personal prestige of Bolívar, exerting its influence even at this great distance, and the unfailing ability and resourcefulness of Santander, saved it from complete anarchy. Overrun with unscrupulous generals—those ignorant men who had been elevated out of necessity on the merits of bravery alone in the early days of the war—the rights of the people were sadly abused. The treasury was empty. Gambling was a universal vice among government officials, and the generals dissipated the public funds.

Anxious as he was to return to the northern countries and set things right, he remained in Lima, working furiously on the constitution which he hoped to have adopted by the Congresses of Bolivia and Perú.

There were a few things, however, that brought him great consolation. On the first of January, 1825, Great Britain had followed the example of the United States and recognized the government of Colombia. Early in 1826 there came to him, through Lafayette, a gift from George Washington Parke Custis, the adopted son of George Washington. It was a gold medallion containing a lock of Washington's hair and bearing a miniature portrait by Stuart. Engraved in Latin were the words, "This portrait of the author of liberty in North America was donated by his adopted son to him who achieved equal glory in South America." The letter from Lafayette, accompanying the gift, read, "My devotion to General Washington could not be better recognized by his family than by honoring me with this commission. . . . Of all men living and even of all men in history, Bolívar is the one to whom Washington would have preferred to send this present. What else can I say to the great citizen whom South America has honored with the title of Liberator, a title that has been confirmed by two hemispheres, a man endowed with a prestige equal to his disinterest, who carries in his heart only the love of freedom and of the republic?"

Bolívar was deeply moved by the honor. He replied to Lafayette, "Words cannot express the appreciation of my heart for this gift. . . . The family of Washington honors me beyond my greatest dreams, for this medal, presented by Lafayette, is the highest of all human rewards. . . ." He wore the medallion around his neck always from then

on and he ordered that every portrait of him show it on
his breast. It has been preserved by the government of
Venezuela in the Bolívar Museum in Caracas.

In studying the voluminous correspondence of Bolívar,
covering such an enormous field of interests and events
throughout the world, one becomes increasingly impressed
with the difficulties of communication of the era and
wonders how anything was ever accomplished with any
sort of timeliness—how contact was maintained between
the various provincial governments, how co-operation was
arranged between army divisions, rendezvous kept, supplies and reinforcements dispatched to reach their destina-
tions at the moment of need. The degree of forethought
and study that these problems required was enormous.
Bolívar and all his subordinates had to consider constantly
not only what the situation was today, but envision as
well what it would be next month or the month after or
six months hence—and to act now in accordance with that
projected picture. Yet, during the whole career of the
Liberator, operations reveal a remarkable adherence to
schedule, a high degree of efficient timing. Very few military or political actions failed because of unforeseen de-
lays. In those countries, in those times, even the shortest
journey, the march of an army or the dispatch of a single
messenger, required the study of innumerable factors—
the time of year, with the accompanying weather conditions, the state of the trails and streams to be crossed, the
clothing and equipment needed, the means for sustenance
along the route as well as the political temper of the inhabitants.

The time elapsing between the writing of a letter and
its receipt was often a matter of many months. The crow-
flight distance between Caracas and Lima, for instance, is
close to 1800 miles; but a communication sent from one
to the other traveled, in those days, nearly 2800. From
Caracas there were two post routes. One was overland by

pack train across the Andes to Bogotá, down to the Pacific coast to the port of Buenaventura, south to Callao by sailing vessel. The other route was by way of Panamá, from La Guaira by sea to Colón, overland across the Isthmus to Panamá, again south to Callao by sailing vessel, bucking the Humboldt Current. It is difficult for the mind of a modern man to conceive the vastly different mental traits and temperaments developed in the people by such conditions—the unlimited patience, the amazing capacity for retaining a composite and detailed picture of events over wide periods of time. He can only be astonished that they accomplished the things they did.

A French admiral, Rosamel, paying Bolívar an official visit in Lima, was astounded at his knowledge of European affairs and found him possessed of information which he himself had supposed were diplomatic secrets of cabinet officers. One of his staff, Van Dokum, said afterwards that he had never before seen the force of intellectual superiority so clearly portrayed and that he felt an almost irresistible desire to bow in veneration before the Liberator.

The constitution which Bolívar wrote in Lima was almost identical with the ones which had been rejected by the Congresses of Angostura and Colombia. His ideas of government for South American countries had never changed. It was again a code based somewhat upon the British system and it contained all his old ideas of life-term president, hereditary senate and a college of censors. The president was to have great powers but could deprive no citizen of freedom or property. It provided for civil liberty, personal security, equality before the law, freedom of speech, press, work and movement. It abolished slavery, prescribed justice through jury and oath and warrant for arrest. The distinguished Venezuelan jurist and historian, Gil Fortoul, says of the Bolivarian Constitution: "Without departing from the sphere of theory . . . it can be affirmed that the constitutional projects of Bolívar, those of Angostura and of Lima, are the most notable philo-

sophic-political speculations of South American history."
Parra-Pérez called it the most liberal constitution in the
world. "Bolívar tried," he says, "to make us gain a hundred and fifty years of history."

When the work was finished Bolívar sent it to Chuquisaca by Ferguson and young Belford Wilson. These
two Englishmen made a notable march across the higher
Andes, a distance of 1800 miles, accomplished in nineteen
days. The Congress of Bolivia adopted the constitution
almost in its entirety and elected Sucre President. He,
however, declined the life term and agreed to hold the
office provisionally for only two years.

In Perú, the political leaders and the people as well
were confounded by the Liberator's determination to
leave the country. Ambitious, scheming and opposed to
his liberal principles as the officials were, they knew that
his influence alone saved them from each other and the
nation from anarchy. They used every device to induce
Bolívar to stay and occupy the executive position. When
the Congress met they adopted his constitution, hoping
to win him over, and named him the first constitutional
president. He was firm, however, refused the office and
Santa Cruz was finally selected to fill it.

To the many critics of the Bolívar Constitution who
characterize it as impractical, visionary, or, as Santander
said, "absurd, a dangerous novelty," the only answer can
be that it never was tried. Perhaps it was all those things;
but no nation ever lived under it, so there is no conclusive proof for anything. In a very short time Sucre's government in Bolivia fell; and within a year after Bolívar
left Perú a revolution broke out there, too, and his constitution was abolished.

Fortoul says, "The destiny of the Bolivarian Constitution was the same as almost all the others of Hispano-
America; it ended in tumult, being replaced by another
that proved inferior in its writing as well as in its efficacy."

Meanwhile, Bolívar's private worries went on. Manuela was alternately a joy and a trial to him. Her escapades sometimes scandalized his nature, grown austere with the years of responsibility, and he had to appeal to his aides. "Do something with her, will you?" he begged young General Córdova. "She's such an idiot. You know her as well as I do." And gradually her hold on him grew tighter, his need for her stronger. Fighting instinctively against the temptation to yield completely to her, he left her or sent her away time and again, only to fly to her once more or call her back. With her he was happy but torn by his struggle against her insidious charm; away from her he was restless, discontented, irritable. After only a few days of such separation he would weaken and write her thus: "Your delightful letters have consoled me and the expression of your affection is my only pleasure in your absence. . . . At the end of this month I am going there without fail. Wait for me at all cost. Have you heard? Have you understood??? If not, you are perfidious, an ingrate and, what's more, an enemy. Your lover, BOLÍVAR."

From María Antonia came word of family troubles, too. Her eldest son, Anacleto, was proving himself a profligate, a perfect rotter. He had gone to Bogotá, leaving his wife and children destitute. There he had created public scandal, brought shame to the illustrious name of Bolívar and had got into political trouble with a group of French spies. María Antonia had paid 1200 pesos of his gambling debts and he owed 8000 more. "Look," she wrote, "what a famous child we have!"

Bolívar sent the erring youth a scathing letter.

It pains me to be forced to address thus one to whom I have always written so affectionately. I am tired of hearing the complaints of your mother and family. If you cannot provide for that family, at least you needn't discredit it as you are doing in Bogotá. I tell you for the last time, if you don't leave Bogotá at once and give up these vices, I shall disinherit you. Your infamous conduct is a shame to you and your family, depriving your poor mother of sums a potentate doesn't spend, abandoning your wife, disgracing your country, honor, family and blood. Is this the reward you give to me who sent you to Europe to be educated, to your mother for trying to make you a good man? Doesn't it shame you to see poor, uneducated llaneros who have had no schooling but that of war become gentlemen and good citizens and learn to respect themselves, solely out of respect for me? Doesn't it shame you, considering that you are my nephew, having for a mother a woman of the finest character, to be inferior to so many poor guerillas who have no other family than the fatherland?

Manuela, away from her lover once more, conceived a trick to teach him a lesson. She wrote that she was considering a trip to London with Dr. Thorne. Bolívar answered in high excitement. "You aren't going anywhere!" he said. "I want to see you and adore you and touch you and feel you and savor you and unite myself to you by every sort of contact. Can it be that you don't love as much as I? . . . I'll teach you to love and you won't go away, not even with God himself!!!" Manuela, understandably, came running.

Conditions in Venezuela were growing steadily worse. The regionalism of the New Granadans and the resentment of the Venezuelan caudillos, the little generals, against the educated and cultured officials from the other half of the republic were creating a hatred between the two peoples. An outright rupture was fast approaching. Páez wrote to Bolívar, complaining of Santander; and Santander accused Páez before the Colombian Congress of insubordination and had him relieved of his office. Though he made every outward effort to preserve the Union of Colombia, Santander, opposed to it underneath, found considerable satisfaction in the trend of events.

When Bolívar wrote him, asking for details, he answered with the statement that the reports were exaggerated, that everything had been smoothed over and that the Liberator's presence wasn't necessary.

But Bolívar wasn't fooled. He was determined to go and see for himself.

As the day for his departure grew near, the people of Lima became frantic in their appeals to him to stay. A few days before the date he had announced for his sailing, the whole population of the city swarmed out to the Villa Magdalena, shouting his name, carrying banners and accompanied by bands. They gave him a great banquet, served out of doors, and the ablest orators pled with him, crying that he was tramping on their hearts and destroying the life he had given them. He replied, expressing his gratitude and explaining that Colombia needed him more than they. "I shall return to Lima," he said, "at least by September of next year to install a new Congress, elected under the Constitution. . . . This will be the end of all my work; and if not, I shall give up the race." Then the women tried their hands. A group of the most beautiful of all those beautiful women of Lima used their blandishments upon him. But even this failed to shake his determination.

On September 4, 1826, Bolívar sailed from Callao northward. His last words to the people were, "Beware the horrors of anarchy." He was never to see that city again, the city that had witnessed the peak of his glory and the beginning of his downfall. As the great Uruguayan writer Rodó said, "Whatever remains of that life is sorrow."

He was in a hurry and he left Manuela behind. He landed in Guayaquil, the southernmost port of Colombia, on September 12 and there he learned of the failure of the Pan American Congress that had convened in Panamá. He smiled sadly at the news and said to his aides, "I am like the crazy Greek who stood on a rocky headland and tried to direct the vessels that sailed around it."

About this time, too, he received, after all these years, a letter from Fanny Villars, who was then fifty-one years old:

Twenty-one years ago today you left Paris. . . . Now, in Europe, all the world proclaims you the first man of the century. . . . Do you remember the tears I shed, how I begged you not to go away? Your will resisted all my entreaties. The love of glory had already possessed you and you belonged to us only superficially, concealing your real purpose, which only time has brought to light.

I remember with pride the confidences you made me about your plans for the future, the sublimity of your thoughts and your exalted feeling for liberty. I had some value at that time, for you found me worthy of your secrets. Your determination to leave wounded me profoundly but today your resolution raises you in my estimation and I place you easily above all men.

I have had, and still have, confidence that you love me sincerely and that in your moments of triumph as well as of danger you knew that Fanny's thoughts were upon you and were invoking Divine Providence to watch over you. . . .

Goodbye, dear friend. I love you. . . . It is not impossible that this is farewell forever; only God and yourself can know that.

Keep my picture. It will be happier than I because, sending it to you, I cannot put my soul into its face. If I could, perhaps you would forget my years.

With his aides and a few soldiers, Bolívar began once more that long and difficult journey along the Andean Cordillera, between the shining, marching peaks. He traveled fast, but now it was an effort for him. The great energy and capacity for endurance which he had expended so freely were beginning to fail him at last. He felt tired now, like other men, after a day in the saddle. In constant pain from his hemorrhoids, he had to drive himself every inch of the way. His old fevers recurred more and more frequently, his body was bathed in sweat at night. Nevertheless, the journey of 500 miles to Bogotá was made in twenty-one days.

Quito, the capital of the southern province of Colombia, had been a hive of political dissension and corruption. With Bolívar's arrival, all disorder disappeared like clouds before the sun. The people forgot their differences and joined in universal acclaim for their Liberator, the leaders came forward and begged for his forgiveness. Addressing them, he said, "I do not even want to know who is at fault. I have never forgotten that you are all my brothers and my comrades-in-arms. . . . Let there be no more regionalism, no more Cundinamarca, no more Venezuela. Let us all be Colombians—or death will cover the deserts left by anarchy." They urged him to remain there and be their dictator. He told them, "I never want to hear the word dictator."

Everywhere it was the same—every village and provincial capital. Cheering crowds, honors, entreaties. Everywhere the dissensions disappeared, rivalries were forgotten. He traversed those mountain valleys like a cleansing ray. But behind him the clouds closed in again almost at once.

Near Bogotá, Santander and the members of the cabinet waited to meet him. On the night of November 14, 1826, Bolívar entered the capital of Colombia after five years' absence. It was pouring rain and only a few people huddled in the doorways. The horses' hoofs clattered on the cobbles and echoed among the dark and empty streets with a dismal melancholy. There were a few banners and arches here and there, but the words they bore were not "Viva El Libertador!" but "Viva la Constitucion!"

Santander had succeeded well in his efforts to convince the people that Bolívar was the enemy of the present Colombian Code and he its champion. Bolívar, tired and ill, didn't care at the moment.

Chapter XXVII

"EVERYTHING FOR GLORY"

❖

BUT even there in Bogotá, where Santander had done so much to undermine his prestige, the old magic charm began at once to do its work. The mere presence of the Liberator in their midst created a stir in the people's hearts. Something went into them like an electric charge and brought the old veneration surging out. Underneath, the common people and the soldiers always, then and after, idolized him.

The change of climate had a good effect on his health. His strength came back and with it some of his old vigor and a renewed will to accomplish the stabilization of the nations he had created. His speeches and proclamations began once more and in only a few days the capital was his, heart and soul—the Congress, the army, the ministers. The foreign representatives, who had always disliked Santander personally and distrusted him politically, were impressed at once by Bolívar, were charmed by his distinguished manners and wrote favorable accounts of him to their governments.

He was ready to make any sacrifice to hold the union together. To Páez he wrote, "Believe me, I do not attempt, nor shall I ever attempt, to make one party triumph over another. I shall not oppose federation; still less shall I demand that the Bolivarian Constitution be adopted. I only want to insure that the citizens are united, that liberty will leave them free to work, that wisdom guides them; and then that they may accept my resignation and let me go far, far away from Colombia."

320

Santander had succeeded in convincing the Congress that Bolívar was opposed to the existing Constitution and intended to force acceptance of his own, an idea which held a degree of truth; and he had also convinced his ministers that the Liberator was determined to foist upon them a monarchy—in which there was no truth at all. Santander had even signed, with his ministers, a manifesto declaring belief in the latter idea and expressing violent opposition. But Bolívar's statements put a quick end to all that. Santander watched with dismay while his own prestige and all the political sentiment he had built up in five years of constant effort dissolved into nothing.

Bolívar once more assumed supreme military and civil powers. He exercised them for only two days—two days of strenuous labor in which he reduced the national budget to conform with income, consolidated and reorganized governmental agencies and made great changes in the army set-up.

All this took place in eleven days' time—the extent of his stay in Bogotá. On November 25 he was in the saddle once more, headed for Venezuela to settle matters with Páez.

The situation in his native land had grown constantly worse and he saw that the fate of all his efforts depended upon his own immediate action. When he had left Venezuela, leaving Páez, Mariño and Bermúdez in command of the three military districts, he had said, "I fear peace more than war"; and his fears had been well founded.

Páez, from the first, had shown his antagonism to the central government in Bogotá—that capital so far away across the Andes—and had assumed privileges and powers beyond his legal authority, coming finally to open defiance. Ambitious, avaricious and dictatorial as he had become, the old llanero was still "an innocent child" at heart; and it must be said in his favor that his actions were mainly the result of the conniving of Mariño, that old enemy of

Bolívar's, and his followers. They urged Páez on, used
the doughty warrior, the none-too-brilliant administrator,
as a dupe to further their own aims. Páez always harbored
a strong personal loyalty to Bolívar; but he sincerely opposed, along with a large faction of the Venezuelan people,
the union with New Granada for which Bolívar fought
so hard. To him and to many Venezuelans, New Granada
was a foreign nation with which they, as people and as a
political entity, had nothing in common.

When Santander accused Páez before the Colombian
Congress and secured an order relieving him of his command and demanding that he appear to answer a charge
of insubordination, the llanero left Caracas and retired
to Valencia in a huff. There Mariño and his followers
whispered in his ear, worked upon his pride and flattered
his ego. An assembly of sorts was set up which declared
against the authority of the Colombian government,
named Páez Supreme Military and Civil Chief and provided for the election of an independent Venezuelan Congress to meet in Valencia the following year. Páez concurred in everything, accepted the position and made a
trip into his beloved llanos to raise an army. Arismendi
and Bermúdez, though they had both intrigued against
Bolívar in the past, were loyal to him now and, in their
separate posts in other parts of the country, declared
whole-heartedly against Páez. Urdaneta, that always loyal
comrade of Bolívar's and veteran of all the early campaigns, prepared to go into action with his troops in
Bolívar's name. There were armed uprisings in Puerto
Cabello, in Cumaná and in Valencia, and patriot blood
was spilled. The government in Caracas, hoping to prevent anarchy throughout the nation, confirmed Páez in
his dictatorship. That was the situation which existed as
Bolívar hurried eastward from Bogotá.

Once more that long, hard journey over the Andean
trails, the scene of so many of his early battles. He had
sent O'Leary ahead to announce his coming and, after

crossing the Venezuelan frontier, he issued proclamations
to the citizens.

Venezuelans!
Already you have stained your glory with the crime of
fratricide. Is this the crown you wish to put upon all your
deeds of valor? Hide your arms; do not destroy the fatherland.
Listen to the voice of your brother and comrade. . . . I pledge
you my word, I solemnly promise to call the people together,
to deliberate with calmness upon their welfare and their sovereignty. . . . The people shall decree their fundamental
laws . . . they shall be masters of their destiny. Not one
powerful man, not a party nor faction, nothing but the will
of the people is sovereign. . . . Venezuelans! I come to you
to put myself between your swords and your hearts. I would
die rather than see you in ignominy, which is worse even than
tyranny. . . . Unhappy those who do not heed my words,
who do not do their duty.

Páez, in the face of the Liberator's coming, flew frantically from one attitude to another like the proverbial
headless rooster. At first he considered resisting and even
took steps to send a force to stop Bolívar at the border;
but he abandoned that project when he saw the sentiment
that was growing among the people. The old spell of the
Liberator was having its effect, even before he entered the
country. The word of his coming spread like wildfire
through the whole nation and everywhere the people began to sing his praises. He had been away nearly six years.
It was time enough to make him a legend. The memory
of his great deeds at arms, his political accomplishments,
his virtues and his wisdom had grown into fabulous tales
told by men to their growing children. His words, repeated a thousand times by the poets of an imaginative
race, had been embellished even beyond their true gran-
diloquence and were spoken with reverence like the words
of a prophet. Accounts of his victories in the far-off and

fabulous land of the Incas had come to them like heroic tales from the age of chivalry.

Páez found the ground cut out from under him. Even his llanero troops were singing the praises of the great man, the old "Iron Arse," who was coming to put things right for his brave ones.

Páez decided upon the opposite tack. From Valencia he issued a proclamation to the people, welcoming the Liberator and promulgating the fiction that he was coming to the aid of Páez himself, to help him with the problems of the country; coming, he put it, "as a simple citizen." "All our troubles are over," the proclamation stated. "The Liberator, from the center of Perú, heard our clamors and has flown to our aid. . . . He comes for our happiness—not to destroy the civil and military authority that I have received from the people, but to aid us with his counsel, with his wisdom and experience; to perfect the work of our reforms. . . . Venezuelans! Forget your troubles: The Great Bolívar is with us."

The Great Bolívar had come from Colombia without any troops at all; but in Maracaibo he took command of the forces of Urdaneta and led them in his march toward Valencia. He was resolved to avoid bloodshed if possible, but he had to be prepared for anything; and he was determined to save his union at any cost.

Páez's new move failed also. It brought from Bolívar a stern rebuke. From Coro he wrote:

. . . I shudder when I think, as I am always thinking, of the horrible calamity that endangers Colombia. I see clearly our work destroyed and the maledictions of the centuries falling on our heads as perverse authors of such lamentable mutations. . . .

Your proclamation says that I am "coming as a simple citizen." And what could I do as a citizen? Who has dissolved the laws of Colombia? . . . Who shall tear the reins from my hands? Yourself! Your friends! The infamy would be a thousand times greater for the ingratitude than for its treason. I cannot believe it. I shall never believe that you carry the ambitions of your friends and the dishonor of your name to this point. It is not possible, General, that you want to see me humiliated for the sake of a handful of deserters whom we have never seen in battle. . . . What do not all owe me in Venezuela? Do not even you owe me your existence?

. . . I have come from Perú to spare you the crime of civil war. I have come that Caracas and Venezuela may not stain themselves with precious blood. And you want me to come without any legal authority? . . . There is no other legitimate authority in Venezuela but mine. I mean supreme authority. . . . You have your command from municipalities, born from three assassinations. There is nothing glorious in this, my dear general.

. . . I want to set myself right. I want to know if you obey me or not and if my patria recognizes me as its chief. May God forbid that my authority is questioned on my own hearth. . . . I will yield everything for glory; but I will also combat everything for it. . . .

Dear General, you will be everything to me, everything, everything. I want nothing for myself. Thus you will be everything, without taking it at the cost of my glory, which has been founded on duty and public good. . . . Be assured of the affection with which I love you from my heart.

The old llanero was again confounded, racking his thick head in Valencia; and meanwhile Bolívar was coming nearer and nearer to force a show-down. Then, on January 1, 1827, Bolívar issued a statement from Puerto Cabello which completely mollified Páez. Amnesty, Bolívar declared, was granted to all concerned in the defection of General Páez, no punishments whatever would be exacted and the General's authority in Venezuela was recognized by the Colombian government through him, its authorized spokesman. It was an astute and politic move—though the Colombian government censured him for it when they heard of it. So great was the relief of Páez that he recognized Bolívar at once as President of Venezuela and ordered that he be given a triumphal entry into Caracas; and then he hurried down the road to Puerto Cabello to meet him in person.

Bolívar was vastly relieved, too, at the peaceful solution. He issued a proclamation to the Colombians that law and order had returned to the Republic, that there were no more domestic enemies, that all were brothers once more. To the Venezuelans he declared that the dominion of evil had ceased. "Let us bury," he said, "in the abyss of time the year 1826. . . . Let it be lost forever in utter darkness. I do not know anything that has happened."

The two old comrades of another day met on the road to Valencia and embraced—Bolívar smiling, loquacious, Páez hanging his great head like a guilty schoolboy. The hilts of their swords became entangled and Bolívar said, laughing, "It is a good omen for the future, General." Together they rode to Valencia and then to Caracas.

For the third and last time the Liberator entered his native city in triumph. Progress had touched the old capital a little and there was a coach for him this time, lent by its owner, a North American named Jacob Idler. The two great heroes rode bareheaded, side by side, through the familiar streets. The coach could hardly move for the throngs that jammed the way and clung to its sides. The bells clamored, the cannon roared, the flowers drifted down from the windows. Bolívar raised his fine and delicate hand in acknowledgment, smiled his mechanical, actor's smile. From balconies old señoras peered intently at the face they hadn't seen for so many years. They found it changed, deep-lined and weary, marked with sadness. The graying hair was still thick and carefully arranged, the teeth still glistening white; but the eyes were sunken deep among lines of suffering and they didn't answer the smile of his lips. Young people ran beside the coach to glimpse the living face of the hero of all those tales they had heard in childhood.

At a banquet held several days after his arrival Bolívar made one of his characteristic dramatic gestures. Taking from his waist the gold and bejeweled sword that had been given him in the capital of Bolivia, he presented it to Páez. The old warrior was completely undone. He wiped the tears from his eyes with his pudgy hand. Then, with his newly acquired and grandiose rhetoric, he tried to speak through the emotion that choked him. Bolívar, he said, was the first-born of fortune, the creator of three republics, the genius of war and peace who came from the Temple of the Sun, armed with an olive branch, to restore life to the fatherland. "He has given me the sword which has liberated a world. . . . How can I preserve its laurels, its glory, its honor? It demands of me strength which only Bolívar possesses. It bewilders me. The redeeming sword of humanity!" He babbled on almost incoherently. "In my hands this sword shall never be other than Bolívar's. His will shall direct it, my arm shall carry it. I shall perish a hundred times and all my blood shall be spilled before it shall leave my hands or ever attempt to shed the blood it has liberated. . . . Bolívar's sword is in my hands. . . . For him I will go with it to eternity."

For all the honors that were heaped upon him, the easy success of his mission and the joy of being with his sisters and kinsmen and his old nurses, Hipólita and Matea, once more, his stay in Caracas was not happy. The old intrigues and dissensions were rife again back in New Granada and the southern countries, just as they had been in Venezuela during his absence. His partisans there were clamoring for him to return, just as the Venezuelans had clamored. He was like a lone man trying to save a great dam that was crumbling fast. No sooner had he stopped a breach in one place than another opened somewhere else —and the distances between them were hundreds of miles.

He was tired and he wanted to rest for a while, to enjoy the company of his family and relax under the loving care of old Hipólita; but his conscience gnawed at him, the old dream refused to die.

He interested himself with the affairs of his properties and his family. From Fernando, at the University of Virginia, came a letter telling of the good grades he had received; and Bolívar wrote him at length, congratulating him and urging him to study still harder.

Felicia, Fernando's sister, the second of the illegitimate children of Juan Vicente whom Bolívar had adopted, was of marriageable age. For a long time General Laurencio Silva, an officer who had fought bravely with Bolívar in his southern campaigns, had been suing for the girl's hand. Silva was a mulatto. Felicia, though a bastard, was proud of her blood and the idea of marriage to Silva was abhorrent to her. Bolívar belittled her objections and urged that she take the mulatto for her husband. He knew Silva's qualities and admired him as a man; but his motives may have been political as well, for he had long believed in the fusion of races, the ultimate development of a South American racial type, a type which would be the hope of the future. He wished to break down as soon as possible the old racial pride and create a homogeneous people combining the intelligence of the Spaniards with the rugged strength of the more primitive races. He felt that an example of mixed union in the family of the country's greatest man would set a good example. Felicia firmly resisted his will; but his determination grew stronger and in the end he forced her with an outright command, threatening to disinherit her. It was one of the few cruel acts of his life. He didn't see it that way, of course. It was the custom of the times for parents to arrange the marriages of their children without consulting their desires at all; and, as head of the Bolívar clan and the girl's foster father, he was entirely within his rights. The matador must dominate the bull, man must dominate woman. Eventually Felicia yielded, and the marriage took place.

Her letter to him, in which she consented to do his bidding, is worthy of reproduction here, in part.

. . . Only the affection and respect which I profess for you induces me to do what you wish. From the year of '14 till the year '21 [the period of the Spanish occupation] I had no other protector than the Supreme Being and I am convinced that He will never desert me. Yes, my Uncle Simón, in this thing, in which I give you the greatest proof of my love, I shall tear from my heart the just resentment against you which your unmerited threat has created. I hope that you will never again give me cause to revive it. . . . I shall correct this fault by submission to your will in everything.

Many years after, when Felicia was an old woman and had borne Silva many children, her grandson said to her, "Where is my Uncle Simón—in Heaven?" The woman replied, "No, child, he is in hell, for having made me marry this negro."

Santander had made the most of the resentment of the Colombian government caused by Bolívar's reconciliation with Páez which killed the charges against the Venezuelan leader. He bent every effort to rebuild his prestige and to establish himself again as "the man of laws" and Bolívar as the enemy of legality. With government money he subsidized a newspaper, *El Conductor,* and through its editor attacked Bolívar openly. Copies of the paper were distributed free among all the provinces. Meanwhile, Santander's letters to the Liberator were full of expressions of loyalty and deep injury over the rumors that were being spread about his activities. But Bolívar wasn't fooled —he had his own sources of information. Nevertheless, he too pretended, for political reasons, to the fiction that all was well between them.

Then from Lima came news of serious trouble there. A New Granadan officer, José Bustamente, having declared against the Bolivarian Constitution, rose in revolt with the troops of the garrison. In this uprising Manuela Sáenz played a futile but valiant part. She had been in Lima ever since Bolívar's departure. Learning of the impending revolt, she dressed as a soldier, gained entrance to the barracks and tried to persuade the men against Bustamente's project. She was put under arrest and shipped away to Guayaquil. The movement went on.

Santa Cruz gathered his troops and drove Bustamente from the country, but the harm was already done. Sentiment had been crystallized against the Constitution—which had never pleased the Peruvians anyway—and it was abandoned. Only six months before, Bolívar had left them with their great lamentations ringing in his ears. Bustamente landed in Guayaquil with some of his followers and there, too, he turned the local government against Bolívar, accusing him of "atrocious conduct." The loyal Colombian Generals Mosquera and Valdez had to flee to the mountains.

Santander was delighted with these doings. When the news reached Bogotá he commanded the bands to play in the streets in celebration, and ordered that Bustamente and all his officers be raised a step in rank.

The foreign diplomats, all on the side of Bolívar, were gravely concerned over the doings in the country their governments had so recently recognized. Through the British plenipotentiary in Caracas, Sir Alexander Cockburn, they reported everything to Bolívar and clamored insistently for his return to Bogotá.

The Liberator was beginning to know hopelessness for the first time in his life. His great optimism was beginning to fail him at last. Sadly, he wrote to Sucre in far-off Bolivia, ". . . I have freed the New World but you cannot say that I have perfected the stability and happiness of one of the nations which compose it. You, my dear friend, are happier than I."

Nevertheless, under the urgent pleading of his friends

he steeled his flagging spirits to another effort. Three months after his arrival in Caracas—it was on July 5, 1827, the anniversary of the Venezuelan Declaration of Independence—he left the city quietly, bound for Bogotá. He sailed with Sir Alexander Cockburn on the British frigate *Druid*. He was never to see his native land again.

Chapter XXVIII

THE PATH LEADS DOWNWARD

✤

IN Bogotá the news of Bolívar's coming threw Santander into the same confusion that had gripped Páez under similar circumstances. The Liberator was bringing soldiers with him. He had landed at Cartagena; and there Mariano Montilla, his old comrade of the early days in Madrid, who had been unswervingly loyal to him since their first dissensions, had greeted him with open arms and turned over his troops for the march to the capital. Now Bolívar was coming up the Magdalena, the scene of his first triumphs, and the people were acclaiming him all along the way. Santander grew more and more apprehensive. He even considered resigning his position and heading an armed revolution; but Soublette managed to talk him out of it. The alarm spread among all the enemies of the Liberator. The editor of *El Conductor* fled the city, and many of the government officials followed his example.

On the tenth of September Bolívar entered Bogotá. He embraced Santander and laughed at his obvious discomfiture. On the same day he was sworn in as President and appeared before the Congress and delivered a lengthy address, explaining all his actions in Venezuela and Perú, defending the expediency of his methods with Páez.

It was the same old story. In the compelling presence of the Liberator all dissension vanished at once, differences were forgotten and the people united once more in his support. There was nothing of fear in that strange surrender. It was the result, in the common people, of a mass hero-worship; in the educated leaders, of their recognition of a superior intelligence, of surrender before the force of a great personality, a tremendous hombría. In them it did not necessarily involve any change of political beliefs.

Word had come from Guayaquil that Bolívar's supporters had combined their forces under Generals Flores and Obando and had delivered a counter-stroke against Bustamente that sent him fleeing back to Perú. The Colombian Congress called for a Great Convention to meet in Ocaña in March of the coming year, to settle for all time the question of a constitution.

Bolívar felt that at last he would have a period of rest. He had missed the companionship of Manuela all these months and he longed for her as he had never longed for anyone before. He wrote to her, "The memory of your enchantments dissolves the frost of my years. Your love revives a life that is expiring. I cannot live without you. . . . I see you always, though I am far away. Come to me. Come, come now. Yours, in soul."

Manuela had been waiting a long time for such a command. To her unfortunate husband, who again begged her to return to him, she wrote a letter that shows more than anything else the kind of woman she was.

No, no, no, never again, por Dios! What do you gain by forcing me to answer . . . no? Señor, you are excellent, you are inimitable—that I shall never deny. But listen, my friend; to leave you for General Bolívar is something; to leave a husband without your qualities would be nothing. Do you think for a moment that I, after being the beloved of this general for seven years and certain still that I possess his heart, would consent to be the wife of the Father, the Son or the Holy Ghost—of the whole Blessed Trinity? I only regret that you are not a still better man, that I should have honored him the more by leaving you. I know very well that I can never be joined to him in what you call honorable love. Well then, Englishman of my heart, I am more honored by being the

mistress of General Bolívar than the wife of any other living
man. I do not worry about the conventions invented by men
for tormenting themselves.

In Heaven you and I shall marry again; but not on this
earth. In Paradise we shall live an angelic, an entirely spiritual life (for, as a man, you are a bit heavy). Everything there
will be in the English manner, for monotony is the exclusive
right of your people (in love, I mean, for none are more enter-
prising in practical things). Their love has no pleasure in it,
their conversation no grace. Their walk is hurried, they get
up and sit down with caution, they do not laugh at their own
jokes. And I, miserable mortal who laugh at myself, at you,
at all this English seriousness, how I shall suffer in Heaven!
Quite as much as though I were to go and live in England
—or Constantinople, perhaps, for the English are tyrants with
women. However, you were never that with me—on the contrary, you were more solicitous than a Portuguese. Am I in
bad taste?

But enough of jokes. Without laughing, with all the sin-
cerity, truth and purity of an Englishwoman, I tell you that
I shall never go back to you again. That you are an Anglican
and I a pagan is the greatest spiritual obstacle; that I am in
love with someone else is a still greater and stronger reason.
You see how exact is my reasoning?

Invariably yours,
MANUELA.

With a small guard of soldiers and her negro maid she
began the long journey north. Traveling rapidly as Bolívar
himself traveled, sleeping in crude native huts or on the
ground on the bleak páramos, she rode to Bogotá to rejoin her lover.

When Bolívar had established the Republic of Colombia
after defeating the Spaniards at Boyacá, the new government had purchased and made him a present of a subur-
ban estate a few miles from Bogotá, called Quinta de
Portocarrero. He always made it his home during his

stays in the capital and he came to love it as he had loved his hacienda at San Mateo, now lying in ruins. Now Manuela came to the quinta to become its mistress.

It was a beautiful home in a beautiful setting. Lying in a green notch between the mountains of Guadalupe and Monserrate, the sharp, crystal sun of tropic highlands tinted its old walls and gave added brilliance to the flowering vines that clung to them. A breeze came down from the cold heights and stirred in the long rows of cypress. Small deer wandered in the parklike shade, nibbling the deep grass and drinking the clear water of the Rio San Francisco that flowed beside the sweeping lawns. The mountain streams had been diverted and dropped over little cataracts into pools, and from two marble fountains they bubbled within the patios of the house itself. There were orchards of fruit trees, and hothouses that provided strawberries and other delicacies of the temperate zones. The buildings themselves were low and rambling, mellowed with age, ornate in the manner of the noble Spaniards.

There, for a few months at least, Bolívar did have a period of rest. His body found new strength; the warm vitality of Manuela did indeed dissolve the frost of his years. He was forty-four and his recuperative powers were still strong.

Bogotá was not Lima, as Manuela quickly learned. She could not indulge there in the public performances she had enjoyed so much in the unconventoinal Peruvian capital. She spent most of her time at the quinta, enjoying her strenuous pastimes among the secluded mountain paths. The gayer officers and political leaders rode out daily with their women, and the quinta became the center of sophisticated society. Its vast salons, gleaming with myriads of candles and a profusion of silver and crystal, were filled nightly with handsome men and beautifully gowned women.

Meanwhile, the business of selecting delegates for the

Constitutional Convention was going on; and Santander, brave once more in the face of the Liberator's lenient attitude, was busy as a bee. He was using every means to stack the convention with partisans of federalism. He went out into the provinces, working for the election of likely delegates and offering them bed and board in his own home in Bogotá. He filled the newspapers daily with propaganda against the policies of Bolívar and with outright charges of monarchial ambitions. To his friends who urged him to suppress the articles and answer the attacks, Bolívar replied, "I have nothing to say. The world knows me. It would be very easy to write articles in my own praise and in scorn of another, but that is not my vocation. I can better use for the good of the country and the general welfare the time that Santander employs in arousing passions—an activity which is highly improper in a magistrate." He contented himself with issuing, through the Minister of the Interior, a circular urging the election of virtuous and intelligent delegates and forbidding interference with the free expression of public opinion. He still had vast confidence in his own hold over the people.

His short period of rest came to an abrupt end. In February of 1828 word came from Páez that a squadron of Spanish warships from Puerto Rico had appeared off the Venezuelan coast and was attempting to co-operate with several groups of royalists who had risen in the country.

Once more Bolívar shook off the lethargy that gripped his failing body, put himself at the head of the army and marched toward his native land. Another long, tiring mountain journey. Happily, on nearing the Venezuelan border, word came that the royalists had been suppressed and the Spanish fleet had sailed away. With vast relief he turned about and started back toward Bogotá; but his satisfaction was brief. Hardly was the army in motion when news came from Cartagena that General Padilla, the patriot commander who had defeated the Spanish fleet in Lake Maracaibo, had instigated a revolt there. Wearily, remarking that he was like Sisyphus, pushing a heavy weight up a hill only to have it roll down again, Bolívar gave the order for the columns to change their route and head for the coast. But once more he was spared the necessity of making war against his countrymen. Halfway to the coast, word reached him that Padilla's uprising had been quelled, the leader arrested and sent to Bogotá for trial. Worn out, Bolívar remained where he was in the village of Bucaramanga.

The Great Constitutional Convention met in Ocaña, ninety miles from Bucaramanga, on April 9, 1828. Well knowing that by its action would be decided the fate of all his dreams for a strong Colombian Union, he resisted all the efforts of his friends to persuade him to attend the meeting in person, and remained where he was. He merely sent a message to the delegates, urging them to consider the good of the Republic and forget all personal considerations. A great pessimism, a spirit of fatalism, had come over him—this, the man who had never faltered in the face of completely hopeless situations. Underneath, a faint hope still lived that his prestige would do its work among the delegates, that the great loyalty of the common people, which had never wavered from him, would influence them in their decisions. With a few of his officers he stayed, inactive, in the quiet village. Daily the reports of the Convention's progress came in.

From the first the utmost confusion reigned at the conferences. Every provincial delegate came with his pockets stuffed with crack-pot plans for a national code; and they supported them with vehemence on the chamber floor. Gradually, however, the factions arranged themselves behind the two main propositions—the federal code supported by Santander and the strongly centralized union of Bolívar. Briceño Méndez, Bolívar's nephew-in-law, and strangely, General Castillo, the brother of the Liberator's enemy of the early days who had sided with Santander on the question of taking Colombian troops into Venezuela,

were the leaders of his faction in the Convention. Santander strove mightily to discredit Bolívar and all his
works; and he packed the assembly with a majority of
his partisans. When, in the turmoil, a proposal was made
that Bolívar be invited to attend in person and present
his arguments, Santander protested violently. "The man
has a blinding and hypnotic presence," he declared. "I
myself have experienced it. Many times, going into his
presence, angry and with well-formed and just proposals,
I have left disarmed and full of admiration. No man living
can oppose Bolívar face to face." He strove constantly to
make the issue one of legality against usurpation and made
the most of the fiction that Bolívar cherished the idea of
a crown. In this he met with little success, for the people
well knew of the propositions that had been made the
Liberator in the past, and of his repeated refusals. Nevertheless, they weren't entirely clear on just what he did
want. Parra-Pérez says, "Bolívar was in reality the defender of the people against future despots, but his
thoughts were tortuously interpreted and gave occasion
for the criticism of those who attributed to him absurd
and ambitious plans."

The Convention did declare from the start the need
for reform in the existing code; and Santander, supporting that idea, could no longer with justification lay claim
to the title, "Man of Laws." He came out openly for
loose federalism.

Bolívar suffered his self-imposed exile in high nervous-
ness, receiving the reports from Ocaña in varying moods
of hope and despair. With a few of his companions he
whiled away the time as best he could. An officer of the
local garrison, Perú de Lacroix, who saw much of him,
recorded his daily movements.

A great change had come over the Liberator. He had
lost to a great extent the self-control and equanimity that
had always characterized him. He had become religious
and attended Mass every morning in the village chapel.

In civilian dress—an old blue coat, white trousers, cavalry boots and a wide hat—he took daily rides alone or in the company of O'Leary and Ferguson. Sometimes he ordered his aides to ride far behind so that he could be alone with his thoughts. He lay in his hammock by the hour, swinging rapidly. Sometimes, when the news was good, there were flares of his old happy spirit; he would sing French songs and tell stories of his battles and discuss the qualities of all his old officers. But he had become irritable as well, his moods unstable. Playing cards, winning, he was all good humor, poking fun at the losers; losing, he became angry, threw down his cards and rose from the table cursing his luck. "Look," he said, "I've lost battles, fortune, friends that I've treasured, I've been betrayed a thousand times; and nothing ever shattered my control as this silly game of cards." Then he'd laugh, apologize, promise to have more patience and sit down to resume the game.

He was always up at daybreak and worked far into the night dictating his letters. He ate very little, drank two glasses of wine at meals—never any more. He exercised regularly, bathed two and three times a day and was meticulous in the care of his hair, hands and teeth.

Normally his expression was pleasant, even kindly; angry, a startling change took place. His face, usually quite fair in color, actually seemed to darken and shadows seemed to form about his mouth, which grew drawn and ugly, the lower lip protruding abnormally. Deep parallel wrinkles formed on the high forehead, the eyes grew very small and flashed fire. His anger centered mostly upon the followers of Santander, whom he called demagogues and rabble-rousers. He said:

Demagogy is like a Hydra; if you cut off one head, a hundred more grow in its place. In '17 the death of one criminal was enough to secure order, but in '28 the death of many hundreds wouldn't be enough. . . . I have the generosity to pardon them. They are all in my hands. A mere signal from me would exterminate them all. Yet, in my place, they would not only give the signal to kill me but also all my friends, partisans and anyone who doesn't hold their opinions. Such are our so-called liberals—cruel, bloody, frenetic, intolerant and covering their crimes with the word "liberty"! They believe themselves justified in their crimes as the Inquisitors and all who have shed human blood in the name of God and religion believed themselves justified in theirs. . . . To the people belongs always the right to write history and to judge the greatness of men. Let the judgment of the people be upon me, then; that is what I want, what I will appreciate, what I believe will make my glory; that, and not the judgment of my Minister of the Interior.

Again he said, "Individual interests, ambitions, rivalries, necessity, provincialism, thirst for vengeance and other miserable passions animate our demagogues and unite them now to overthrow existing forms; but afterwards they will only separate, and establish their partial sovereignties, and govern the people as slaves and with the old Spanish system."

There is no doubt that he did have the power to destroy his enemies, as he declared. The army was his and the backing of the people. But he remained supine, letting the Convention function freely, even knowing that it was packed against him. His fear of the opinion of the world and of history was even greater than the desire to see his dreams fulfilled.

Meanwhile, in Bogotá, Manuela was engaged in valiant but foolhardy efforts in behalf of Bolívar's cause. There were clamorous meetings of his partisans nightly in the quinta, and Manuela led them in planning all sorts of wild and impracticable actions. Luckily, nothing came of them. On one occasion an effigy of Santander was burned on the grounds of the estate and the cry was raised, "Death to the traitor!" The disturbance was so loud that city authorities came and placed a young officer under arrest. Another time Manuela came upon a group of Santanderists in the plaza, scrawling abuse against Bolívar on the walks. Spurring her horse, she dashed among them, striking about with her heavy crop, shouting revilement. The police had to break up that disturbance, too.

Méndez and Castillo worked assiduously in the Convention for the adoption of the Bolivarian code. Failing to induce Bolívar to attend in person, and seeing that the faction of Santander was growing and preparing for final action, they decided in desperation upon a last move. On June 2, with all their loyal delegates, they walked out of the assembly, declaring the deliberations to be useless and dangerous. Without a quorum to take any legal action, the assembly was forced to adjourn. So the Great Convention accomplished nothing at all. Worse, in fact, it left the country without any code whatever, for it had declared the old Constitution unsuitable.

In this situation an assembly of citizens and ecclesiastic authorities met in Bogotá and called upon Bolívar to return and assume control. He came on June 24 and was declared dictator until another convention should meet in 1830—two years off.

The city greeted his arrival with another great spontaneous demonstration of acclaim; but his response was dispirited, his smile weary, his gestures more mechanical than ever. Addressing the people, he said, "I shall not talk to you of liberty because, if I fulfill my promises, you will be more than free—you will be respected. Under a dictatorship who can talk of liberty? Let us pity both the people who obey and the man who rules alone."

He took up his residence in the governmental palace and Manuela came in from Quinta de Portocarrero to live with him. He drove himself to the tasks of creating a semblance of order out of the chaos left by the Convention. He formed a council, suppressed the military courts and sought to reorganize the nation's finances. His great-

est problem was what to do about the partisans of Santander. The city was full of them, angry over the debacle
of Ocaña, taking out their spleen in secret plottings.
Armed with his dictatorial powers, he could have dealt
drastically with them, of course; but he did nothing at
all. Perhaps he was beyond caring. He went on now out of
long habit, out of that old force which had driven him to
action for many years in the face of impossible odds. His
heart didn't care now but his spirit went on of its own
inertia. To get rid of Santander he appointed him Minister to the United States. His old antagonist accepted the
post but delayed his departure day by day—waiting, perhaps, waiting. . . .

It was late in the night of September 25, 1828. Bolívar
had felt ill and Manuela had read to him until he had
fallen asleep. Their room was on the first floor of the
palace, only a few steps above the level of the street. The
Liberator was wakened suddenly by the barking of the
household dogs. Manuela was already sitting up in bed,
listening. The sounds of a confused uproar came from the
palace corridors beyond the heavy door, grew louder, resolved into the angry shouts of men; and then there were
pistol shots. Bolívar and Manuela leaped from bed, Manuela lit a candle and Bolívar pulled his trousers on up
over his nightshirt and grabbed his sword. The uproar
was closer now—the sounds of fighting, the clash of sabers.
Soon words could be heard, the voices of men shouting,
"Death to the tyrant! Death to Bolívar!" Bolívar went to
the door, prepared to fight for his life. Manuela ran ahead
of him and pushed him back.

"You can't fight them!" she cried. "You'll be killed!
There are too many of them. They've overcome the guard
and they're almost at the door. You'll be killed!"

"What does it matter? I'm going to fight them!"

"You can't, I tell you! I won't let you!"

She glanced frantically about the room and her eyes fell

upon the wide window, only a few feet above the street. "There!" she cried. "The window!" She pushed him back and he yielded, protesting. The sounds were at the door now, the clash of arms in the foyer and the voice of young Ibarra, the guard, crying out in pain. Manuela saw Bolívar safely through the window and over the low rail of the little balcony, and then she caught up a sword and ran to face the assassins. The door broke in with a crash and there in the feeble candlelight Manuela charged upon the mob of men, brandishing her sword like an angry goddess, crying maledictions.

"Where is Bolívar?" the men demanded.

"He isn't here. He's at the Council Hall."

"You lie! He's here all right, and we'll have his head!" They disarmed her roughly, pushed her aside and searched the room. Seeing the open window, they went to it and glanced up and down the street; but Bolívar was nowhere to be seen. "He's at the Council Hall!" Manuela insisted. "He's been there all night!" Cursing her, the men stamped out to search the rest of the palace. Manuela rushed after them into the corridors. Seeing Colonel Ferguson running in, she tried to warn him; but he declared he would die doing his duty. A moment later he was shot dead. Ibarra had his arm nearly severed, and several other palace guards were wounded or killed.

Later Manuela told of the affair laughingly. "He wanted to defend himself!" she said. "My God, imagine him standing there in his nightshirt, sword in hand! Don Quixote in person! If I hadn't made him jump from the window, he was a dead man."

In the dark, deserted street, Bolívar was joined by José Palacio, the head servant of the palace household. Together they stole along the sidewalk, hugging the shadows of the buildings. From all parts of the city came sounds of fighting—shots and the shouting of men. Lights appeared here and there in the windows of houses and people called out to neighbors. Approaching the bridge across the Rio

San Agustín at the foot of the street, Bolívar saw the dark
figures of armed men, running. There was no way of knowing if they were friends or enemies. Palacio urged Bolívar
down into the darkness under the stone arches of the
bridge, beside the gently flowing stream.

They huddled there for two hours. The noise of fighting became louder and spread everywhere; soon there was
skirmishing on the very bridge above their heads. The
shouts came to them clearly: "Viva Santander!"—"Death
to Bolívar, the tyrant!" There was no way of knowing the
extent of the uprising or the way the battle was going.
Bolívar didn't even care. He was heartsick, sunk in the
very depths of despair.

Actually, the movement had been a widespread plot in-
volving nearly all the battalions in the various barracks
of the city. One battalion, the veteran Vargas, had remained loyal to Bolívar and rushed out to battle. Gradually they dispersed the scattered forces of insurgents, drove
them from the streets and arrested their leaders. General
Padilla, the man who had revolted in Cartagena and had
been captured and sent to Bogotá, had engaged in the plot
from his prison cell. A party of insurgents released him
and he shot his guard, José Bolívar, a kinsman of the
Liberator, dead.

The two men hiding under the bridge learned at last
from the words of the people above them that the loyal
friends of Bolívar had triumphed. As dawn was breaking
the Liberator dragged himself wearily from his hole. He
went to the plaza, where the troops of Urdaneta, shouting
with joy, surrounded him.

Santander, Padilla and most of the leaders of the plot
were arrested that same morning. All of them were tried
and sentenced to be shot. Bolívar, uncaring and fatalistic
now, pardoned all save those who confessed their guilt.
Santander protested his innocence violently; but the tribunal, with the testimony of many witnesses, found that

though he had taken no active part in the conspiracy, he had known of it and given it his approval and counsel. Bolívar commuted his sentence to exile. Santander was escorted to Cartagena and put aboard a vessel; and thus the Liberator's long-time enemy went out of his life.

After Bolívar's death, Santander returned to Colombia and became President of the Republic.

Young Ferguson had been preparing to marry a girl in Cartagena. Bolívar wrote to the girl's father, communicating the news of the Englishman's gallant death: "Colonel Ferguson has confronted the fury of the enemy in a hundred battles. His gallantry has always answered the call of duty and loyalty. The patria has lost one of its noblest servants and your daughter a husband beyond compare."

Fourteen of the conspirators, of the hundreds who were guilty, were shot in accordance with the sentence of the court. Once Bolívar would have exterminated all his enemies ruthlessly—for he had railed against the government of the First Republic for failing to do just that and had blamed its leniency largely for its downfall. But now he had gone far down the road to despair.

He felt almost as though he actually had been assassinated. "My heart is broken," he said, "and the prestige of my name is gone." And again, "I am morally assassinated. Their daggers have penetrated here," he said, pointing to his heart. "Is this the reward of my services to Colombia and to the cause of independence? How have I offended against liberty and against these men? Santander has caused it all. I will be generous nevertheless, for my glory demands it."

Chapter XXIX

"THE GREAT GENTLEMAN
OF COLOMBIA"

✤

SUCRE, as President of Bolivia, had had his troubles from the first. Gil Fortoul says, "His government was illustrious, progressive, liberal—and weak." Though a stern and determined commander in battle, the noble Sucre was far too gracious a character for a civil magistrate in those times. He exercised none of the powers allowed him under the strong Bolivarian Constitution. He reduced the standing army to only fifty men and the country became shot through with dissensions in the face of his apparent weakness. Only a few months after he took the oath of office an assassin, one Valentín Matos, entered the palace and attacked him with a knife. Matos was tried by the courts and sentenced to death; but Sucre commuted the sentence to exile and gave the man 200 pesos out of his own pocket to pay for his journey. Shortly afterwards he pardoned the man entirely.

Finally, in April of 1828, a serious revolution broke out. There was fighting on the city streets and Sucre was severely wounded in the right arm and head. To climax the catastrophe, troops from Perú crossed the border into Bolivia with the intention of bringing the new nation back into the dominion of the Lima government. There had long been considerable resentment among the Peruvians over the separation of one of the old viceroyalty's richest provinces.

Utterly discouraged in the face of all this, Sucre resigned his office on August 2, 1828. Shortly before, he had

346

married a beautiful girl of Quito, María Carcelán y Larrea, Marquesa de Solanda. He left the nation he had served as its first president and went to Quito to live in retirement.

After his departure Bolivia had three presidents, two of whom were killed, in five days.

Word of these affairs struck Bolívar like the dull blows of a hammer that had already beaten the sense of feeling out of him. The blows were falling constantly and from all directions. General Obando, the Spanish commander whom Bolívar had won over in Popoyán and who had fought with him valiantly ever since, raised a revolt in his old province. Then General Córdova, the hero of Ayacucho, the gallant young officer who had given the inspiring command, "Step of conquerors," formed a rebellion against Bolívar in the province of Antioquia. The movement was suppressed by O'Leary, and Córdova was assassinated. The man who confessed to the crime was a British legionnaire, Colonel Hand, and he hinted that he had acted on orders from a high authority. Many writers aver that this fact points to Bolívar as the author of Córdova's murder; but there is no evidence to support the charge. It doesn't seem likely that, having pardoned Santander and so many really important and dangerous enemies, he would have ordered the death of young Córdova.

From Venezuela, too, came word of new dissensions, more clamoring for secession from the Colombian Union.

Bolívar, harassed, ill and disillusioned, resorted at last to repressive measures. He became, for the first time in his life, the stern dictator that his enemies had always claimed him to be. They had at last forced the rôle upon him. He silenced the press, suppressed the freedom of speech and public assembly and disarmed the citizens. Growing ever more religious, he gave the Church, for the first time, a part in the affairs of government and placed the archbishop on his Council. "My countrymen," he declared, "who failed to kill me by stabbing, now seek to assassinate me morally with their ingratitude and calumnies. In times past they honored me as a God, now they try to soil me with their venom. When I cease to exist these demagogues will devour each other like wolves and the edifice which I built by superhuman force will decay in the slime of revolution."

Then, early in 1829, the Peruvian General La Mar invaded Guayaquil with 8000 troops and declared war on Colombia. Bolívar made a final desperate effort. He was very ill now, taken with incessant violent fits of coughing. The flame had at last consumed the oil. He mobilized his army and began once more the long journey southward along the Andes; but he who had been called "Iron Arse" by the toughest horsemen in the world could now stay in the saddle only a few hours at a time.

Meanwhile, Sucre had come out of his retirement, organized an army and marched against La Mar. He defeated the Peruvian forces at Tarquí on February 28 and forced the surrender of La Mar. When Bolívar joined him in Quito the semblance of peace reigned once more. The Liberator went to Guayaquil and remained there the whole summer, resting.

To O'Leary, whom he appointed to replace Santander as Minister to the United States, he wrote, "Considering what I have been all my life, it is incredible the state I am in. . . . A universal calm, an absolute indifference has taken possession of me and dominates me completely."

From Páez, who at the time was also growing weary of struggling against the dissensions in Venezuela, he received an affectionate and touching letter. The old llanero proposed that the two of them retire to his hacienda in far Apure and pass their lives in peace, "like simple Roman citizens." Bolívar replied, in part, "I remain, my beloved general, your grateful friend. The idea has moved me greatly. Would to God I could enjoy the rest of my life in your companionship."

ly a month later the various provincial governments
nezuela separately declared absolute secession from
nbia. Practically all the old loyal comrades of Bolívar
l the articles. Páez went before the Congress and
that war be declared against the Colombian govern-

anwhile, word came to Guayaquil that Bolívar's cabi-
ı Bogotá had formed a plan for a monarchy. The
ıtor was to be kept in power as president until he
ınd then a European prince would be invited to
to Colombia and occupy the throne. Already the
plan had been communicated to the ministers in France
and England and news of it had spread throughout the
country. The nation was split into a hundred factions
over the proposition. Wearily Bolívar wrote his cabinet
to desist in their efforts and to leave the matter of government to the Congress that was soon to convene.

In December he started north for Bogotá. The citizens
of Guayaquil, feeling the old spell of his presence, exerted
even in his present state of collapse, begged him to stay
and be their president for life; but he refused and bade
them good-by forever.

The Congress, under the presidency of Sucre, convened
in Bogotá on January 20, 1830. Bolívar opened the first
session and delived an address, resigning his dictatorship:

Fearing that I am regarded as an obstacle to establishing
the Republic on a firm base of happiness, I remove myself
from the high office to which you were good enough to elevate
me. . . . Never, never, I swear to you, has the ambition for
a monarchy soiled my mind. My enemies have invented that
idea to destroy me in your good opinion. Undeceive yourselves. My one desire has been to contribute to your liberty.
. . . The Republic will be happy if, accepting my resignation,
you name a president beloved of all the nation. . . . Hear

my prayers. Save the Republic. Save my glory, which is Colombia's.

The Congress deliberated for five months while Bolívar rested in his quinta under Manuela's care. But not even her never-failing gaiety and affection could lift the shadows that had fallen upon him now. The Congress elected Joaquín Mosquera President and the Constitution which they adopted was a complete triumph for Santanderism. It was exactly the sort of loose federal code which Bolívar had fought against all his life. He hadn't even bothered to present one of his own for their consideration. The Congress also proclaimed him the first citizen of Colombia for all time and voted him an annual pension of 30,000 pesos. He was penniless but he refused the pension. There was small comfort for him in such things. His dreams had been for something infinitely greater.

His mind had been made up for some time. He was determined to leave the Republic forever. Where he would go he didn't know—France, England, the Antilles, perhaps. "Independence," he said, "is the only thing we have acquired and that at the cost of everything else." He could have made a happier statement had he given up five years before. He had won his military war against the Spaniards and he had lost the political one against his countrymen, the one he found so hateful.

To the Congress he declared, "I am reduced to the private life which I have so greatly desired, and if the Congress wishes a special proof of my blind obedience to the Constitution and the laws, I am ready to give any that it may ask of me."

He wrote to the husband of one of his nieces in Caracas to hasten the sale of the mines of Aroa, his last remaining property, and urged him to forward the money as soon as possible. He was going to live abroad, he said, and his needs would be small, for he was accustomed to a bare, military way of life. He must, he said, leave Colombia in time to save her the disgrace of ordering his exile. In this his foresight proved itself still keen, for only shortly afterwards the Venezuelan government refused to treat with Colombia so long as Bolívar lived within her borders.

Manuela must remain behind. His plans were indefinite, he had no money, he didn't know where he was going. After, when the money came from Venezuela and he was settled, he would see.

On the eighth of May he rode out, for the last time, from the capital of the Republic he had created. Thousands of people lined the streets, weeping as he passed. The foreign ministers, nearly all the government officials and hundreds of citizens rode with him to the outskirts. There they dismounted and he embraced them one by one. He climbed into the saddle with a great effort and disappeared down the road toward the coast. Standing there watching, Colonel Patrick Campbell, a British legionnaire who had become his nation's minister, said, "He is gone—the great gentleman of Colombia."

He had left without saying good-by to Sucre, probably intentionally, to spare himself the pain. The valiant officer whom he loved as a son and who had helped more than anyone else to achieve his glory sent a letter hurrying after him:

My general, when I went to your house to go with you I found you gone. Perhaps it is well, for it has spared me the sorrow of a last farewell. Right now my heart is empty. I do not know what to say to you.

I have not the words to tell you easily the sentiments of my soul regarding you. You know them well, for you have known me a long time and you know that it has not been your position but only friendship which has inspired in me the deepest affection for your person. I shall conserve it no matter what the fate which befalls us and I beg of you to conserve for me the appreciation you have always bestowed upon me. I shall try in every circumstance to deserve it.

Good-bye, my general. Receive as a token of my friendship the tears which I am shedding at this moment. Be happy, wherever you are going, and be sure always of the devotion and gratitude of your most loyal and passionate friend.

ANTONIO JOSÉ DE SUCRE.

Postlude

THE PATH ENDS

✤

H IS route lay down the valley of the Magdalena, along the river where, as a young man untouched by glory, he had commanded his little fleet of flatboats and driven the Spaniards before him, tasting his first triumphs. Guamal, Banco, Mompox, where his glory was born . . . but he didn't ride in glory now. In profound melancholy, he rode slowly, his emaciated body slumped forward in the saddle; and almost daily the blows fell upon his bowed head in a relentless rain. Quito and Guayaquil seceded from Colombia and formed the independent Republic of Ecuador. Venezuela was torn with frightful dissensions. Páez, who only a few months before had invited him to retire and live in peace with him in his beloved llanos, now declared, "The existence of Bolívar is a menace to the Republic and his name deserves to be condemned to oblivion." Bermúdez proclaimed him "a despot, a false prophet of republican principles, an aspirant to monarchy, a man of criminal designs and vile ambitions." Arismendi declared him "the tyrant of Colombia, an ungrateful son of Caracas, a creature of evil purposes."

He arrived in Cartagena on June 24. The money from his mines in Venezuela had never come. Almost penniless, desperately ill, he went to live in a little cabin on a hillside overlooking the walled city. There the heaviest blow of all fell with terrific force. Sucre had been murdered. The only son he had ever known, his right hand—Sucre, the undefiled, the white knight. Riding down that long mountain range from Bogotá to Quito where his wife and

353

month-old daughter waited for him, Sucre had been way-
laid on a forest trail in the land of the Pastusos and shot
from ambush. The news wrung a cry of anguish from
Bolívar: "They have killed Abel!"

Then word came from Bogotá that the government of
Mosquera had fallen and the capital city was in the throes
of disorder. Out of it arose a movement that, in another
day, would have sent him hurrying back to begin all over
again his pursuit of glory. A group of army officers and
the troops of Bogotá and several other provinces formed
a coalition headed by Urdaneta and proclaimed Bolívar
the Chief of the Republic, vested with supreme authority.
The ministers of the United States and Great Britain
wrote to Bolívar, urging that he accept the proposal and
put an end to the turmoil. In Cartagena, too, the troops
rose in revolt and begged the Liberator to head them in
a movement to form a new government. Then María
Antonia wrote him from Caracas that large factions
throughout the country were clamoring for his return;
that in spite of the efforts of the political leaders, the people and the soldiers still loved him. "The country districts," she wrote, "are full of armed deserters who say
that they care for no one but their old man and father,
the Liberator."

But Bolívar was through. Fate had beaten him down at
last.

He wrote to a friend, "I am about to die. My cycle is
completed; God calls me. I must prepare to give an account and my account will be terrible, for the agitations
of my life have been terrible." "I have scarcely strength
enough to support the last days that remain of my miserable life," he said. He begged his friends to leave off their
efforts, declaring, "I see no salvation for the country. I
believe everything is lost forever. If there were a single
sacrifice I could make—my life, my happiness or my honor
—believe me, I would not hesitate; but I am convinced
the sacrifice would be useless. Since I am unable to secure

the happiness of my country, I refuse to rule it. Further, the tyrants have taken my native land from me and therefore I have no longer any country for which to make a sacrifice."

In final abject disillusion, he wrote, "All who have served the Revolution have ploughed the sea."

The heat that lay over the landlocked city was intolerable. The rain fell in dismal monotony; steam rose in billows from the sun-hardened earth. His illness and the heat created in him a feverish impatience, a frantic need to get away—anywhere, far, far away. He must get away from this land that had disowned him. His money was almost gone and still none had come from Venezuela. He moved down the coast to Barranquilla, hoping to escape the heat; but there was no relief there, either. For two months he lay in that place and then, in November, still without funds, he boarded a frigate bound for Jamaica. Perhaps the sea voyage would do him good, the heat be less intense on the British island. But the motion of the little vessel made him violently ill and they had to return to the Colombian coast at Santa Marta. There Bolívar was carried ashore in a litter, too weak to stand. He could never escape now from his homeland.

The people of the village were very kind to the little bundle of bones that had been the greatest man of South America. A few friends had come to him now—Mariano Montilla, Laurencio Silva, José María Carreño and his nephew Fernando Bolívar. With him, too, was José Palacio, the servant who had hid with him under the bridge of San Agustín that awful night in Bogotá. The village doctor, a Frenchman named Alexandre Révérend, attended him night and day. An American doctor from a ship in the harbor confirmed Révérend's diagnosis of tuberculosis of the lungs and left what medicines he had. When Mariano Montilla, that old companion of Bolívar's in Madrid and in the Patriotic Society (and later, for a while, his enemy), heard, in private, the doctor's opinion, he burst into tears.

Seven days dragged slowly by. Bolívar lay still, his head burning, his hands and feet cold as ice. He was racked with long spells of coughing and vomiting but he said he felt no pain. On December 7 they carried him on a litter five miles out to the small hacienda of San Pedro which belonged to a local officer, Joaquín de Mier.

His periods of fever came more frequently and brought delirium with them. In the lucid moments between he was very calm. He spoke to Dr. Révérend in his own tongue. "What did you seek in this land, doctor?" he asked him once. "Liberty, sire," Révérend replied. "And have you found it?" "Yes, my general." "Then you are more fortunate than I."

One evening he felt better and asked if he might have music. Some peons of the neighborhood came into his room and played their fifes for him until he fell asleep.

The next day the Bishop of Santa Marta visited him and heard his confession, and the local curate, attended by Indian boys who served as acolytes, holding candles and giving the responses in Latin, administered the Blessed Sacrament and Extreme Unction.

That evening all his friends and all the villagers who could find space crowded into the room where Bolívar lay on his bed. A notary began to read them the Liberator's last proclamation to the people of Colombia. Halfway through, everyone was in tears, soldiers and civilians alike. Dr. Révérend had to leave the room and the notary couldn't go on. Manuel Recuero, the army auditor, finished the reading. Bolívar had written:

Colombians! You have witnessed my efforts to plant liberty where tyranny reigned before. I have labored with disinterest, sacrificing my fortune and my own peace. I resigned from command when I saw that you had no faith in my disinterest. My enemies took advantage of your credulity and trampled upon what is most sacred to me—my reputation and my love of liberty. I have been the victim of my persecutors, who have led me to the gates of the sepulcher. I forgive them. On disappearing from among you, my affection tells me that I should declare my last wishes. I aspire to no other glory than the consolidation of Colombia. All of you must work for the inestimable good of the Union: the people obeying the government in order to avoid anarchy; the ministers praying to Heaven for guidance; and the military using its sword in defense of social guaranties.

Colombians! My last wish is for the happiness of the patria. If my death contributes to the end of partisanship and the consolidation of the Union, I shall be lowered in peace into my grave.

In the silence that followed the reading of these words, Bolívar said in a low voice, "Yes, to the grave. That is where my countrymen have consigned me. I forgive them. If only I could take with me the consolation that they would remain united!"

He made a will leaving whatever was left of his property after his debts were paid to be divided among his sisters and the two children of Juan Vicente. His servant, José Palacio, was to have 8000 pesos, Sucre's sword was to be delivered to his widow, his books were to go to the University of Caracas. To Sir Robert Wilson he sent his gratitude for the faithful services of his son Belford.

He lingered on for seven more days, coughing blood and babbling in delirium. "Let us go!" he cried out. "They have no use for us here! José! Bring the luggage. They do not want us here!"

Bolívar had come at last to the end of his path of glory.

At one o'clock in the afternoon of December 17, 1830, he died. He was forty-seven years old. The day was the eleventh anniversary of the founding of his beloved Republic of Colombia. . . .

At the village of Teneriffe on the Magdalena a blue-eyed French woman had been waiting for seventeen years for the glamorous person who had touched her life for a brief moment. Hearing that he was lying ill in Cartagena, she gathered her few belongings into a bundle and hurried there; but when she arrived he had sailed and they said he was in Santa Marta. She waited for eight days, hoping for a boat to carry her there; but none came and she set out on foot. With her bundle under her arm she walked sixty miles through the jungles along the rugged coast. In Barranquilla she lay ill in the hut of a kind peon, and when she was well again she found passage on a small fishing vessel; but she did not arrive in Santa Marta until the day after the Liberator had died. She looked into his face at the customhouse where they had laid him, and she followed his body to the grave in the little cemetery.

In Bogotá another woman hurried toward Santa Marta when she heard that Bolívar was dying. Manuela Sáenz had started down the Magdalena when the news of her lover's death reached her.

She remained true to the memory of Bolívar for the rest of her life. When Thorne died he left her his estate and she refused it. Years later she was in the little town of Paita on the Peruvian coast, selling cigars for a living. The government found her there, granted her a generous pension and decorated her with the Order of the Sun. In 1858 the great Italian patriot Garibaldi visited her in Paita and found her a bedridden but still lovely lady. She entertained him for hours with her lively and intelligent conversation and her memories of Bolívar, the consuming interest of her life. In his memoirs Garibaldi said that she was the most gracious lady he had ever known.

On a December day in 1842, twelve years after the Liberator died, a great fleet of war vessels crowded the harbor of Santa Marta. Besides the colors of all the nations he had liberated, the flags of England, France and

Holland hung from their staffs at half-mast. The town was crowded with the representatives of foreign countries. To the slow boom of cannon and the roll of drums, the remains of Bolívar were placed on a barge and rowed out to a waiting vessel. Soon the whole fleet raised anchors, hoisted great sails and moved eastward.

On December 17 the body of Bolívar came home to his native city. Caracas was draped in mourning and arches had been built over the streets. Under them rode a long procession of great men of many nations and behind, drawn by black-shrouded horses, came a huge catafalque hung with wreaths, garlanded with flowers and draped with black silk. The people stood in silence as the procession passed to the beat of slow music. María Antonia had died in the midst of preparations for the trip to Santa Marta; but Hipólita and Matea, the black nurses of the Liberator, were there to do him honor. It was Páez, the old llanero chief who had injured him so much during his life, who arranged these honors for him now, after he was dead.

Bolívar had come at last to find the place he had sought in the hearts of his people and in history.

AUTHOR'S NOTE

✤

THERE is no figure in English or North American history that exists today in the consciousness of the people as Simón Bolívar exists in the consciousness of millions of South Americans. For them he is no mere vague, heroic character from the pages of books; he is a living entity, a divine, compassionate, omniscient being who dwells apart somewhere and guides their destinies. He is practically a deity, and his adulation almost a cult. Half-naked Indians and ragged peons who could not decipher his name in print repeat his words as though they were spoken yesterday—whisper them in reverence and with a strange air of confidence that his words alone have the power to cure their ills and to protect them from oppression. In the South American cities statesmen and scholars raise their hats at the mention of his name. They have named the building in Caracas, where his body lies, the "Pantheon"; and the president of Venezuela is said to go there and pray for guidance. South American writers speak constantly of Bolívar's "apotheosis." I remember seeing once a litany written to Bolívar and it had some of the mystic quality of the Litany of the Blessed Virgin, that strange, beautiful prayer with its haunting phrases— Mirror of Justice, Seat of Wisdom, Vessel of Honor, Mystical Rose, Tower of David, Tower of Ivory, House of Gold, Gate of Heaven, Morning Star. The Litany to Bolívar was scarcely less comprehensible to the uninitiated mind.

This quasi-deification of Simón Bolívar by the citizens of the lands he liberated from Spain obviously places very formidable obstacles in the way of the dispassionate biographer. It would be quite possible (in fact, it is rather difficult to do otherwise) to portray him as the all-time great romantic hero, the possessor in superlative degree of every human virtue and of unequaled military, political, intellectual and literary talents, and have, for every bit of evidence contributing to the, portrayal, legitimate authority in the statements of eminent historians as well as from the primary sources of Bolívar's own words or the words of his companions. Unfortunately, this picture of the Liberator cannot be accepted in its entirety by one of rather skeptical nature, such as this observer. It is just too good to be true. Human beings simply aren't made that way. The unreservedly admiring historians of Bolívar, eminent though they may be, have simply overdone it; they have awakened doubts by their very zeal and certainty. Even a writer of the stature of Rufino Blanco Fombona will go off the deep end with a statement like this: "History has never known a warrior whose charger has traveled farther nor whose theater of war was more extensive. Not the European captains, Gonzalo de Córdoba, Carlos XII and Frederick the Great, nor the fabulous warriors of Asia, Genghis Khan and Tamerlane, have trod in triumph such vast lands as he." Yet there is considerable basis for Fombona's statement and it might even be entirely true; it would be difficult to prove otherwise. Nevertheless, it will be looked upon with skepticism by most historians. Certain it is that the areas of Bolívar's operations are incredibly vast and his marches well-nigh unbelievable, even disregarding the nature of the terrain. One becomes dizzy tracing his movements back and forth across the map of South America. The Colombian writer, Fernando González, says, "I have acquired from the Yankees the deplorable habit of classifying things as the biggest or the best or the greatest in the world. Well, I give you the man who has ridden horseback the most in the world—Simón Bolívar."

In 1906 the American statesman, Hiram Bingham, be-

BOLIVAR'S SOUTH AMERICA

Scale of Miles

0   100   200   300   400

Caribbean Sea

Atlantic Ocean

Pacific Ocean

Sta Marta
Barranquilla
Mompos
Tenerife
Ocaña
Cúcuta
Merida
San Cristóbal
Rio Apure
Bucaramanga
Boyacá
PARAMO DE PISBA
Santa
Buenaventura
COLOMBIA
(NEW GRANADA)
Bombona
Popayán
Pasto
Pichincha
Quito
ECUADOR
Riobamba
(QUITO)
Guayaquil

I. CURAÇAO
I. COLOMBIA
Pto Cabello
Coro
Carabobo
Maracaibo
La Guayra
Valencia
Caracas
Trujillo
San Fernando
Achagua
Orinoco
Angostura
I. MARGARITA
Cumaná
Barcelona
Cariaco
Maturín
I. TRINIDAD

BRITISH GUIANA
DUTCH GUIANA
FRENCH GUIANA

R. Amazon

B   R   A   Z   I   L

Trujillo
Pativilca
Junín
Callao   Lima
Ayacucho
P   E   R   U

TITICACA
BOLIVIA
La Paz
Arequipa   (ALTO PERU)
Arica
Chuquisaca
Potosí

CHILE   ARGENTINA   PARAGUAY

Area Included
in the
Larger Map

R.E. Falconer.

ing a bit skeptical of the oft-described difficulties of that terrible, heroic march of Bolívar's from Angostura across the Andes into New Granada, determined to see for himself and to retrace the footsteps of the patriot army. He made the journey nearly a century after Bolívar. What he encountered filled him with stark amazement and left him with utter incomprehension of how Bolívar's march had ever been made.

The fact of Bolívar's greatness and the heroic proportions of his achievements cannot, of course, be denied. There they are, unassailable—solid truth. Where this account is at variance with those of Bolívar's unequivocal admirers is mainly in the interpretation of his personality, in a denial of his infallibility and invariable moral virtue and unfailing military and political sagacity.

Bolívar's detractors, what few there are, have also defeated their purpose by their excessive zeal—and to a much greater degree. The sheer venom and personal animosity of their words open them at once to the suspicion of deliberate calumny. The two principal ones, the Englishman, Hippisley, and the Frenchman, Ducoudray-Holstein, both of whom wrote in English, were disgruntled army officers who served with the Liberator for only a short time and left him under unsavory circumstances. The same holds true for Brown, Hackett and Chesterton, lesser-known Englishmen who wrote derogatory accounts of Bolívar. Hippisley and Ducoudray-Holstein even contradict each other. Ducoudray-Holstein goes to the ridiculous length of accusing Bolívar of physical cowardice while Hippisley says, "Personal courage he is gifted with, even to a fault." The uniformly unpleasant impressions of the South American people and their customs that Ducoudray-Holstein gives in his work need only be compared with those of his contemporary writer, the American, William Duane, in his *Visit to Colombia in 1822 and 23,* to mark Ducoudray-Holstein for an unregenerate misanthrope. This author has rejected largely the evidence of these men. Against them can be weighed the evidence of other European associates of Bolívar—Daniel Florence O'Leary, Irishman, aide-de-camp and private secretary of the Liberator and long in his service; Francis Burdette O'Connor, Irish patriot and general in Bolívar's army; Belford Wilson, son of Sir Robert Wilson and long an aide of Bolívar; Admiral Charles Cochrane and General William Miller, Britishers. The works of O'Leary alone, comprising his memoirs and a vast collection of documents and letters of the Liberator, fill thirty-two volumes.

A modern Spanish writer, Carlos Pereira, has attempted by very exhaustive research to disprove nearly every quality and achievement of Bolívar universally accepted as fact and, while he has unearthed some interesting and pertinent material, his undeniable bias, his distortion of logic to sustain his premise and disregard of evidence which would refute it, condemn his work almost entirely.

In regard to Perú de Lacroix's much-disputed work, *Diario de Bucaramanga,* this author feels that the new edition, in which the apocryphal additions of Bolívar's nephew Fernando and other persons have been nosed out and certain discrepancies and errors in the original are ably commented upon by Monsignor Nicolas E. Navarro, can be accepted fully for what it is—a fairly true picture of the Liberator during one phase of his life by a minor officer who was not really so much in the confidence of his chief as he pretends to be.

There are many stories and legends written and told of Bolívar, things in the nature of the "Washington and the cherry tree" story, for which there is no documentary substantiation. Those of them which have been repeated in this volume are not necessarily given credence by the author but are included because they conform to the popular picture of Bolívar as well as to the author's own. In every case they have been pointed out as merely legendary.

So much, then, for this author's attitude toward prime source material in general on Bolívar. From secondary sources he has tried to select such opinions and observations as seem to him entirely just and logical. The picture of the Liberator which he draws is as true to his honest conception of the man as he could make it with words; and he hopes he has not offended too much the South American people for whom he has a deep affection. There is still plenty of glory left to their hero, even after the attempt has been made to transform him from a god to a human being by showing his human weaknesses and failings.

And glory was what Bolívar desired above all else—glory through the world, through the ages, after he was dead. In 1825, when they proposed to erect a statue of him in his native city, he said, "Wait until after my death, in order to judge me without prejudice. Then you can accord me whatever honors are thought suitable. Monuments should never be raised to a man in his lifetime; he may change, he may betray. You will never have to charge me with that; but wait, wait, I say again."

ACKNOWLEDGMENTS

✤

A GAIN, as in *Gómez*, I must thank Mr. Rudolph Dolge of Caracas for his interest and advice. During his many years' residence in Venezuela Mr. Dolge has gained the respect and affection of the people and has done more, perhaps, than any other individual to establish good will toward the United States. I must thank also Mr. E. E. Boylan of Caracas and Judge Frank Feuille for their help and counsel. None of these, however, are to be held responsible for any statement or opinion appearing in this work.

My thanks also to the staff of the splendid Columbus Memorial Library of the Pan American Union.

THOMAS ROURKE.

BIBLIOGRAPHY

✤

IN 1933 the Columbus Memorial Library of the Pan American Union in Washington, D. C., published, in commemoration of the one hundred and fiftieth anniversary of the birth of Simón Bolívar, a very complete bibliography of the Liberator which is available for the use of any interested person.

This author does not feel that it is necessary to give here a list of material which he has obtained from private sources, because such material would not be accessible to most people, but will confine himself to those works pertaining to Bolívar which are to be found in the United States either in the Library of Congress or the Columbus Memorial Library.

Abreu y Lima, José Ignacio de, *Resumen Histórico de la Ultima Dictadura del Libertador Simón Bolívar.* Rio de Janeiro, 1922.

Academia Nacional de Historia, *Archivo Santander.* 24 vols. Bogotá, 1932.

Academia Nacional de la Historia, *Documentos para los Anales de Venezuela,* vols. 1-7. Caracas, 1889-90.

Adam, William Jackson, *Journal of Voyages to Marguaritta, Trinidad, and Maturin . . . in 1819 and 1820. . . .* Dublin, 1824.

Agosto Méndez, J. M., *El Médico del Libertador.* (In *El Universal,* Caracas, September 13, 1930.)

Alamo-Ybarra, Carlos, *La Constitution de Bolívar pour la République qui Porte Son Nom. . . .* Geneva, 1922.

Andara, J. L., *The Bolívar Doctrine.* (In *Inter-America,* New York, October, 1920.)

André, Marius, *Bolívar y la Democracia*. Barcelona, 1924.
Angell, Hildegarde, *Simón Bolívar, South American Liberator*. New York, 1930.
Antuña, José G., *Bolívar, el Más Alto Símbolo del Continente*. (In *El Universal*, Caracas, September 1, 1932.)
Arias, Harmodio, *The International Policy of Bolívar*. (In *Inter-America*, New York, October, 1918.)
Arocha Moreno, Jesús, *Bolívar Juzgado por el General San Martín*. Caracas, 1930.
Arrocha Graell, C., *El Libertador en Guayaquil; Entrevista con el General San Martín*. Panamá.
Atlántida, Barranquilla. Special Bolívar issue, December, 1930.

Baralt, Rafael María y Díaz, Ramón, *Resumen de la Historia de Venezuela desde 1797 hasta 1830*. Paris, 1841.
Barbagelata, Hugo David, *Bolívar y San Martín*. Paris, 1911.
Bates, Lindon Wallace, Jr., *The Path of the Conquistadores*. London, 1912.
Bayo, Ciro, *Bolívar y Sus Tenientes*. Madrid, 1929.
Becerra, Ricardo, *Vida de Don Francisco de Miranda*. Madrid, 1927.
Belaúnde, Víctor Andrés, *The Political Ideas of Bolívar*. (In *Bulletin of the Pan American Union*, Washington, D. C., December, 1930.)
Bellegarde, Dantés, *Pétion et Bolívar*. (In *Revue de l'Amérique Latine*, Paris, December, 1924.)
Bermúdez, José Alejandro, *La Quinta de Bolívar en Bogotá*. (In *Boletín de la Academia Nacional de la Historia*, Caracas, January-March, 1931.)
Billiken, Caracas. Special Bolívar issue, December 20, 1930.
Bingham, Hiram, *Address in part before the United States Senate on Simón Bolívar*. (In *Bulletin of the Pan American Union*, January, 1931.)
——*The Journal of an Expedition across Venezuela and Colombia, 1906, 1907*. New Haven, 1909.
Blanco, Eduardo, *Venezuela Heroica*. Caracas, 1935.

Boletín de la Biblioteca Nacional, Caracas. Special Bolívar issue, December 17, 1930.

Bolívar, Simón, *Cartas de Bolívar, 1799-1822.* Prólogo de José Enrique Rodó y Notas de R. Blanco-Fombona. Paris, 1912.

—— *Cartas de Bolívar, 1823-1824-1825.* (Con un Apéndice que Contiene Cartas de 1801 a 1822.) Notas de R. Blanco-Fombona. Madrid, 1921.

—— *Cartas de Bolívar, 1825-1827.* Notas de R. Blanco-Fombona. Madrid, 1922.

—— *Cartas del Libertador Corregidas Conforme a los Originales. . . .* 10 vols. Caracas, 1929-30.

—— *Discursos y Proclamas;* Comp., Anotados, Prologados y Publicados por R. Blanco-Fombona. Paris, 1913.

—— *Papeles de Bolívar,* Publicados por Vicente Lecuna. 2 vols. Madrid, 1920.

Brandt, Carlos, *Universal Peace, the Work of Bolívar.* (In *Inter-America,* New York, October, 1924.)

Bulnes, Gonzalo, *Bolívar en el Perú.* 2 vols. Madrid, 1919. *Historia de la Espedición Libertadora del Perú (1817-1822).* 2 vols. Santiago, 1887-88.

Camacho, Simón, *Recuerdos de Santa Marta.* Caracas, 1842.

Chaves Mata, José María, *El Libertador.* Guayaquil, 1928.

Churión, Juan José, *El Humorismo del Libertador. Cien anécdotas. . . .* Caracas, 1916.

Civilización, Barranquilla. Special Bolívar issue, December 15, 1930.

Clay, Henry, *Works of;* edited by Calvin Colton. New York, 1897.

Cleven, Nels Andrew Nelson, *Readings in Hispanic American History.* Boston, 1927.

Cochrane, Charles Stuart, *Journal of a Residence and Travels in Colombia during the Years 1823 and 1824.* London, 1825.

Correa, Luis, *El Libertador en el Perú.* (In *Boletín de la*

Academia Nacional de la Historia, Caracas, April-June, 1928.)

Cova Maza, J. M., *Mocedades de Simón Bolívar.* Barcelona, Ven., 1924.

Cromos, Bogotá. Special Bolívar issue, December 13, 1930.

Cruz, Ernesto de la; Goenaga, José Manuel; Mitre y Carlos, Bartolomé; Villanueva, A., *La Entrevista de Guayaquil.* (*El Libertador y San Martín.*) Prólogo de Rufino Blanco-Fombona. Madrid.

Cuervo, Luis Augusto, *La Monarquía en Colombia.* Bogotá, 1916.

Dalencour, François, *Alexandre Pétion devant l'Humanité; Alexandre Pétion et Simón Bolívar; Haiti et l'Amérique Latine. Et Expédition de Bolívar par Marion Ainé.* Port-au-Prince, 1928.

Duane, William, *A Visit to Colombia in 1822-23.* Philadelphia, 1826.

Ducoudray-Holstein, H. Lafayette Villaume, *Memoirs of Simón Bolívar, President Liberator of the Republic of Colombia and His Principal Generals; Secret History of the Revolution and the Events which Preceded It, from 1807 to the Present Time. . . .* Boston, 1829.

El Commercio, Quito. Special Bolívar issues, December, 10-15 and 17, 1930.

Eurindia, Mexico City. Special Bolívar issues, Nos. 7 and 8, 1930.

Gil Fortoul, José, *Historia Constitucional de Venezuela.* Caracas, 1930.

Goenaga, José Manuel, *La Entrevista de Guayaquil.* Bogotá, 1911.

González, Juan Vicente, *Biografía del General José Félix Ribas.* Madrid, 1918?

González, Fernando, *Mi Simón Bolívar.* Bogotá, 1928.

Graham, Robert Bontine Cunninghame, *José Antonio Páez.* London, 1929.

Guzman Blanco, Antonio, *El Libertador de la América del Sur.* London, 1885.

Hasbrouck, Alfred, *Foreign Legionaries in the Liberation of Spanish South America.* New York, 1928.

Hippisley, G., *Narrative of the Expedition to the Rivers Orinoco and Apure in South America.* London, 1819.

Jiménez Arraiz, Francisco, *Camino de Gloria.* Caracas, 1925.

La Nación, Santiago de Chile. Special Bolívar issues, December 17 and 18, 1930.

La Prensa, New York. Special Bolívar issue, December 17, 1930.

Lafond, Georges y Tersane, Gabriel, *Bolívar et la Libération de l'Amérique du Sud.* Paris, 1931.

Larrazábal, Felipe, *La Vida y Correspondencia General del Libertador Simón Bolívar.* New York, 1878.

Lecuna, Vicente, *Papeles de Bolívar.* 2 vols. Madrid, 1920.

Le Gouhir y Rodas, José, *Historia de la Republica del Ecuador*, vol. 1 (1809-1860). Quito, 1920.

Lembcke, Jorge Bailey, *La Verdadera Manuelita Sáenz.* (In *El Universal*, Caracas, September 9, 1927.)

Lemly, Henry Rowan, *Bolívar, Liberator of Venezuela, Colombia, Perú and Bolivia.* Boston, 1928.

Libro de Oro del Centenario de Bolívar. Barranquilla, 1931.

Lockey, Joseph Byrne, *Pan Americanism: Its Beginnings.* New York, 1926.

López, Ismael, *Las Amadas de Bolívar.* (In *Variedades*, Lima, December 6, 1924.)

López, Manuel Antonio, *Recuerdos Historicos de la Guerra de la Independencia. Colombia y el Perú. 1819-1826.* Madrid, 1919.

López Contreras, Eleazar, *Bolívar Conductor de Tropas.* Caracas, 1930.

Lozano y Lozano, Fabio, *El Maestro del Libertador.* Paris, 1913.

374   BIBLIOGRAPHY

Mahoney, William D., *Campaigns and Cruises, in Venezuela and New Granada, from 1817 to 1830.* . . . 3 vols. London, 1831. (Authorship also attributed to Ricardo Longueville Vowell.)

Mancini, Jules, *Bolivar et l'Emancipation des Colonies Espagnoles des Origines á 1815.* Paris, 1912.

Miller, John, *Memorias del General Miller al Servicio de la República del Perú.* . . . Traducción por el General Torrijos. . . . 2 vols. Madrid, 1918?

Mitre, Bartolomé, *The Emancipation of South America.* London, 1893.

—— *Historia de San Martín y de la Emancipación Sud America.* 3 vols. Buenos Aires, 1887-1888.

Monsalve, José D., *Estudios sobre el Libertador Simón Bolívar.* Bogotá, 1930.

—— *El Ideal Politico del Libertador Simón Bolívar.* Bogotá, 1916.

Moses, Bernard, *The Intellectual Background of the Revolution in South America, 1810-1824.* New York, 1926.

Mosquera, Tomás Cipriano de, *Memorias sobre la Vida del Libertador Simón Bolívar.* New York, 1853.

Niles, John Milton, *A View of South America and Mexico . . . by a Citizen of the United States.* H. Huntington Hartford, New York, 1826.

O'Connor, Francisco Burdett, *Independencia Americana. Recuerdos de Francisco Burdett O'Connor.* La Paz, 1915.

O'Leary, Daniel Florencio, *Memorias del General O'Leary.* 32 vols. Caracas, 1879-88.

Páez, José Antonio, *Autobiografía.* 2 vols. New York, 1871.

Palma, Ricardo, *Bolívar en las Tradiciones Peruanas.* Madrid, 1930.

Pan American Union, Bulletin of the, Washington, D. C. Special issues, December, 1924, June, 1926, June, 1930, December, 1930.

Parra-Pérez, C., *Bolívar, a Contribution to the Study of His*

Political Ideas. Translated by N. A. N. Cleven. Pittsburgh, Pa. 1930.

Paulding, Hiram, *Paulding's Visit to Bolívar in His Camp* [1824]. (In Meade, Mrs. Rebecca (Paulding), *Life of Hiram Paulding.*) New York, 1910.

Penzini, Hernández, J., *La Guerra a Muerte y el Abrazo de Santa Ana.* Trujillo, 1930.

Pereyra, Carlos, *Bolívar y Washington: Un Paralelo Imposible.* Madrid, 1915.

—— *La Juventud Legendaria de Bolívar.* Madrid, 19—?

Pérez, Diaz, M., *Estudio Médico-Psicologico de Bolívar y Análisis Psiquiátrico de Sus Ideas y de Sus Actos.* (In *Gaceta Médica de Caracas,* October 15, 1915.)

Pérez y Soto, Juan Bautista, Comp., *Defensa de Bolívar.* Lima, 1878.

Perú de Lacroix, Louis, *Bolívar Jugé par un Officier de Napoleón.* (In *Mercure de France,* Paris, September 16, 1913.)

—— *Diario de Bucaramanga.* Edited by Monseñor Nicolas E. Navarro. Caracas, 1935.

Petre, Francis Loraine, *Simón Bolívar "El Libertador."* New York, 1910.

Pineda, C., Manuel Antonio, *Bolívar ante la Historia.* Cartagena, 1930.

Pinilla, Sabino, *La Creación de Bolivia.* Madrid, 1917.

Ponte, Andrés, *Bolívar y Otros Ensayos.* Caracas, 1919.

Posada, Eduardo, *Apostillas á la historia colombiana.* Bogotá, 1926.

Posada Gutiérrez, Joaquín, *Memorias Histórico-Políticas.* 3 vols. Madrid, 1920-21.

Pradt, Dominique de Fourt de, Archbishop of Mechlin, *Congrés de Panamá.* Paris, 1825.

Recollections of a Service of Three Years during the War of Extermination in the Republics of Venezuela and Colombia. By an officer of the Colombian navy. 2 vols. London, 1818.

Restrepo, José Manuel, *Historia de la Revolución de la República de Colombia.* 10 vols. Paris, 1827.

Révérend, Alejandro Próspero, *Diario sobre la enfermedad que Padece S. E. el Libertador, Sus Progresos o Disminución y Método Curativo Seguido por el Médico de Cabecera.* . . . Boletines 1-33. (In *Boletín de la Biblioteca Nacional,* Caracas, December 17, 1930.)

Rivas Vicuña, Francisco, *Las Guerras de Bolívar.* Caracas, 1921-22.

Robertson, William Spence, *History of the Latin-American Nations.* New York, London, 1925.

Rodó, José Enrique, *Bolívar.* Panamá, 1918.

Cinco Ensayos. Madrid, 1917.

Rodríguez, Simón, *Defensa de Bolívar.* Caracas, 1916.

Rojas, Arístides, *Estudios Históricos.* Caracas, 1926-27.

Rojas, José María, *Simón Bolívar.* Paris, 1883.

Saavedra Galindo, José Manuel, *Colombia Libertadora.* Bogotá, 1924.

Samper, José María, *Apuntamientos para la Historia Política y Social de la Nueva Granada desde 1810.* Bogotá, 1853.

San Martín, José de: *Su Correspondencia 1823-1850.* Madrid, 1919.

Santana, Arturo, *La Campaña de Carabobo (1821).* Caracas, 1921.

Sevilla, Rafael, *Memorias de un Official del Ejercito Español.* Madrid, 1916.

Sherwell, Guillermo, *Simón Bolívar (el Libertador) Patriot, Warrior, Statesman, Father of Five Nations.* . . . Washington, 1921.

Sucre, Antonio José de, *Cartas de Sucre al Libertador (1820-1830).* 2 vols. Madrid, 1919.

Tavera Acosta, Bartolomé, *Anales de Guayana.* 2 vols. Ciudad Bolívar, 1913-14.

El Tiempo, Lima. Special Supplement, December 9, 1924.

Torrente, Mariano, *Historia de la Revolución Hispano-Americana.* 3 vols. Madrid, 1830.

Torres Caicedo, José María, *Unión Latino-Americana, Pensamiento de Bolívar para Formar una Liga Americana.* . . . Paris, 1865.

Urdaneta, Rafael, *Memorias del General Rafael Urdaneta.* Madrid, 1916.

Urrutia, Francisco José, *El Ideal Internacional de Bolívar.* Quito, 1911.

Vallenilla Lanz, Laureano, *Críticas de Sinceridad y Exactitud.* Caracas, 1921.

Vaucaire, Michel, *Bolívar, the Liberator.* . . . Boston, New York, 1929.

Velasco Ibarra, José María. (In his *Estudios varios*) Quito, 1928.

Villanueva, Carlos A., (*La Monarquía en America*). Paris, 1912.

Vivano, Carlos A., *La Conjuración del 25 de Setiembre.* . . . Quito, 1929.

Wendehake, José Rafael, *The Master of Bolívar.* Colón, 1930.

Ybarra, T. R., *Bolívar, The Passionate Warrior.* New York, 1929.

INDEX

❖

Printed in the United States
781000001B